P9-CQN-987

Humphrey Tonkin

Jane Edwards

# THE WORLD IN THE CURRICULUM

## Curricular Strategies for the 21st Century

Change Magazine Press

This book is part of a series of publications by the Council on Learning, which established its Education and the World View Program in an effort to encourage the nation's colleges and universities to widen their international components in their undergraduate curriculum. This program has been funded by the National Endowment for the Humanities, the United States Department of Education, the Exxon Education Foundation, and the Joyce Mertz-Gilmore Foundation. The various activities under this endeavor have been guided by a national task force of 50 leaders out of public life, the academy, and industry. Other volumes in this series are listed at the end of this volume.

**$6.95**

**THE WORLD IN THE CURRICULUM:
Curricular Strategies for the 21st Century**

© 1981 by Change Magazine Press
271 North Avenue
New Rochelle, N.Y. 10801

April 1981
Change Magazine Press
271 North Avenue
New Rochelle, N.Y. 10801

ISBN 0-915390-28-0
LC #80-69765

$6.95 each; $5.95 each for 10 or more copies.

# Contents

## V—Communicating With the World: Language

## VI—Meeting the World Halfway: Study Abroad and International Exchanges

## VII—Living in the Academy and Living in the World: Actors and Constituencies

## VIII—The World on the Campus: The Campus as an International Environment

# IX—College and Community

# X—Financing International Programs

# XI—Change and Transformation

# References

# Organizations

# Foreword

Throughout Man's painful journey into contemporary times—from his stone age cave existence through his development of nation-states to a planetary life now made suddenly critical by the flash-point compaction of new and old forces—the distance of our consciousness has stretched from a few thousand feet to the outer markings of our world and the planets and stars beyond. To live in and more fully understand this new global life is to cope and survive it. The once distant hustings of the world, be they hostile or friendly, strange or familiar, open or closed, now to wit are set in our backyard. There is to be no further retreat to our protective caves of Paleolithic times.

Undergirding those necessary visions for a global century lie the pragmatic and down-to-earth abilities which will enable us to traverse this new world with any degree of success. How are we to be attuned to the new necessities of survival? That is the question. In this useful book on curricular strategies for undergraduate institutions, Jane Edwards and Humphrey Tonkin have done their important and very necessary work in describing what must inevitably take place: To remove international education from much of its exhoratory and peripheral past and to put it full flush into the mainstream of American education. In higher education and elsewhere, professionals understandably prefer larger conceptual canvasses to the nuts-and-bolts business of the underlying process. But visions will not convert to realities until we are willing to get our hands dirty. There is enough in this book of practical value to satisfy that vast array of needs and practices of our colleges and universities across the country. The test is in the doing.

Educational change never takes place in a vacuum. It is only right to ask whether the national mood will add or detract from academic efforts to make their institutions more global enterprises. The return of our hostages from Iran has created a new mood of patriotism and pride that has not been seen on these shores since the second world war. But whatever one's politics, it can no longer be a matter of nationalism versus internationalism, but a matter of intelligent world leadership versus one conducted by the seat of our pants. An enlarged national consensus on America's place in the world has become a sine qua non of our survival. Only to the degree that we develop a larger citizen sophistication about global issues, and understand those necessary contextual relationships of histories and cultures and events, will we make certain that we will navigate as a nation with the best advantage to ourselves and the rest of mankind.

This book is one of the many outcomes of the Council on Learning's project on Education and the World View. This project has combined a number of fact-finding efforts with recommendations for action and the development of useful tools. All will enable institutions and faculties to pursue the objective of stretching students toward some post-Galilean visions of their world. We are grateful to the authors for the practical nature of the recommendations. They answer how our encroaching world can be reflected in sound and affordable campus strategies. They have not underestimated the difficulties, and the practical modesty of the necessary incremental steps they recommend make their larger vision all the more possible.

*George W. Bonham*
*Council on Learning*

## About the Authors

Humphrey Tonkin has a doctorate in English and is Professor of English at the University of Pennsylvania, as well as Coordinator of International Programs at the University. He is the former Vice Provost for University Life. Jane Edwards has a doctorate in folklore with a regional interest in Latin America. She is Foreign Student Advisor at the University of Pennsylvania's International Programs office. Both authors received part of their education in England.

# Acknowledgments

We brought to the task of writing this book a strong sense of the breadth of our subject and of our own inadequacies. It is no mere lip service to state our indebtedness to others whose knowledge in this area is greater than our own, and it is with pleasure and gratitude that we acknowledge their assistance.

We would like to thank those colleagues who gave us information related to specific topics. Ann Busch, Henry Ferguson, and Paul Griffith, of the state education departments of Maryland, New York, and Illinois, gave us both information and insights about the policies of their states on international education. Weber Donaldson of Tulane University explained the Tulane language requirement. Seymour Fersh, formerly of the American Association of Community and Junior Colleges and now at Brevard Community College, Florida, not only set us straight about community colleges but provided a wealth of ideas about teaching international subjects. Frederick Frey at the University of Pennsylvania talked to us about government employment of area specialists. Australian Ambassador to the UN Ralph Harry gave us information about language competence in the Australian Foreign Service. And A. Ronald Walton of the National Association of Self-Instructional Language Programs explained that method and other aspects of language teaching.

Thanks are due to those who discussed the project and made suggestions in the planning stages, particularly James Harf of Ohio State University; Rose Hayden, until recently of the U.S. International Communications Agency; and David Jordan of the University of California at San Diego.

We also would like to express our gratitude to those who read our drafts and gave us their comments, in many cases extensive and in all cases valuable. These include our colleagues here at the University of Pennsylvania: Roger Allen, Peter Conn, Hilary Conroy, Barbara Freed, Richard Lambert, Martin Meyerson, Norman Palmer, and Henry Teune. In other corners of the country we imposed on Richard Brod of the Modern Language Association of America; Archer Brown, Hugh Jenkins, and Jack Reichard at the National Association for Foreign Student Affairs; Basil Karp and Craig Millar of Pennsylvania State University; Margaret Lonzetta of the World Affairs Council of Philadelphia; Paul Watson of the University of Pittsburgh; Jonathan Pool of the University of Washington; Frederick Rudolph of Williams College; Judith Torney-Purta of the University of Illinois-Chicago Circle; Frederick Starr of Tulane University; and Burns Weston of the UCLA Law School.

We are grateful to the staff of the Council on Learning for their support and assistance, particularly George W. Bonham, the originator of the Education and the World View project and our editor, and Robert Black, project director. We owe special thanks to Barbara Burn of the University of Massachusetts, Amherst, formerly executive secretary of the President's Commission on Foreign Language and International Studies, whose early suggestions and extensive and informative comments on the manuscript were as invaluable to us as her recent book on a topic closely related to our own; and to Robert Leestma of the U.S. Department of Education for giving us so much information and so much of his time and, above all, his encouragement. We hope that they and all our commentators will understand that where we failed to act on their suggestions it was not without considerable soul searching.

Finally, we must apologize to the staff of the Office of International Programs of the University of Pennsylvania for our occasionally erratic behavior over the past few months and thank them for their forbearance. We are particularly grateful to Elva Power, without whom we would probably never have managed to produce a comprehensible manuscript, and to Ann Kuhlman, who helped us, in spite of her own extensive commitments, in a dozen different ways.

The length of this list is some indication of the greatness of our debt. For any errors or inconsistencies that remain, we are solely responsible.

*Humphrey Tonkin*
*Jane Edwards*
*March 1981*

*O wad some Pow'r the giftie gie us*
*To see oursels as others see us!*
*It wad frae mony a blunder free us,*
                    *And foolish notion*

                              Robert Burns

# Introduction

In the darkest days of World War I, when German U-boats were harassing the coasts of Europe and America and the world looked grim, Will Rogers sent a letter to Washington. "I have an answer to the U-boat problem," he wrote the Secretary of War, "and would like to come and tell you about it." That august statesman was overjoyed. Summoned into his eager presence, Rogers explained his plan in a single sentence: "Fill the U-boats full of seawater." "But how in heaven's name can we do that?" asked the puzzled Secretary. "What do you want from me?" replied Rogers. "*I* had the idea. *You* work out the details."

All too frequently texts on international education remain fixed at a level of generality that does not tolerate descent to the details of execution. Pious hopes for a better understanding of the world, and for surer political decision making based on informed public opinion, touch responsive chords among educators but are unaccompanied by the particularities of programs and curricula and the necessary administrative arrangements. Alternatively, facts and figures may chill the blood or elevate the soul, but they lack the required sense of purpose and philosophical direction. In this book we have tried to avoid these shortcomings, offering both a rationale for the procedures we recommend and a set of very specific programmatic and administrative prescriptions. There is room for disagreement on the diagnosis, but we believe that the specifics of the book are likely to prove useful to most people wishing to increase the international dimension in undergraduate education, if only as a starting point for their own ideas and prescriptions.

The book begins with a relatively simple premise. In recent years the world has been overtaken by a series of fundamental changes in technological, economic, and political realities. Some of these changes have been good, some less good. In either case they have had a profound impact on the shape and functions of national and international institutions and on the aspirations of the world's four billion people. These changes will continue, bringing with them new opportunities and new problems and obliging us to continue to modify our thinking and our ways of doing things.

Although not alone in this regard, the American system of higher education has been relatively slow to react to these new developments. In important respects events in the world are outstripping the ability of our educational, as well as other national, institutions to respond to them. Yet it may not be overdramatic to suggest that our success in shaping these educational institutions in response to changing times will determine whether the United States, as a world leader, can have a benign effect on the world, help avert global destruction, and create a better future for coming generations.

We shall concentrate on the undergraduate curriculum—an educational arena in which the general goal of educating the citizen about the world intersects with the need to train specialists in international affairs. The book calls for a more systematic effort to internationalize the curriculum, in order to bring it into line with new global conditions. To an ever increasing degree we are entering an era in which decisions will have to be arrived at collectively— among citizens, both in the U.S. and abroad, better versed in the complexities of foreign affairs and conflicting value systems, and among the representatives of those citizens acting in concert on a worldwide scale. One fundamental key to this process is education.

When we talk of internationalizing the curriculum, we generally have in mind two goals: first, increasing the number and quality of programs, courses, and other opportunities for the study of international and global affairs; and second, infusing the entire undergraduate curriculum with a sense of the international and global, so that a growing number of courses and programs, in whatever subject, can better reflect the realities of an increasingly interconnected world. The first is necessary because the steady increase in our contacts with other countries, and in the growth of areas of human activity that essentially transcend national boundaries, makes it essential that we prepare more specialists in international affairs and provide them with better training.

But the second purpose may be even more important: Every citizen, not just the international specialist, must understand how our local and national concerns relate to the larger world and how realities dictate that our own aspirations be harmonized with those of other nations and peoples. The democratic principle of consent has always made it essential that Americans understand what they are voting for. Only if we have an informed citizenry can we influence and support our leaders to follow a wise course in their dealings with the rest of the globe. Today, when a single military command can trigger the destruction of our entire civilization and when both local and national decisions have a strong impact on the world beyond our own boundaries, it is imperative that the public better understand what values and what human necessities are at stake in our foreign relations and in our international conduct.

While this book focuses on the undergraduate curriculum, its authors are well aware of the larger context of that curriculum. There is a direct and organic relationship between undergraduate and graduate programs on the one hand and the education that students receive in elementary and secondary schools on the other. Nor does a curriculum exist independently of people, financial resources, and physical settings. And the students who participate in that curriculum have lives extending beyond the classroom. We take these connections into account, offering a prescription not for curricular reform in an isolated setting but for the gradual realignment of entire institutional structures.

In so doing, we are very conscious of two considerations. First, an institution wishing to bring vitality to its global and international efforts must have the collective will to formulate and act upon its plans. This requires leadership and skills to mobilize human and financial resources effectively. Second, strong and well-established institutions have a sense of their own direction and a set of values, however imperfect or imperfectly perceived, that preclude radical and sudden departures from established behavior. Hence change must be gradual, well planned, and intellectually satisfying, preserving what is good and providing a sense of direction derived at least in part from an institution's existing strengths and traditions.

Ideally these changes will come about through, or be accompanied by, action at the highest level in the leadership of a college. Such action might be triggered by determined faculty or by the declared aspirations of students. Without the support of the institution's leadership the effort is unlikely to succeed. The model that we suggest for this initiative is that of collective decision making, encouraged and backed by determined leadership. We suggest that a college wishing to internationalize its curriculum establish its own committee or task force to generate discussion at all levels and thus to shape plans for action. This "international committee" can determine, either directly or indirectly, the priorities of the institution with respect to international studies and how the institution's resources will be adapted to take these new priorities into account. Above all, the committee, and everyone else involved in this planning process, must be acutely aware of the fact that successful change only comes about from a perception of shared interests. One cannot successfully change an institution, particularly an educational one, by forcing behavior patterns on its members. But progress cannot be expected through serendipity alone.

We begin with a general consideration of the reasons for internationalizing the curriculum, looking briefly at how the world, and America's role in it, has changed in recent years. We then consider the constraints and opportunities presented by different kinds of institutions of higher learning, stressing the fact that internationalizing the curriculum means different things in different settings and will have different outcomes. This takes us to the heart of our discussion—the reform of existing programs and the introduction of new ones to increase the attention given to the international aspects of education and their centrality in the undergraduate curriculum.

We supplement our discussion of programs with a consideration of the people involved in them and the constituencies they serve, and go on to consider how the entire undergraduate environment can be made more obviously global and international and how undergraduate programs and the international facilities of the institution in general can better relate with the public at all levels. We conclude with a chapter on the financing of international programs.

Throughout the book we stress what is to us a particularly important reality: internationalization is already with us and all around us. The revolution in communications of recent years puts us in easy and instant contact with the rest of the world. That world intrudes on us in a thousand different ways and its messages require answers. Increasingly, Americans deal directly with people from other countries and with foreign institutions on a daily basis in what has in effect become an interactive world system. Hence our need for knowledge about the world is not confined to the need to have an impact on our leaders to shape foreign policy. In our various ways we ourselves are making such policy, in our communities and in our daily lives, and we must be enabled to do so more wisely.

We are not espousing some internationalist cause or calling for a weakening of our international leadership. The issue for us is simple: Because people's lives are already in large measure internationalized, they must internationalize their educational institutions as well. All of us must learn to attune ourselves to this communication and interaction with the rest of the world, and to make creative use of it to avert disaster and increase the chances for humanity.

We should add a word about our own sense of the relationship between this book and the Education and the World View project in general. Ours is not a consensus document, not an attempt to sum up the views of the initiators and leaders of this project. Our assignment was to take a critical look at the orientation of American undergraduate education, to ask questions about the aptness of the preparation offered today's students, and to suggest both rationale and strategy for change. Our own institutional experience has been primarily in a research university, and this bias may reveal itself along with other shortcomings. But we believe that much of what we have to say is readily applicable to the broad range of American colleges. If we do not always give credit to those aspects of the educational system that are deserving, it is because we are here concerned with areas where it is apparent that change is most called for. The role of the United States in the world of the twenty-first century will be, however defined, a leading one, and it calls for our increasing sophistication in understanding complex global issues. The young people in college today will have difficult decisions to make about their lives and about the life of their country. They deserve the best understanding of the world that we can provide.

# 1

# A World of Interconnections

# A World of Interconnections

## 1. Our fate is bound up with the fate of others....

In a world that is full of risk and challenge, education has no easy tasks. In some necessary fundamentals educators must be more conservative than much of the rest of society. Old human and intellectual values and ways of thought need preserving amidst transitions. But at the same time educators must be more revolutionary than the rest in order to oblige society, and especially the young, to face up to the fact that circumstances are changing and that still greater changes are on the way. Thus the educator must be historian and prophet, preserver of the past and foreteller of the future.

At one time this mediation between the old and the new—the adaptation of society to changing opportunities—was easily associated with the idea of progress: If we educated ourselves well, we could advance our society to new heights and achievements. Science seemed an absolute good; industry brought prosperity and the good life; a higher standard of living helped raise many of the world's poor out of misery. True, even then we were aware of blemishes in this picture, but the choice rested between education and progress on the one hand and ignorance and stagnation on the other.

Today the case is significantly altered. We are more conscious of the fact that there are risks involved in the advance of science and technology, that there are peoples in the world (including members of our own society) who do not share the traditional American enthusiasm for material advances, that even our traditional beliefs in democratic institutions may be perceived differently by others. We are faced with the massive and ongoing problem of adapting to circumstances in which our own values cannot be considered absolutes. Not only is it right and decent to act on our doubts as well as our certainties; we must also learn to live with those around us whose views are different from ours. The very science and technology that brought our society to its present peak of achievement have also inexorably brought us into competition with the other peoples of the world for raw materials and markets and productive capacity. Science and technology, of course, have also brought us new opportunities for human advancement and, conversely, new dangers of nuclear annihilation.

The critical choice is no longer between stagnation and progress, but between destruction and survival. Whether, through education, we can go beyond survival to forge a new sense of ourselves and others as global partners remains to be seen. Though occasionally the situation might look bleak in this regard, we should remember that thinking on such matters has advanced by leaps and bounds through the 1960s and 1970s. Today, whether Republicans or Democrats, leaders in the nation's foreign policy establishment speak increasingly of the need to avoid a simpleminded nostalgia for a past that cannot be recalled. "To advocate 'nationalism,' as if it represented a workable alternative to 'internationalism,' " wrote Elliott Richardson in the *Wall Street Journal*, "can only lengthen the lag between reality of change and our adaptation to it.... In the end, instead of riding the wave of the future, we shall be overwhelmed by it." Cyrus Vance, looking back over his years at the State Department, refers specifically to the dangers of this new nostalgia, which, he maintains, can only lead "to simplistic solutions and go-it-alone illusions.... Our real problems are long-term in nature. It will not do to reach for the dramatic act, to seek to cut through stubborn dilemmas with a single stroke."

Secretary Vance's plea for a lowering of expectations and a new realism and reflectiveness strikes home with particular force at colleges and universities. One can easily read it, and Elliott Richardson's warnings, as a recipe for indecisiveness—the capitulation of the intellectual entrapped in his own cogitations. But if the problems themselves are too complicated for simple solutions, it is precisely the task of the academy to make sense of these complexities so that humane and decisive action can issue from such understandings. Americans need educational institutions more than ever before: The proper relationship between thought and action that they ideally can provide is essential not simply for our local or national survival, but that of people everywhere.

Although these problems are great and perplexing, the American education system is in many respects well set up to deal with them. Over the years it has shown itself remarkably adaptive to the changing needs of the communities it serves. Unlike the educational systems in many other countries it is not hidebound by central control, not monolithic in its structure. Local and regional control makes experimentation still possible and makes specific changes easier to institute. On the other hand, the very fact that it is bound closely to the needs of local communities increases the difficulty of convincing those constituencies controlling it to look beyond their immediate boundaries. This is true not only of elementary and secondary education but of the sector that is our particular concern in this book: undergraduate higher education. Here too, local and national biases are apt to prevail. In undergraduate education the traditional guiding principles have been education for productive citizenship and participation in American institutions. While higher education has a good record in certain aspects of international education, the area has for the most part taken second place to other concerns.

In many ways the pace of change in the world is faster than the pace of change in higher education. Academic institutions are not keeping up with changing needs. Consider, for example, the matter of integration of national economies. Between 1960 and 1977 direct foreign investment in this country rose by 77 percent and our investment abroad by 123 percent. Imports of goods and services went up 246 percent and exports 202 percent. As Richard Lambert points out (1980: 160), "Direct investment in the United States from abroad is well over $30 billion. Foreign banks in the United States have assets exceeding $250 billion. Foreign ownership of manufacturing units within the United States is growing apace." At issue here is not whether foreign investment in the United States is a good thing or whether U.S. trade with the rest of the world creates stability or destabilizes our economy (though they are questions that citizens ought to be able to debate with some grasp of the issues), but the simple fact that these changes are taking place in the world around us. Not just Economics I but the entire curriculum, the entire professoriat, had better pay attention to what is going on.

Consider the matter of global human contact—both transportation and electronic communications. In the brief space of 30 years or less they have revolutionized our lives: The first regularly scheduled jet service across the Atlantic dates from 1958, a year after the launching of the world's first artificial satellite. In 1965 only 5 countries possessed satellite antennas; by 1979 114 countries had antennas in the Intelsat satellite system (UNESCO 1978: 41; 1980: 62-3). While in 1950 Americans made 900,000 overseas telephone calls, 25 years later that annual figure exceeded 60 million. Neither aircraft nor satellite systems could function without computers—and today computer networks dominate international communications to an ever increasing degree. Yet the first computer—filling an entire room and capable of only relatively simple operations—was invented just 35 years ago.

To what extent has American education adapted to these new realities? We refer not only to the need to teach American students how to use these new machines but to the need to consider the changes they have wrought on human institutions, the new institutions that will be needed in the future to exploit and regulate them, and the implications they carry for the organization of societies and individual freedom.

We speak of competition for natural resources. Americans, who make up 5 percent of the world's population, consume 27 percent of the world's production of raw materials. Of the 30,000 gallons of petroleum consumed worldwide per second, the United States uses 10,000. The natural resources of the world are finite, though we may disagree on just *how* finite. A 1977 report of the United Nations concluded that the world could run out of certain minerals such as lead and zinc as early as the year 2000. Half of America's recoverable oil reserves have probably already been used. What do these facts mean, not only for Geology I, but for political science, economics, biology and psychology, and above all for Ethics I (where such a course still exists) and Education I?

We speak of raising the poor out of misery. Yet human misery goes on. The world cannot feed its people. An annual increase in food production of 4 percent would be necessary to ensure that by 1985 the world was adequately fed, but actual food production increases only in the neighborhood of 2 percent. Of the 4.5 billion inhabitants of this planet, probably some 1.3 billion remain chronically undernourished. There are 250 million children in the world who have never seen, and will probably never see, the inside of a classroom. Quite apart from the massive human cost involved (a cost almost beyond our ability to comprehend), misery breeds instability, despair breeds violence, and no belief in the decency of democratic institutions can prevail against the imperatives of personal, human survival. This is no new problem, but it is one that strikes at the very heart of our way of life in a world in which the United States, like all the other nations in their various ways, can no longer so easily call the shots or predetermine the outcomes.

Our fate is bound up with the fate of others. The acid rain that falls on Scandinavia is primarily produced in the industrial plants of Britain and the Low Countries. Our own nuclear testing in the South Pacific during the 1940s so damaged the homeland of the people of Eniwetok that not even the biggest cleanup project ever attempted, at a cost of over $100 million, could restore the island to habitability. In the Baltic Sea the residuals discharged by many bordering countries have already come close to destroying the sea's ecology. Only an unprecedented cooperative effort from nations encompassed by the Mediterranean seems likely to prevent that body of water from dying. Every nation is at fault because every nation has tended to put its own concerns first. Yet to a greater and greater extent we are discovering that it is in our best interest to consider others' interests and to create instruments and institutions of cooperation to take the place of the confrontation politics of the past. What do Economics I and Government I and Anthropology I and Biology I have to tell us about the dynamics of this new world and about the threats and risks involved in cooperation as well?

Perhaps out of a certain American penchant for guilt, perhaps because of a belief in the imminence of apocalypse, which brought many of the first settlers here—or perhaps simply because we sense that we can at least *do* something about American institutions —there is a tendency to see the faults of the world as reflections of our own. Or to assume, first, that it is only our own house that is out of order, and second, that by putting our own house to rights we shall thereby do the same for everyone else's. The fact, however, is that though the world has made immense progress in recent years in governing itself and in husbanding its resources—in the face of growing difficulties and complexities—the road is rutted with failures on all sides. For every dollar spent on education worldwide, 60 are spent on armaments. Nuclear confrontation, across the Bering Strait and arching over Europe, continues. It has been joined by a problem that promises to increase in urgency—that of nuclear proliferation. The trade in so-called conventional weapons feeds dozens of local wars. In 1975 5.5 percent of the world's gross national product was devoted to military expenditures and, while the ratio is dropping slightly in the industrialized world, it is rising in the developing nations. New wealth generated by foreign investment and aid in the developing countries has been slow to filter down to all levels of the population. In fact, it may have done more to raise the expectations of the poor through the contiguity of riches than to fulfill these expectations. And some of the best-intentioned efforts have had their undesirable side effects. The much vaunted Green Revolution, which raised crop yields dramatically, did nothing to address the problems of food distribution and tended to put agriculture at the mercy of machines and fossil fuels (Ehrlich 1977; Ruttan 1977; Christensen 1978). While aid pours into Southeast Asia from the industrialized world to ward off starvation for millions of people, that world continues to sell infant formula to Cambodian refugees, though formula feeding in unhygienic and impoverished surroundings may actually contribute to infant mortality.

These problems are in no sense the exclusive fault and burden of

the United States. Nor will a dramatic improvement in our awareness of the world bring change overnight. But there is much that we
can do to increase our awareness, and our students' awareness, of
such issues. It may be the single most important task now facing
higher education. In effect we must help our students come to grips
with what is increasingly perceived to be a single set of interlocking
concerns of almost indescribable complexity. Are our fragmented
knowledge institutions and modes of thought adequate to the need?

We should remember that the increase in international contact
over the past 30 years has been accompanied by unprecedented
growth in the scope and impact of international institutions. It has
even included some voluntary surrender of sovereignty on a regional
basis—in the European Economic Community, for example. In this
regard the importance of the massive consultative and cooperative
mechanism born in the United Nations Charter of 1945 should not be
underestimated. The UN may not always do what we would like it to
do, and it may sometimes seem a mere political talking-shop. But talk
is better than war, and relations between states are, by definition,
political. The elimination of smallpox was the work of a "political"
body, the World Health Organization, but that in no sense dimin-
ishes the importance of the task or the need to support it (Muller
1976). Supplementing such formal organizations as the UN or the Organization of American States or the Organization of African Unity
is a host of less formalized structures promoting the free exchange
of information across national boundaries and supporting international cooperation in myriad ways. These are structures in which all
participants have a stake, and which to that extent help diminish
conflict and promote dialogue.

## 2. As Others See Us

We may choose to divide world affairs into numerous problem areas
—war and peace, hunger, disease, illiteracy, and so on. But we
should not forget that these problems manifest themselves in human
populations. Our subject is people. Indeed, we ourselves are often
actors in the problems we study. Not only have the problems of the
world changed in scope and complexity in recent years, and not only
have advances in technology created new difficulties and helped
solve old ones, but the ideas and aspirations of much of the world
have changed—our own included. One of the greatest challenges
facing education in world affairs is the cultivation in our students of
an understanding of the motives of other people and of the social and
psychological (and historical) settings that cause them to think and

act as they do. Unmitigated malevolence is a poor motivator: Most people, even when they do wrong, think they are doing right. We must learn to understand others' motives, as well as our own, with greater sophistication.

As technology flows outward from the industrialized nations, and as knowledge of these nations becomes more widespread in the developing countries (accelerated by advances in mass communications), the aspirations of the developing peoples grow to keep pace. This should come as no surprise, nor should it necessarily be a cause for dismay. But it is the biggest single change in the complexion of world power in the last 20 years and it is a process little understood in this country. American education and the American media have exposed the leaders of many of the developing nations to the riches of this country. Their reaction has not always been an easy acquiescence to the status quo. In fact, the emergent self-awareness of many of the new nations has produced a riptide, an undercurrent, in the flow of knowledge and technology from the developed to the developing worlds. Are we not victims, these nations ask, of a new colonization, in which technology now plays the role of the colonial army and we continue to serve the needs of foreign economies? There is talk of a New International Economic Order, based (according to the declaration accepted by the United Nations in 1974) "on equity, sovereign equality, interdependence, common interest, and cooperation among all States." The so-called NIEO is in certain respects a political stick with which to beat the industrialized nations, but the aspirations it expresses are also serious ones, which we must learn to understand.

There is a dilemma at the heart of these new stirrings of political will. On the one hand, the new nations want to share in the wealth of the industrialized countries. On the other, they are eager to preserve many of their traditional values. Sometimes it serves the interests of those in political power to stress technological advancement and modernization. Sometimes they see in their own traditional cultures features that are politically useful. But in a larger sense, a sense transcending the political predilections of this or that ruling elite, the arguments for the preservation of a measure of diversity are very strong.

This stress on cultural autonomy and interdependence is in part a result of recent spectacular advances in communications technology —a field in which the United States continues to dominate (Tunstall 1976, 1977). Currently this country controls more than half the world market in computer hardware and its hold on the software market is still greater. Two of the world's four major news agencies are American and the other two are in the hands of ex-colonial powers. Films and television series earn $200 million in exports annually for this country and four of the five largest record distributors are American. The United States also dominates in the production and use of artificial satellites. It is argued by many in the developing world that the flow of communications is all in one direction —from the developed to the developing world. The new nations feel tied to the intellectual apron strings of the old and they resent the intrusion of Western, and particularly American, ways of thinking on societies that have their own values and ways of doing things. In the nations' wish for a new order of communication, the subject of intense debate in UNESCO and elsewhere in recent years (Masmoudi 1978; El-Oteifi 1979) is a desire to create and preserve a separate identity, and not to succumb to the same values as those that prevail in the industrialized countries. To what extent is such an aspiration right and proper? To what extent is it legitimate to restrict the flow of communication? To what extent are such restrictions mere excuses for political repression? The West is deeply skeptical of the motives of the developing countries; a similar skepticism toward the West prevails among the developing nations.

We allude to this sometimes acrimonious debate because it is a good example of the way in which politics and moral imperatives are intertwined in our dealings with the Third World. The very fact that the debate can be conducted at all is one indication of how international relations have changed over the past 30 years or so. The new states have found a voice in the United Nations, and the best endowed among them have also discovered economic power.

Nevertheless, the predominance of economic power in the world continues to lie on the northern side of the world, among the large industrialized nations. Here, too, the situation has changed dramatically in recent years. At the core of Western Europe, in the European Community, lies a partially integrated economy, pulled this way and that by internal rivalries but integrated in many respects. The Community is now expanding to take in new members. Its external trade is increasingly enmeshed with the nations of Eastern Europe, who have pulled away from the Soviet Union and now pursue often independent courses, though constantly held in check by their master to the east. Japan, South Korea, Singapore, and others have taken their places among the major industrialized powers. China, the great enigma, clouds the foreign policy considerations of everyone. And through it all the rivalry between the United States and the Soviet Union goes on, and the squabbles and quarrels of individual nations take place in the constant shadow of the nuclear threat.

Though the East-West rivalry may be a constant in the world array of power, recent events have shown with startling clarity that neither grouping of nations is monolithic. Nor is the Soviet Union winning the hearts and minds of the developing world. In fact, there is every indication that a new pluralism, a new polycentrism, is entering the relations among states. The old residual alliances are breaking up and a new pragmatism is appearing. This fact in itself only confirms the importance of an understanding of people and their motives. At the best of times one nation can only hope to have an inkling of the motives behind the actions of another. We must learn to understand how people feel about us, about one another, about their places in the world; and we must act on this understanding, whether as specialists in world affairs, as leaders and opinion makers, or as ordinary citizens.

## 3. The Response of the United States

When we turn from consideration of other countries' attitudes toward the United States (and they are obviously far more complex and diverse than our brief comments could suggest) and look at our own attitudes to the rest of the world, the record is mixed. The 1970s have been puzzling years for this country, beginning and ending with events of ironic significance. The decade began with our invasion of Cambodia, which broke on April 30, 1970, as the United States tried vainly to contain the war by expanding it. On December 29, 1979, the Soviet Union invaded Afghanistan, prompted by motives seemingly as self-contradictory as those of its archrival 10 years earlier. In 1970 the United States vetoed in the Security Council the economic isolation of Rhodesia; in 1980 it actively supported Zimbabwean independence. And in November 1979 53 Americans were taken hostage in Tehran and suffered 444 days of captivity.

While there are those who delight in pointing to the ineptitudes of the United States in one country after another, our record is no worse, and may be considerably better, than that of other nations. But the fact remains that we are insufficiently prepared to cope with the complexities of the new world order that is gradually and inexorably coming upon us. Keller and Roel (1980: 81) point out that "studies in television suggest that Americans receive less exposure to foreign countries than any other people in the world" with the possible exception of China. Content analysis of the popular press produces comparable results. In 1945 some 2,500 staff correspondents from the American press were stationed abroad; 30 years later the number had dropped to 429. There may be many reasons for this, not all of them indicating a decline in interest or quality, but the figures are disturbing.

Educational statistics are also worrying—at every level. The teaching of foreign languages in elementary schools, an expanding sector in the midsixties, has now more or less stopped altogether. While 24 percent of American high school students were studying a language in 1965, by 1976 the figure had fallen to 18 percent. Between 1968 and 1977 enrollment in college language courses fell by 17.7 percent. Nor do the statistics show a rise in interest in other aspects of international studies. As for the federal government, its funding of international studies in colleges and universities has declined steadily over the past 10 or 15 years—in fact, by as much as 50 percent in real dollars over a 10-year period (Pres. Comm. 1979: 6).

It is curious that this lack of awareness of international affairs and international expertise is taking place at a time when the need is greatest. It has negative effects in many ways. First, there is a shortage of skilled experts in international affairs—experts trained in leading universities, with specialized knowledge of particular fields or geographical areas. Second, relatively little attention is given to the international dimension in the general education of our school and college students. This means that the public is less conscious than it might be of the degree and nature of America's involvement with the world beyond its borders and of the options and constraints involved. Third, and related to this, the relative lack of attention to world events in the mass media tends to reinforce and compound the problem.

With respect to each of these areas—specialized education, general education, public opinion—there is a growing uneasiness on the part of many Americans about our readiness to grapple with the problems of today and tomorrow. That in itself is encouraging. Keller and Roel, quoted earlier, prepared their report at the behest of the Modern Language Association of America, whose task forces on language and public life have done much to alert the nation's intellectual leaders to the gravity of the situation. Within months of the establishment of the MLA task forces came the decision to establish a President's Commission on Language and International Studies, which filed its report in late 1979. Legislation on Capitol Hill, stirrings among curriculum planners at all educational levels, growing interest in the problem among business leaders—all these factors suggest that now is the time to bring about some change of direction and priorities with respect to the role of international awareness and international studies in this country.

The problem of educating and effectively utilizing experts in foreign affairs is an old one. The activities of the United States in international commerce, for example, have gone on for the most part out-side the intellectual reach of university-trained specialists in inter-national affairs. Given the extent to which emphasis is placed on the college training of future business people in this country, and the ex-tent to which commerce does indeed call on the assistance of univer-sity-trained specialists in management and finance, this relative failure to reach beyond management into the international fields seems puzzling at the least.

Likewise it is a common cry among legislators, government offi-cials, and outside critics that so many of our foreign policy decisions are made without adequate consideration of local conditions or without adequate recourse to specialist knowledge. Despite numer-ous studies on the matter and a great deal of righteous indignation, the precise nature of the problem remains unclear. There is evi-dence that on certain subjects and areas there simply exist no spe-cialists, or so few as to make little difference. In other instances the experts exist but they are not consulted. In yet other cases the ex-perts exist and are consulted but their advice is ignored. Of course, universities and governments are engaged in very different enter-prises, and establishing effective working relationships between the two will always be difficult. It is the function of academics to raise complex questions, and it is the function of people in government or commerce to provide clear answers. The questions have a way of in-terfering with the answers: Sometimes one can come up with neater-sounding solutions to problems by ignoring (either consciously or un-consciously) the accumulation of evidence. Occasionally large bu-reaucracies may work out complex mechanisms to circumvent the "messy" questions altogether. The fate of U.S. China specialists dur-ing the Cold War is one example of this process: Their views con-flicted with the preconceptions of senior policy makers, so they were labeled subversive and shunted aside (Koen 1974: 113-94). McCar-thyism did untold damage by limiting the flow of objective informa-tion and by exacting penalties, explicit or tacit, for the use of such objective information as did get through.

The view is widely held that, in the aftermath of the McCarthy era, the United States misjudged the situation in Vietnam out of ig-norance of local conditions. Our collective knowledge of the Viet-namese language and people was certainly marginal at the onset of the war. Even at its end the number of experts remained small. But courses in Vietnamese were being offered as early as the midfifties at Cornell, Michigan State, and the universities of Washington and Hawaii. There is little evidence that the expertise so generated was ever fully used. Officials in Washington chose to ignore the advice of

Foreign Service officers in the field, who were largely opposed to the kind of involvement subsequently undertaken; decisions were apparently made primarily on the basis of priorities already set, having to do with European politics and the alliance with the French, rather than on any clear understanding of the political or social reality in Southeast Asia (Luce 1972; Chaliand 1972; FitzGerald 1972). In Iran we may have made many of the same mistakes. Barry Rubin's recent study on that country shows how, as in Indochina, policy decisions tended to shape people's perceptions rather than the other way about (Rubin 1980: 208). There continue to be startlingly few speakers of Farsi in the Foreign Service or Iran experts in government in general (despite the existence of strong programs on Iran in our universities).

Recent events in Iran, Afghanistan, and Southeast Asia have made clear once again that the existence of a cadre of experts in the universities does not necessarily imply their utilization by our political leadership. The fault may not lie exclusively with government officials or politicians: Much of this expertise may be in topics or in approaches not easily accessible to the formulators of foreign policy. Mechanisms for increasing the responsiveness of universities to national needs are probably required and a broader sense of those national needs on the part of government would clearly help. Foreign affairs agencies do not always make effective use of the specialists they recruit: Career executives are encouraged to become generalists, not specialists (Berryman and others 1979: 45). And many experts, for one reason or another, are never recruited at all.

The use of specialists in international affairs by government and business is only the tip of a very large iceberg. Specialists do not exist in a vacuum, but their employment results from a felt need on the part of generalists and, in some less direct sense, on the part of the public. Only when the electorate insists that foreign policy decisions be made on the basis of all available evidence, and only when the public is willing to consider available options, will the foreign policy expert, the area studies expert, the linguist, be used as he or she should. This leads again to the problem that is our main concern in this book—that of general education.

For numerous reasons this is not an easy problem. Historically, as many scholars have pointed out, our American society is assimilationist and integrationist. Over the years we have absorbed a vast range of nationalities and races whose overriding desire has been to become American, to differentiate themselves from those they left behind and break the old ties. This process of absorption has led inevitably to a concentration on American ideas and values

(Rudolph 1977: 65)—ideas and values which, because of the very fact that they are not the natural heritage of many of those who espouse them, must be repeatedly articulated, written down, recited, and reaffirmed.

This long melting pot tradition may now be weakening. We place more emphasis on ethnicity than we once did—with results disquieting to many who value a sense of American cultural homogeneity. Our society to an increasing degree recognizes the importance of cultural diversity and differing personal roots. There is at least some effort to learn more about the countries from which our ancestors came, and even to revive and maintain their customs and languages in the new American setting. Of course, ethnicity may simply produce what Bruce LaBrack (1980), in a different context, has called "dual ethnocentrism"—dedication to the imagined virtues of a single nation or people in addition to the United States. Nevertheless, it does admit the possibility of diversity and can lead us to appreciate diversity in others. With 12 million native speakers of Spanish in our midst, most of them born and raised in this country, we are one of the world's largest Spanish-speaking countries (Hayden 1977), but it is only in recent years, through the bilingual education movement (with all its own vicissitudes) and an increasing awareness of the legal rights of Spanish speakers, that we have begun to appreciate this fact.

Aiding our efforts are other factors. More Americans are traveling abroad. More and more foreign visitors are coming to this country. The influence of other nations on our economy and our way of life is observable at every turn. To a greater and greater extent we are obliged to deal with other peoples as equals. It is not exactly that the United States is shifting from a condition of isolation into active participation in world affairs, but that it is learning, or must learn, how to become a partner rather than a dominant power. What Senator William Fulbright (1966) called the "arrogance of power"—a sense of manifest destiny concerning America's role in the world—has probably always been an improper way of handling our international relations, but it has now become impractical as well.

Education is not the only element needed in the adaptation of the United States to this new view of the world, but it is one of the most important. If educators do not take the lead in making the public more aware of the world and in creating a sense of world responsibility and global values among our citizens, it is difficult to know who will. And if our schoolmasters are not ourselves, they may ultimately prove to be our rivals, whose mode of education is more abrupt, more painful, more demoralizing. The place to start, then, is in school and college curricula, in the attitudes of educators, and in their prescriptions for their students.

## 4. Beyond Nostalgia

As Secretary Vance pointed out, the United States may feel nostalgic for the old simplicity, for a time when supposedly the nations were uncomplaining and the old spirit of expansion was still alive, but it cannot be brought back. Indeed, we more than anyone else were responsible for its demise. Naked force is no answer. Technology largely developed in the United States now ensures that the miseries of war flash instantaneously on television screens all across the world. It is partly due to American leadership that the smaller and weaker nations are able to raise their voices in the chambers of the UN. The dimension of human psychology and human understanding now has its place firmly established in the art of war as well as the art of peace. As one student of the science of military strategy puts it, "Bad anthropology makes for bad strategy" (Bernard Brodie, quoted by Howard, 1980).

It is fashionable, and has been for a number of years, to suggest that the world is becoming increasingly complicated. But such a view is an oversimplification. It is not that the world is more complicated but that we have cultivated a more complicated approach to it, as we become more aware of the limits of power and as greater participation in decision making (again, largely a consequence of the revolution in communications) gives more voices the power to be heard. Above all, the ever present awareness that we possess the power to destroy ourselves, through environmental as well as nuclear catastrophe, adds to each decision a new dimension of agony. "A democracy," wrote de Tocqueville, "cannot get at the truth without experience, and many nations may perish for lack of the time to discover their mistakes." We would not be the first to attribute to de Tocqueville an uncanny clairvoyance: What was once true of nations is now true of humanity itself. As was noted by a recent Club of Rome report, arguing for a new type of learning, we can no longer hope to learn only from experience, for the experience may be fatal (Botkin, Elmandjra, Malitza: 1979).

Many feel that the old battles of national sovereignty are, or ought to be, outdated and that world loyalties will gradually outstrip national loyalties. But another, largely unspoken, attitude sharpens resistance to this view. Many people fear that the inculcation of "global" values, of a world view of things, will somehow weaken the national resolve of our own society and expose us to the manipulation of other nations. But neither innocence nor ignorance provides protection against manipulation. Lack of knowledge may on occasion make action easier, but it also heightens the probability that such action will prove self-defeating. We must have the courage to seek out, and act upon, the international facts of life.

The realities of interdependence are with us all. Interdependence is not so much an ideal as a very simple fact. Even those who fear it must learn to understand it, if only to set limits to it. At issue is whether we shall manage interdependence effectively, not whether we have the collective capability to wish it away.

# 2

## American Higher Education and the World View

# American Higher Education and the World View

## 1. The American World of Learning

Is the American educational system ready for the changes implied in the notion of the United States working in cooperation with other nations, given today's complexities? Any generalization about the American higher education system is dangerous: It has been distinguished by nothing so much as diversity. Nevertheless, if we look back at the history of higher education in this country, we find that the curriculum has, on the whole, adapted remarkably well to the changing needs of American society—at least as those needs were perceived at the time. The propelling reasons for this adaptation were not for the most part intellectual: The American educational system has been less than successful in distinguishing the enduring and important from the transitory and less important. The reasons arose largely from the fact that throughout much of its history American higher education has kept pace with, or even outstripped, the demand for its services. In fact, there has been a surplus of college places, and perhaps of colleges, over the stretch of the history of American institutions. The present condition, in which colleges are threatened with shrinking enrollments, was familiar indeed to many college administrators in nineteenth-century America (Rudolph 1977: 172-3). The student has always been an important determinant of college curricula.

Furthermore, American colleges and universities have always regarded themselves as social institutions and, to a greater or lesser extent, a part of the broader political fabric of the nation. Almost from its beginning Harvard College trained administrators as well as young men for the ministry, and the colonial colleges educated that small elite that ultimately would kick over the British traces. The great expansion of higher education in the nineteenth century was in large part a product, and a cause, of the opening of the Midwest and the West. Many new colleges and universities were geared to the immediate practical concerns of a nation in need of teachers, engineers, and specialists in agriculture. And the system was not hidebound, as it was in Britain, for example, by centralized control or the need for government approval; if there was a felt need, someone moved in and filled it.

Many of the colleges were, of course, founded and run by the states themselves. Others benefited from private philanthropy, again frequently of a practical bent, emphasizing social usefulness. In our own day the system would collapse without the active support of governments at the local, state, and federal levels. The largesse of the federal government is in no sense disinterested, and since the Second World War governmental influence in higher education has grown steadily more pervasive. It has entered the field after the fact, as it were, and has concerned itself not with the establishment of institutions of higher education but with the purchase of a wide array of services. In short, interventions from outside education have in many respects controlled the educational purse strings. On the other hand, though much of the system is tied closely to public agencies, it still gives at least the appearance of independence.

This independence, the sense that much of the system of higher education is its own master, coupled with that moral strain that has been part of American culture and society from the beginning, has caused American educators to wonder repeatedly about the higher goals of their calling and the institutions they serve. Perhaps because of that utopian awareness that they were building institutions from the ground up and were free to shape them untrammeled by the constraints besetting their European counterparts, the founders of colleges felt more of a need to explain themselves. The idea of the liberal arts, transplanted from European classicism, became the justification for what was essentially a new kind of civic education, derived from moral philosophy but in tune with the developing nation-state. "Unless a general acquaintance with many branches of knowledge, good as far as it goes, be attainable by great numbers of men, there can be no such thing as an intelligent public opinion," declared Charles William Eliot in his inaugural address at Harvard, "and in the modern world the intelligence of public opinion is the one condition of social progress." His sentiments have been echoed and were to be restated to the point of platitude in the succeeding century. In this sense the American system of higher education has had at its very center the high ideals of the American Constitution and the practical realities of the country. In so far as these constitutional ideals coincide with the aspirations of all humanity, the American system can be regarded as already international in spirit. "The profoundest and most wide-seeing minds of Greece and Rome," remarked Alexis de Tocqueville, "never managed to grasp the very general but very simple conception of the likeness of all men and of the equal right of all at birth to liberty."

But it is this conviction of common humanity, which de Tocqueville identified in the American spirit, that in certain respects makes change difficult. The belief that all the rest of the world is like us, though this belief may be derived from the most laudable of principles, makes for a certain inflexibility in coming to terms with the aspirations of those who do not share these ideals, whose background and culture and upbringing have been different, or who have inherited a different set of social structures. American enthusiasm for human decency, defined in American terms, can be variously potent, touching, or oppressive. Precisely because of the close link between the espousal of these principles and the country's institutions, even American virtue becomes a kind of national institution. It forms alliances with other, less palatable institutions, and the whole becomes eminently exportable. This must surely be the only nation in the world where automobile manufacturers produce commercials claiming that they have helped guarantee the constitutional right to freedom of movement.

Although the American college or university has proven its adaptability, and although it has been hospitable to (indeed, derived from) ideas from abroad, it is not by nature or history a disinterested and expansive international institution. The countries of Western Europe had universities before they became fully aware of themselves as nations, with national needs and priorities. Bologna, Paris, Oxford, Cambridge—these institutions served what was in effect an international clientele. Later they became parts of what could be described as national systems of higher education and in several cases have become more ethnocentric today than many American universities. Nevertheless, the United States lacks this particular international legacy. The builders of Johns Hopkins or Catholic University or Clark University—institutions created in the late nineteenth century essentially as graduate and research universities—had the model of the German universities in mind, but in practice they created elements in a national system, with national priorities.

Because of its interest in technology, to which it was more receptive than many of its European counterparts, and its interest in research, the American university has had a profound effect on the economies and thinking of large parts of the world. The United States is the world's greatest supplier of education as a commodity. It plays host to an enormous number of education-related visitors —researchers, students, faculty members—from every corner of the world. As noted earlier, the foreign student is frequently the agent of change in the developing world; returning home, he or she shapes new countries in terms and in forms familiar to the inhabitants of the old. Through this process of educating and returning, the influence of Western technology and Western institutions expands. But despite their numbers, foreign students have relatively little effect on the institutions at which they study. They come essentially as clients on our terms. Though we do worry from time to time about the adjustment of our system to suit the needs of the foreigner (e.g., Myer 1979), the fact of educating large parts of the globe has not led to the articulation of an international mission in a larger sense: We perceive as our first mission the service of our home ground.

We are confronted, then, with a paradox: The United States educates a larger number of foreign nationals than any other country. Yet, institutionally, it remains largely oblivious to this fact. One of the tasks before us is to create a greater sense of reciprocity, learning from our foreign visitors as well as teaching them, and modifying our thinking about ourselves and our place in the world. The truth is that while American education has, by its concentration on the particulars of technology, changed in a fundamental way the daily lives of much of the globe, it has been less successful in setting these extraordinary advances in an ethical, human context. It is not so much that we have internationalized the American system through this process as that we have Americanized the international system; much of the international organization of knowledge, particularly in the social sciences, has taken on an American cast, dominated by the English language and by American thought patterns. As America's share in the world economy lessens, it may prove impossible to sustain this American world of learning and we may be forced to adapt to new pressures and modes of thought. Yet we may not be ready to do so.

## 2.  Obstacles to the World View

The history of American higher education is the history of the interaction of its clients. In each case—private philanthropy; students; local, state, and federal governments—a clearly definable investor bought into the system and affected its policies and direction. The colonial colleges laid the groundwork for the development of a very different set of institutions in the Midwest as that area opened up. These institutions grew in parallel with the research universities. The country moved gradually from colonies to national development to national maturity. But the next stage—from national to international status—lacks an obvious patron. Thus, transforming a nationally oriented educational system into one that takes into consideration, to a degree proportional to recent shifts, the importance of an international approach will be difficult at best. At the moment its main ally is an altogether dubious one—the federal government, whose concern, when all is said and done, is not necessarily with committing higher education to an international perspective but with strengthening America's role in the world.

It is an uneasy alliance, not least because much of it goes on, at least as far as international affairs are concerned, in an atmosphere of crisis. The federal government's involvement in higher education, of course, goes back to the early nineteenth century (Mayville 1980). The Morrill Act of 1862 made possible a decisive expansion of the commitment of the states to higher education. But the federal government's direct involvement in curricular matters came about initially as a result of the crash programs devised during the Second World War to provide specialists in international affairs urgently needed at the time. The Second World War, in fact, stands like a great watershed between a world centered on Europe and North America and today's polycentric world. It is not exactly that the Second World War opened up the rest of the world, but that the rest of the world intruded on trade patterns traditionally controlled and managed by the powers of Europe and North America. A European war became truly international at that point when Japanese planes crossed the Pacific—when distance was conquered by technology. This process has been accelerating ever since.

In the 1950s and 1960s the United States could afford, at least in some measure, the eccentricities of a State Department devoted to a Manichaean approach to foreign affairs. The country's hold on foreign markets stood firm, its industry prosperous, its resolve, despite Korea, largely unchallenged. And the Korean War was different from the war in Vietnam—much closer, in fact, to the model of the two world wars, with clearly defined fronts and opposing armies. With little need for knowledge of other peoples, in the period following the Allied victory, the United States did relatively little to adapt its training to accommodate its changing world role.

Voices were raised even in the fifties to deplore this state of affairs. The launching of the Ford Foundation Area Fellowship Program in 1952 marked the beginning of what was to become the heyday of foundation funding for international programs—in which Carnegie, Rockefeller, and others soon joined. And the vision that created the United Nations, that went into the writing of the Universal Declaration of Human Rights and into the Constitution of UNESCO, with its ringing declaration that "since wars begin in the minds of men, it is in the minds of men that the defenses of peace must be constructed"—this vision certainly led to important efforts at curricular reform and the introduction of international elements into the curriculum. There was a marked increase in interest, for example, in the need to train Americans in other languages. During this period significant international courses entered the curricula of government and political science departments and began to appear in economics programs. Programs in international relations multiplied all across the country.

But it was no homegrown crisis or local Cassandra that precipitated the biggest change. The launching of Sputnik in 1957 did more to advance American awareness of the need to compete educationally than any other single modern event. What before had appeared as primarily a political and military rivalry between the United States and the Soviet Union took on the appearance of a scientific and educational rivalry, and government, at least, rose to the occasion. The National Defense Education Act of 1958 helped lay the groundwork for a shift in U.S. interests overseas, as attention moved from the rebuilding of Europe to the development of the newly independent nations of Africa and Asia. In this respect it paralleled similar initiatives in our foreign aid programs. By putting new resources into high schools and colleges, the act led to a positive explosion of interest in area studies. Although NDEA can be seen as an effort to outflank the Soviet Union in a bid for the economic and political spoils of the crumbling overseas empires of Europe (the parallels with Britain and Russia and the Turkish Empire in the 1870s are striking), it contributed to a growing acknowledgment of pluralism and a general optimism about the ability of the United States to improve the condition of the developing nations—an optimism that also helped lead to the creation of the Peace Corps in the early 1960s.

The opening of area studies centers on many campuses had an indirect, though important, effect on undergraduate programs, extending the range of electives to take in new parts of the globe and giving increased attention to the non-European world. New courses in comparative development or in comparative political systems began to appear; there was an increase of interest in non-Western religions (though the causes of this were complex); there also occurred a notable increase in the range of geographical interest on the part of history departments.

But essentially this process constituted a kind of filtering down from new graduate programs, and such subjects were not so much taken into account by the planners of the curriculum as added on in a period of rapid expansion of resources, facilities, and faculty. Although undergraduate rather than graduate enrollments were in the majority from the beginning (Lambert 1974: 375-87) and NDEA had made allocations for undergraduate programs from the start, then as now, graduate programs determined hiring decisions and most internal resource allocations, inevitably shaping the nature of undergraduate courses and programs offered. The reality is that, even if the options increased, the basic curricula of colleges remained essentially unchanged. It would be mere carping to suggest that the federal money invested in area studies and related activities during this period did not have as much effect on undergraduate education as it should have. In any case, the primary aim of the funding was to create specialists, not generalists, and to train graduate students, not undergraduates.

But, as with the State Department China hands, we can only regret that the existence of knowledge and resources, made possible by the government, was limited in its effect by inhospitable structures: The integration of area studies programs into the universities, earnestly desired by many in the academy, was neither as rapid nor as complete as it might have been. In fact, the very existence of outside money allowed specialists in area studies and international studies to carry on their work under the aegis of universities without having to confront these universities directly on intellectual grounds and bring about a change in their thinking. When, 10 or 12 years later, the expansion slowed and retrenchment ultimately set in, most of the old curriculum had survived. It was often the new arrivals that withered and died, never having felt the necessity to secure a place for themselves in the center of the academic enterprise.

We might contrast this with the experiences of an earlier era. The departmentalization of the research universities was primarily a product of the particular needs of the natural sciences and, to a lesser extent, of the social sciences. The humanities followed this trend primarily to secure equal treatment in an increasingly rigidly divided structure. In fact, the humanities, primarily in the twenties and thirties, entered what might best be described as a pseudoscientific period, in which they imitated the methodologies of the sciences and sought an exactness that it was probably never their nature to achieve. But one of the consequences of this sacrifice of integrity—this espousal of a method in many respects alien to them— was their acceptance into the departmental structure and their ensuring of their future. One might argue whether the results of such security were beneficial or detrimental. Did a field like English really prosper by the application of methods that vested every literary text with importance and led to a virtually endless proliferation of scholarly studies based on what were in many instances texts intellectually unworthy of the loving attention they received? Regardless of our answer, it was the creation of a discipline of English, the demarcation of a piece of intellectual turf, that assured the future of the field. It is this process of institutional socialization that has been lacking in the development of area studies programs and centers. They have never been obliged to engage the central concerns of the academy in direct intellectual debate, and their priorities in which those concerns are ordered have largely remained unchanged.

For reasons such as these many specialists in international studies now find themselves in difficult straits. Inevitably they look to the federal government for further sustenance. The recent report of the President's Commission on Foreign Language and International Studies devotes much attention (understandably, perhaps, given its charge) to ways in which the federal government should support international studies—but in today's context what is ultimately far more important is the definition and articulation of the goals and priorities of the entire community of teachers and scholars engaged in aspects of international education. The challenge is less financial than intellectual: The academy at large must come to terms with the implications of international education, and it is probably only the international education community that can bring that about.

It is perhaps ironic that the great crisis in the disciplines came later, at a time when, in the agonies of the late sixties and early seventies, colleges and universities were accused of functioning as a kind of invisible government and condoning the foreign policy of the United States. At the same time, the full-blown expansion of higher education had made tough intellectual decisions about the nature of the disciplines themselves and about their philosophical priorities unnecessary, or avoidable. In fact, the very structure of knowledge in terms of so many disciplines, inventions for the most part of the nineteenth and early twentieth centuries, was called into question, and their apologists were ill equipped to defend them.

Some of this dispute has now died down, in part because many dissidents have chosen to leave the academy, and in part because the imperatives of job security and advancement, to say nothing of the need to prove to students that they can move easily into the job market, have brought an uneasy conformity. But for all that some academics might wish it, there can be no going back. The world of 1950 and 1960 has gone; we live in a fool's paradise to think otherwise. We are left with the task of building new structures, or adapting the old, to deal with a world in which the United States no longer holds sway, and in which the received values of the past can no longer prevail without scrutiny.

The college administrator or faculty member attempting to expand an institution's commitment to the teaching of international affairs must nonetheless come to terms with what might be called the ideological block of learning about the world. It appears in many forms in the academy. We naturally recoil from unpalatable truths and there is much about today's world that we would rather not confront. Even education, devoted to the pursuit of knowledge and motivated by the desire to understand, is not immune to such psychological obstacles. It may not be enough to counter with the observation that knowledge of the world acquaints us with challenges as well as disasters, opportunities as well as fearsome truths, but the point is nonetheless worth making. Of course, opposition to change seldom takes the form of direct address on the issues. Efforts to increase attention to international matters in the curriculum will be blocked not so much by arguments about their irrelevance as by problems of scheduling, and money, and by appeals to the need to maintain existing courses and programs—and to the need for intellectual rigor. These arguments are important, but they need to be looked at dispassionately and with care. It is sometimes better to face these issues head-on—to ask ourselves questions about priorities and to proceed by substitution rather than addition.

Even among those who believe the attention to international matters in the average college curriculum is inadequate, there will exist sharp differences of opinion on how such lacks should be remedied. We must distinguish here between efforts to understand the world on our terms—in order to increase our control over it, or to function more effectively in it—and efforts to understand some part of the world or section of its population in the terms of those who are studied. In short, we must recognize a potential conflict between those who feel that international affairs must be taught more diligently to preserve America's position in the world and those who espouse the need to find global solutions to human problems—what Robert Johansen has termed the contrast of national interest and human interest. This conflict of goals has, of course, always existed in American education, most sharply since the federal government became involved in area studies and related fields. As noted earlier, the impulse behind the National Defense Education Act was the need to strengthen the United States in its dealings with the rest of the world: The emphasis was on *defense* and *nation* as well as on *education*. Behind the thinking of Congress was not altruism but the building of an educational Maginot Line. When, eight years later, the International Education Act came before Congress, the speeches in its favor were eloquent indeed; but, for whatever reason, its programs were never funded.

Though many would deny the existence of this conflict of views, it seems inescapable. The alternative is to suppose that what is good for America is good for the world—as though the national interest is never in conflict with the international. The lobbyist for international education may occasionally tend toward such arguments, but they rest on shaky premises. Yet if these two views lead to very different conceptions of curricula and priorities, they agree on one point: international affairs needs greater attention in the undergraduate curriculum. Either way, American survival depends on it.

## 3. The Current Situation

If we examine the present state of international education in our colleges and schools, we are likely to come away somewhat depressed. In recent years several studies have drawn attention to the often glaring inadequacies in students' international knowledge and awareness at all levels of education. We are told that students lack basic information—who rules what country, where it is situated, and so on. We are also told that they lack the ability, or knowledge, to interpret information on international affairs.

Aside from the new Council on Learning assessment of college students, perhaps the most significant study on this subject was one carried out in 1974 and published by the U.S. Office of Education in 1979 under the title *Other Nations, Other Peoples*. The study examined some 600 students in fourth, eighth, and twelfth grades in 27 states. It revealed that no less than 61 percent of the twelfth-grade students thought that non-European countries were members of the Common Market, and that about a quarter of the eighth and twelfth graders believed that either China or India extended into Europe. Back in 1974, the Middle East, according to the researchers, was "a relatively unknown, undifferentiated area for most students." As for their knowledge of American affairs, only 49 percent of eighth and 70 percent of twelfth graders recognized the intent of the Bill of Rights, and large numbers of students (50 percent and 41 percent respectively) thought that the United States spent more on its space program than on defense. The most quoted answer on this survey related to Golda Meir, who, declared 32 percent of the eighth graders and 27 percent of twelfth graders, was the President of Egypt.

A more recent survey, by John H. Petersen, who looked at attitudes of junior and senior high school students in Kentucky, is less pessimistic. Petersen suggests that the students he surveyed are "far from being unsophisticated parochials" on international matters, despite their relative isolation in the heartland. Their views—a rejection of isolationism, support for the United Nations, and belief that conflict will continue to play an important role in world affairs —suggest a degree of thoughtfulness and realism about international relations at considerable variance with at least some of the findings of the Office of Education survey.

We should in any case beware of taking such findings too seriously. They may tell us considerably less about developing attitudes
among students than we think. It is ironic that the very advocates of
an awareness of pluralism in world affairs tend to forget about the
pluralism of the American educational system. Many countries possess standardized public examinations, or prescribed curricula, or
even prescribed textbooks. This country does not. There are good
schools and bad schools, knowledgeable teachers and deplorably ignorant teachers. The system's pluralism tends to bring out the ex-
tremes: The good teachers are unconstrained by uncongenial textbooks, the bad teachers are unredeemed by the crutch of a standard
curriculum. Then again, so much depends on the way in which sur-
veys are carried out and, particularly, on the way in which questions are asked. Taking survey findings out of context is a doubtful
undertaking at the best of times, and quoting answers without quoting questions verbatim may also be misleading.

More could be done to foster international attitudes in children
—especially in lower grades, where students are more receptive to
learning about other peoples. Research indicates that middle child-
hood, before the onset of puberty, may be the critical period for developing a global perspective, before prejudice and stereotyping
create barriers and negative attitudes (Torney 1979: 68; Carnie
1972). Such efforts are especially important in a large country like
our own. A cross-national study sponsored by the International Association for the Evaluation of Educational Achievement, which explored the knowledge acquired by 10- and 14-year-old students from
9 countries about the international political system, found that children in countries like the Netherlands, with a high level of international contact, were more internationally minded than children in
countries like the United States (Torney 1977: 15).

Clearly, part of the mission of teachers should be to keep young
minds open while at the same time increasing their ability to make
sophisticated judgments—no easy task under any circumstances.
Teachers themselves often lack a sophisticated awareness of the
outside world. In many respects this is hardly surprising. Trained in
an atmosphere that pays little attention to international affairs (except, of course, for those specializing in languages and social
studies), teachers do not naturally come to see international matters
as important. Many passed through college in the late sixties and
early seventies, when Americans had turned away from the outside
world and concentrated on domestic issues. This is not to suggest
that teachers are incapable of retraining themselves or updating

their knowledge. But they are inclined to reflect the values of their society unless efforts are made to stress the importance of moving beyond those values. Unless and until a knowledge of the world is given prominence in the curricula of teacher training programs and in state certification requirements, teachers' parochial attitudes may prove one of the largest stumbling blocks to broadening pupils' attitudes.

While this statement may seem harsh, there is some evidence to support it. The Council on Learning's ambitious survey of college students in 1980 (Barrows et al.) examined "what college students actually know and perceive about global relationships" and measured "their comprehension of current global complexities." The survey, like that described in *Other Nations, Other Peoples*, was carried out by the Educational Testing Service and funded by the federal government. Asked to answer a complex and sophisticated test on global awareness, education majors scored lowest of all fields—including fields normally regarded as remote from international affairs, such as the natural sciences. This may simply reflect the relative sophistication of students who study education; many of the better teachers, at least at the high school level, major in other fields and pick up teacher certification along the way. But it does confirm our impression that a greater level of global awareness among teachers is imperative if we are ever to rise above the current restricted view of the nature of international affairs.

Some problems with this method of teaching global awareness have already been discussed. But for the most part the picture revealed by the Council on Learning survey is by no means as depressing as some prophets of doom had predicted. There are serious gaps in students' knowledge and sophistication, to be sure. But the eighth graders who had difficulty in distinguishing between Egypt and Israel (a mistake, some would say, more pardonable today than then) scored significantly well, six years later, on numbers of questions related to the role of the United States in world affairs. Nevertheless, "even able students," say the authors of the new college survey (Barrows et al. 1981: 20-1), were confused by the following:

- The degree to which U.S. dependence on foreign oil increased during the 1970s and the vulnerability of our economy to increases in oil prices or decreases in the supply.
- The membership of OPEC and why it can raise oil prices.
- The causes of inadequate nutrition as a global problem.
- The United States' record on signing human rights treaties adopted by the United Nations and the major accomplishment of the Helsinki Accords.

- The comparative world membership of Islam and Christianity and the countries in which Islam predominates or has a significant minority.
- The difficulties connected with either national self-sufficiency or dependency in a world of interdependent nations.
- The historical origins of the Western sovereign territorial state and the modern state system and the emergence of nationalist movements as significant political forces in European history.
- The patterns of world birth and death rates today.
- The pattern of the world's past and possible future consumption of fossil fuels.
- The reasons for the lack of substantial progress toward world peace during the twentieth century.
- The main purpose of the recently completed multilateral trade negotiations, and the demands of representatives of developing countries in the North-South talks.

There may be many reasons these weaknesses showed up on the test—some possibly relating to aspects of the test itself. (Is it that students did not know the significance of the Helsinki Accords, or that they had no notion of what the Helsinki Accords were, or that perhaps they did not agree with the Western-oriented value judgment on what aspects of the Accords were important? The last, we admit, is unlikely—but the whole issue is problematic.) The fact remains that the "informed citizenry" we would like to create is still far from existence—particularly if we bear in mind that these students are among the better informed of our younger citizens.

Offering prescriptions is no easy task. As any student of curricular reform knows, all good ideas have already been tried somewhere—and have generally failed. Yet there is always room somewhere for a new idea, a new experiment. Perhaps the biggest difficulty facing the reformer of higher education, at least at the undergraduate level, is the vertical organization of most large colleges and universities—by departments and schools. As Jencks and Riesman have pointed out (1968), and as Veysey (1965) and others have shown historically, over the years professional loyalties have largely replaced institutional loyalties among the professoriat. Teachers are first and foremost members of departments and disciplines, devoted to the training of graduate students and to the advancement of a scholarly career within a discipline. In such a configuration of priorities, reform, at least that of the general education of undergraduates, tends to take second place to the strengthening of graduate programs.

This contention has surfaced again recently in the debate over the Harvard core curriculum. In a sharply worded critique of the Harvard proposals in *Change* Magazine, Barry O'Connell (1978) points out that, primarily because of the dominance of disciplines and departments developed 70 or 80 years ago, "Harvard's conception of the essentials of a good education in 1978 is limited to subjects most scholars in 1900 would have regarded as the core." The statement is not entirely fair since, as Archimedes might have said, physics is physics is physics, and there is much about the world of 1900 that deserves to be preserved and studied in the world of 1978 or 2000. But O'Connell's central argument carries the weight of logic: Processes of communication, ways of looking at the world, the uses and abuses of technology, issues of war and peace, are significantly different today and they require a different approach, and probably a different conceptual framework, from that offered by a simple but uneasy coalition of the old disciplines. An observation by the researchers responsible for the Council on Learning's ETS survey may also be relevant here:

> The relative standing of seniors on the test was most directly related to their scores on parts of the test that dealt with arts and culture, war and armaments, race and ethnicity, relations among states, and international monetary and trade arrangements—topics usually encountered in traditional fields of undergraduate study. Topics such as environment, population, energy, human rights, health, and food, which fit less readily into the established framework of the academic disciplines, produced patterns of performance that were less similar to the pattern of the total test.

In short, many of today's problems require a new approach. But can educators, socialized in traditional disciplines, provide it? The structures of those disciplines may militate against the detailed study of some of the topics mentioned by the Council on Learning study. If so, we face a complex problem of academic organization, as well as an intellectual issue, in working them into the curriculum.

In this regard James Q. Wilson's response to O'Connell (1978: 42) may be less than totally reassuring. Referring to the processes of change in large institutions, he writes:

> The admirable features of a faculty are readily apparent. Individuals are left alone, no one presumes to have the authority to commit someone else to action without that someone's consent, inequalities (at least among the tenured members of the faculty) are slight...and deans govern more by indulgence than by command. The costs of this form of social organization are no less apparent. Change is slow and requires endless discussion; bold visions of an ideal curriculum are subjected to skeptical scrutiny; coordinated action is difficult to achieve; and the kinds of decisions most easily

made by bureaucracies either do not get made at all or are made
contingent on their winning a broader acceptance.

It is not surprising that most commentaries on the new curriculum at
Harvard stress the process whereby protracted discussion and compromise among an assortment of vested departmental interests finally brought forth a document on which everyone of authority could
agree. Given the strength of the departments at a research institution like Harvard, the achievement is remarkable; but one cannot escape the conviction that the *structures* of the institution are in important respects at odds with its educational objectives, at least as
far as undergraduate education is concerned.

## 4.  What Knowledge Is Enough?

The experience at Harvard has important lessons for would-be reformers. The present structure of departments and disciplines and
professorships, with all their vested interests, is a fact of academic
life. It would be irresponsible to prescribe their abolition—a task
probably impossible and perhaps not even desirable. We prefer to
recommend that the reformer work with and through them to shape
them to the ends of international education. It is a difficult, but not
impossible, undertaking—and it is this gradualist philosophy that informs most of what is said in the pages that follow.

We start with the assumption that all institutions, no matter how
forward-looking and how attuned to contemporary realities, can improve. We make no specific intellectual prescriptions, argue for no
core, specific major program, or mode of organization. We try instead to provide practical suggestions about processes of reform
and change, all directed to one end—increasing undergraduates'
awareness about the international dimensions of their world, encouraging them to transcend the confines of their own national point
of view or local preoccupations. We do, however, make certain assumptions, not so much about the content of education at any level
as about the skills and sensitivities a graduating American student
should have acquired. These include a sense of relativity as a human
being and as an American, of the relativity of one's own values
(though not so as to exclude an ability to distinguish between right
and wrong or to prefer and defend certain principles over others),
and an ability to adapt to a world of interlocking dependencies, in
which sharing becomes an essential part of survival. Clearly, a
knowledge of world problems—war and peace, hunger, literacy, disease, the right to a decent life, natural resources, environment—is
one essential element. So is a knowledge of foreign peoples and lan-

guages. In reply to the question "What global knowledge is enough?" George Bonham (1979b) and the task force on Education and the World View have enumerated three essential ingredients:

- A fundamental understanding of the key elements of global and national interdependence, as taught through the major fields in humanities, the social sciences, the pure sciences, the applied sciences, and the professional disciplines. This understanding should equip college students to analyze and respond intelligently to domestic and international developments. Such competence should be evidenced by a student's independent analysis of the most important strands of the new global circumstances and comprehension of the United States' increased interdependence with other nations for its survival and economic growth.
- A deeper knowledge and understanding of another culture, as seen through its history, language, literature, philosophy, economics, and politics. Student perceptions of another culture will substantially enhance the ability to understand the United States' needs and changing world position, and enable intelligent consideration of highly complex developments on the world scene. Sensitivity to other cultures; increased capacity to analyze issues, having learned other viewpoints; and enhanced tolerance of differences contribute to a citizenry better able to cope in the twenty-first century and to approach conflict resolution.
- General competence in a second language as a basis for the fuller comprehension of other cultures and of one's own in the global context. Language skills are becoming increasingly essential for communication in a wide range of contexts. Students' access to effective language instruction is therefore necessary to the college experience in the 1980s and beyond.

The three ingredients in this definition are unequal. The third is a skill—an ability to handle a total system of linguistic communication other than the student's own. The second should depend on the third: Only by knowing its language can a student gain comprehensive access to another culture. But the other two must ultimately rely on the first. A student must be somewhat at home in the larger world—equipped with the basic competencies to understand its complexities (and these competencies should include fact as well as opinion, data as well as the ability to analyze data, and, above all, the ability to distinguish between what is known and what is merely surmised; the catchy statistic is the bane of global studies). At the same time a student must learn how the disciplines can contribute to this understanding—how they interlock, supplement, sometimes even distort. This interrelationship of the disciplines is something frequently neglected in the conventional undergraduate education.

And the American student must be able to relate these matters to his or her own country, to make intelligent and ethical decisions about the present and the future, and to contribute to the management of an interdependent world in which the United States is a partner. He or she should know something about processes of institution building, and about international as well as national institutions that govern national and international relationships.

Some would argue that even this prescription is inadequate to the need. They would suggest that a fundamental change in consciousness is required if we are ever to adapt to the needs of the future. While we are nagged by the feeling that a fundamental change in consciousness may itself be a somewhat naive Western concept, and that our globalization should be less demonstrative and more gradual, we must acknowledge that in many respects the advocates of this position are right. Robert Hanvey, in a particularly sensitive presentation of the issues, suggests that an attainable global perspective should consist of five elements:

- **Perspective Consciousness**, "the recognition or awareness on the part of the individual that he or she has a view of the world that is not universally shared."
- **"State of the Planet" Awareness**, "awareness of prevailing world conditions and developments, including emerging conditions and trends."
- **Cross-Cultural Awareness**, "awareness of the diversity of ideas and practices to be found in human societies around the world."
- **Knowledge of Global Dynamics**, "modest comprehension of key traits and mechanisms of the world system."
- **Awareness of Human Choices**, "some awareness of the problems of choice confronting individuals, nations, and the human species as consciousness of the global system expands."

Most of this knowledge, even that prescribed by Hanvey, is already present in our colleges and universities. While the structures have been slow to change, American colleges have grown by addition and accretion, new courses attaching themselves to old curricula and new programs appearing at the peripheries of the old. The present undertaking calls not so much for the creation of new structures as for the realignment of the old—for an emphasis on new priorities among these options and a shifting of authority from some areas to others.

Even more important, and relatively underemphasized in the task force definition, is the need to diffuse throughout the curriculum, *overall*, a new sense of the global implications of knowledge. Most students take no undergraduate courses that are international in focus (except for straightforward language courses). Even if we strengthen the quality and quantity of programs and courses in international studies, we shall hardly affect most of the undergraduate population. As Richard Lambert puts it in his survey (1980: 156), "If we really want to make a dent upon the outlook of a substantial number of our students, we will have to reach more of them, and this means adding an international component to a large number of courses, including those that are currently entirely domestic in their subject matter." At the same time we must work to change the environment in which undergraduate education takes place. Making undergraduate education genuinely international in scope will require an effort of collective will that transcends matters of curricular reform and tinkering with courses. A broader view of the enterprise of undergraduate education itself is needed. Inevitably, and particularly at a time of limited resources and competition for students, institutions, like their clientele, look to the immediate pay-off—the landing of a job, at a good salary. But the educational system must lead as well as serve the job market and must look beyond immediate needs to those of the nation and the world of the future.

# 3

# Where Learning Happens: The Limits of Physical Settings

# Where Learning Happens:
# The Limits of Physical Settings

Since we are concerned above all with practical suggestions on internationalizing the undergraduate curriculum, we must give attention not so much to ideal curricula and comprehensive reform as to incremental change and subtle shifts of emphasis. Certain types of reform are possible in certain settings but cannot succeed in others. We begin, therefore, by looking at the types of American higher education institutions and their needs and possibilities. We shall pass from this examination of setting to a consideration of specific programs. We then shall look at the actors—those who advocate and staff and approve the programs. These programs in turn require particular structures if they are to be realized. Finally, we shall look at the environment in which academic programs are carried on—both the institutional environment and society beyond the campus.

Early in its work in the seventies the Carnegie Commission on Higher Education (1973) drew up a classification of institutions to aid in comparative analyses of types of educational setting. The commission distinguished five types: doctoral-granting institutions, comprehensive universities and colleges, liberal arts colleges, two-year colleges and institutes, and professional schools and other specialized institutions. This last category covered a multitude of miscellaneous establishments, ranging from medical schools and medical centers through schools of business and management to teachers' colleges, theological seminaries, various health professional schools, schools of engineering and technology, schools of law, and schools of art, music, and design.

This taxonomy is a useful starting point for consideration of the settings of international programs and international education generally. We might, however, supplement this horizontal classification with a vertical one in terms of the living patterns of the students and the geographical setting of the institution. Certain kinds of international programs are only possible in a residential institution. At Yale, for example, the educational potential of the residential college system has been reinforced through the establishment in 1968 of a program of seminars, given with full credit within each of the 12 residential colleges. These highly praised and popular courses are offered in a range of rarely taught subjects. Such a structure is particularly appropriate to topics of international interest designed to expose undergraduates from all fields to material they may never otherwise encounter in an informal, nondepartmental, and nontraditional setting.

Other programs can be carried out in urban settings but are less successful on remote campuses. The proximity of different kinds of institutions and a greater number of students and faculty with varying interests make such projects relatively easier in cities. These might include those taking foreign students into school systems, like the International Classroom project of the Philadelphia area; or the sharing of facilities, including library resources, where institutions are located within easy distance of each other. Courses in less taught languages have a greater chance of success where credit can be given to students from colleges with limited staff. They may study languages that would otherwise be unavailable to them.

Some programs possible in large institutions would flounder in small ones; others depend on the intellectual cross-fertilization that is characteristic of small colleges. Only after Western Kentucky State College became Western Kentucky University, with an increase in students from 2,000 to over 13,000, did curricular changes with an international emphasis become possible. These included undergraduate curricula in Latin-American and Asian studies, technical assistance projects overseas, and student and faculty exchanges. But such integrated international education programs as the one developed at Earlham College, Indiana, would be totally different without the requisite intimacy of a small liberal arts college.

## 1. The University

The Carnegie classification includes under doctoral-granting institutions four subcategories, ranging from major research universities like Michigan or Princeton to those awarding at least ten PhDs a year, like Bowling Green and the University of Portland. The departmental structure is strongest in institutions of this kind and frequently undergraduate programs are overshadowed by the emphasis on graduate study. With but one exception, all of the area studies programs financed by the federal government, which include a graduate component, are housed at universities in this list (which includes 173 institutions).

These are the institutions at which the largest share of research on international studies takes place. They are well suited for specialized language programs and for the drawing together of faculty around area studies concentrations or programs focusing on specific world problems. Probably the most successful undergraduate programs involving elements of international studies will be offshoots in some way of graduate programs. In light of the priorities of such institutions and the political framework in which they operate, it is difficult to create undergraduate programs, or cooperation across department boundaries at the undergraduate level, without some close association with graduate activities. However, the sheer range of resources available at the graduate level makes possible, with imaginative planning, the creation of numerous stimulating options for undergraduates.

But it is also in such institutions that conflict between the emphasis on specialization that is characteristic of graduate programs and the more general needs of undergraduates can result in difficulties in establishing satisfactory courses at the undergraduate level. There are ways of reconciling these two sets of concerns, however. Seminar programs have been developed with various degrees of success at, for example, Brown, Stanford, and Harvard, in an effort to fortify the general component of the undergraduate program. At Stanford a high percentage of seminar staff are from areas that do not teach undergraduates, thereby providing a unique experience for both students and faculty. In general, however, the seminar programs launched at many institutions in the early seventies are languishing for lack of structural support.

This conflict between generalization and specialization manifests itself not only with respect to international studies but in other ways. Many general education programs, modeled after those developed by such institutions as Harvard in the forties, have floundered over the years because the specialized departments have refused to teach courses primarily designed for the nonspecialist. "When a faculty reached the agreement necessary to change the curriculum in any fundamental way," writes Frederick Rudolph of the period since the Second World War, "specialization was the most likely beneficiary" (1978: 253). The notion of a core curriculum or general education program tends to give way to some system of distributional requirements, whereby students take specialized courses in different areas and are expected to perceive the relationship among these disparate elements and create out of them a sense of general education. As Rudolph goes on to point out, the worst failure in this system occurred in the sciences: "Why professors of science developed few courses that were appropriate to the general education of nonscientists was a mystery, but the evidence would suggest that they did not care, that they had carved out prestigious territory of their own, and that, with the help of professional societies and graduate and professional schools, they had been able to use outside influence to support for themselves departures and exemptions from the course of study as generally stated."

The increased need for specialists in our technological society means, paradoxically, that general education is increasingly important to provide a basis of common knowledge sufficient to surmount differences in vocation. However, those carrying out a survey of 26 4-year institutions in the early 1970s concluded that none of the programs examined succeeded in providing bridges between different areas of knowledge, as opposed to offering courses that merely provide a nodding acquaintance with yet another area of specialization (Levine and Weingart 1974). Here international studies may have a special role. Since the field is by nature cross-disciplinary, its subject matter provides an ideal vehicle for the effective integration of the disciplines. One of the great challenges and opportunities confronting the organizer of curricula in major research universities is the development of general courses in international studies along such lines. Not only will they help the general education of the undergraduate but they may attract the student who otherwise might never take a course involving international matters.

As we shall suggest in chapter 5, the teaching of languages to undergraduates runs into particularly complicated and often unsatisfactorily resolved problems of organization in the research university. Trained as specialists in literature and culture, faculty in departments charged with the teaching of languages frequently have little interest in imparting elementary knowledge of languages to reluctant students who must fulfill a requirement—yet they are sorely aware that their livelihood depends on it. There are two approaches to this problem. One is to draw out the language faculty, linking them with other departments and convincing them to adapt their language programs to suit not only students interested in literature but those interested in the more practical uses of the language.

A second approach is to separate the teaching of literature in other languages from the teaching of elementary language. At Dartmouth, for example, deemphasis on literature in association with language instruction accompanied the introduction of John Rassias's well-known Dartmouth Intensive Language Model, which uses a combination of dramatic techniques and frequent oral practice to induce confidence in speaking (Luxenberg 1978; Schulz 1979: 30-6). The number of students choosing a language major quadrupled during the eight years following its introduction. About 40 other institutions are using this method. There may even be growth in lit-

erature course enrollments as competence and interest in language
learning increase (Simon 1980: 43). Though faculty may not enjoy
teaching basics, most departments of language and literature are reluctant to give up so immediately visible a reason for their existence;
but there are examples of such a separation. At the University of California at San Diego language and literature are organized into two
separate departmental units: All language courses are offered
through the language department, while all literature courses are
taught within a single literature department. This approach serves
the dual function of breaking down the perceived limited application
of the language major and encouraging a comparatist approach to
the study of literature. Literature majors must take upper-level
courses taught substantially in the relevant language, and two areas
of specialization are required.

Large research universities often include undergraduate professional schools in such fields as business and engineering. One of the
challenges before the academic planner is to open such schools to
the influence of the liberal arts—or (since the resistance often
comes not from the professional schools but from the liberal arts faculty) to convince both sides of the usefulness of such cooperation.
The advantages to the professional schools of proximity to liberal
arts resources are obvious: strong language programs, the presence
of political scientists and economists whose skills can provide a context for hard-core business and engineering subjects, and the availability of courses in such fields as anthropology and sociology. While
it may be hard to tap these resources because of scheduling and
budgeting, or because of psychological resistance on both sides, it
can be immensely beneficial. Nor is the benefit all on one side: There
are few better ways of drawing language professors or anthropolo-
gists out of their shells than by confronting them with a specific and
practical need in a preprofessional curriculum.

## 2.  Comprehensive Institutions

The Carnegie Commission's second category is comprehensive universities and colleges. These 453 institutions award few or no doc-
toral degrees but may have master's programs; all include not only
programs in the liberal arts but at least one professional program.
Here again, the social sciences and humanities can be brought to
bear in imaginative ways on the professional programs to increase
their attention to international affairs. Even where projects considerably less ambitious than the Foreign Area Studies Program of Pacific Lutheran College are envisaged, the introduction of programs
such as theirs—using specially designed modules to internationalize

the teaching of business administration—is workable, and with co-operation can be expanded to other professional and preprofessional programs wherever the impetus exists. Language programs can be adapted to students in professional schools. Links can be made between professional school faculties and those in the liberal arts to focus on major world problems such as health, literacy, food, or the environment.

The so-called comprehensive universities and colleges are one of the largest suppliers of teachers to the elementary and secondary schools. Hence they represent particularly important elements in our larger national agendas. Building links between international specialists in the liberal arts and faculty in education schools should be one of the main priorities in these institutions. However, except where a small body of faculty supported by student interest and administrative cooperation simply starts programs of its own, the very size of the student body and standardization of curricula can stifle initiatives (Taylor 1969: 67). Concern for reform of teacher education often includes, encouragingly, interest in world education; and where those in charge of teacher education, such as the Teacher Education Committee at the University of North Carolina at Charlotte (an institution, nonetheless, in our first category), take an initiative in developing an international studies curriculum, student teachers are likely to greet it with enthusiasm (Gray 1977: 50).

### 3. The Liberal Arts College
Generalization about the 719 liberal arts colleges included in Carnegie's third category is close to impossible. There are nevertheless certain types of programs that flourish in smaller institutions with a strong tradition in general undergraduate education. Faculty frequently have broad interests and are willing to work together across what are often ill-defined departmental lines. The smaller college provides the best setting for comprehensive efforts to internationalize entire institutions; some of the most internationally minded institutions in this country belong in this category. For example, Adams State College in Colorado, as the second stated goal of its general education, encourages students "to exercise responsibility in the local, national, and world communities." For a rural college with fewer than 3,000 students Adams has built an extraordinary array of international and multicultural programs. Its activities range from providing headquarters for an extensive Brazilian exchange program to sponsoring Vietnamese refugee students. Since most small liberal arts colleges are residential, various types of living-learning programs, focusing on a language or on world problems, can be developed.

There are some striking examples of major efforts at internationalization in private liberal arts colleges. We have already mentioned
Earlham College in this regard. With its Quaker affiliation, Earlham
emphasizes practical service, good informal organization for faculty, and community and responsibility among students. A commitment
to international understanding and experience demonstrated in the
past by excellent language teaching and carefully coordinated
study-abroad programs gave rise to a sequence of courses in peace
and conflict studies that is now being worked into a more generalized four-course series in global studies. This will form one part of
an effort to provide an integrated international program designed to
increase awareness of global issues and develop skills for understanding and confronting them. Such efforts as that of Mills College
in California, which in the 1960s consistently expanded social science offerings in non-Western areas (Gumperz 1970: 103), are likely
to be the result, unobtainable in many other kinds of institutions. Administrative leadership here combines with the concern of a faculty
which knows that teaching excellence is valued above prolific publication and good citizenship above prestige.

## 4.  Community and Junior Colleges

Some of the most interesting developments in international studies
are taking place in community and junior colleges. After World War
II, when the two-year college emerged as a comprehensive, vocation-
al, and public institution, the mission of community colleges was perceived to be incompatible with the interests of an international dimension. What was to be offered was relevant education for residents who planned to remain in the community. This is often still the
mandate, but the world increasingly forces itself upon even the local
community; many community colleges are ready to come halfway to
meet it rather than allow their students to remain unprepared to
deal with global differences.

In response to what is seen on some community college campuses
as a major challenge, consortial arrangements have grown nationwide. The International/Intercultural Consortium of the American
Association of Community and Junior Colleges (AACJC) was established in 1976 and has 50 member colleges. The consortium office
mediates between members and representatives of governmental
and private agencies seeking assistance with international projects,
helps identify funding sources and arrange meetings and conferences, and publishes a bimonthly newsletter. Furthermore, the
AACJC has an Office of International Services, begun with a grant
from the Ford Foundation. Its activities include assistance with for-

eign student placement and curriculum development, and organizing national conferences.

It is of course on the campus itself that the extent of college commitment becomes apparent. The growth of international education in community colleges in recent years is clear from the wide range of programs and efforts listed in response to a 1976 survey of two-year colleges (Shannon 1978). It is not only that many community colleges have study-abroad programs comparable or superior to those in four-year colleges. (Rockland Community, New York, offers more than 50 study-abroad options in 34 countries and sends 300 students abroad every year.) An increasing number are engaging in technically oriented programs in cooperation with such institutions in other countries: Asnuntuck College, Connecticut, has a broad-based cooperative arrangement with Chien-Hsien Junior College of Technology in Taiwan. Community Colleges for International Development Inc. (formerly the Community College Cooperative for International Development), directed from Brevard Community College, Florida, has negotiated exchanges with Taiwan and Surinam.

Above all, the community college reaches an enormous number of students whose horizons might otherwise never extend beyond their community. The effort to introduce an international dimension into courses in business, nursing, or social work is thus particularly important. Community college students also need to gain confidence in themselves, to develop the ability to become self-educating, and to transcend their cultural conditioning. Cultural and ethnic studies can be of great assistance in this framework (Fersh 1979: 17).

A major factor in the internationalization of the community college campus is that the number of foreign students continues to rise; though only 16.3 percent of all foreign students in the U.S. were enrolled in community and junior colleges in 1978-79, this represents a significant increase since 1970-71, when it was 10.6 percent. Furthermore, the number of foreign students in two-year institutions shows a 14.9 percent increase over 1977-78, a larger increase than the 11.5 percent for four-year colleges. As the cost of American education rises, and as less developed countries become increasingly aware that they can fill their needs for technically qualified personnel through shorter programs in community colleges, such campuses may become more international in both population and programs. Here more than anywhere else foreign students are, by their very presence, a kind of adjunct faculty. And since they are often engaged in programs at least partially tailored to their needs, an awareness of some issues of technology transfer is brought directly to the campus. Many Nigerians have been sent here by their government expressly to enroll in two-year colleges. A program in Seattle offers students from Surinam specially designed technical training. Community colleges have flexibility because their special aim is to respond to their students' needs; by the same token, the experience of foreign students in community colleges is likely to be rich in terms of student and community interaction.

The other side of this coin is that community colleges also depend largely on local and state agencies for funding, and the constraints under which they work may hamper efforts to introduce an international dimension. Foreign enrollment quotas, and different perceptions of program priorities, can create a climate that precludes innovations that are possible in other classes of institutions. The extent to which some community colleges have developed an international dimension, however, shows what can be achieved with determined leadership.

The quality and shape of international programs at junior and community colleges, as at other kinds of institutions, varies enormously. Some have not experienced the kind of international awakening we describe here. Perhaps to a greater extent than in other types of institutions, much depends on the quality of college leadership and on the faculty's entrepreneurial spirit and willingness to try new things. Where leadership is lacking, international studies faculty—especially language teachers—may feel irrelevant or demoralized (Schulz 1979: 52ff).

Difficulties aside, the potential importance of community colleges in the effort to advance citizen education about international matters was recognized by the President's Commission on Foreign Language and International Studies:

> Our more than 1,000 community colleges, which constitute a widely dispersed network committed to accessibility and community education, and whose students reflect the social, economic, ethnic, and occupational diversity of American society, should have a central role in the commission's charge to "recommend ways to extend the knowledge of other citizens to the broadest population base possible." The enrollment in noncredit adult and continuing education courses at colleges and universities in 1977-78 was 10.2 million; of this number, 5.2 million were at the community colleges.

## 5. Professional Schools

The Carnegie Commission's fifth category covers professional schools and other specialized institutions. An interest in international affairs has not traditionally been a feature of most American professional schools. Since their curricula are comparatively rigid and specialized, internationalizing their curriculum may prove difficult. It is often hard to add faculty with expertise in this area when all positions are already committed to existing specialties. Nor is it always possible to convince students to change their priorities so that they give greater attention to international matters.

This is, however, more true in some professional areas than in others. Students in the health sciences, for example, tend to study in programs geared to the community. But schools of law, engineering, and business each present special possibilities for a different kind of internationalization. The Rand report to the President's Commission on Foreign Language and International Studies in 1979 (Berryman et al.) indicated that employers sensed a growing need for qualified graduates in these fields who also had language and area skills. Holders of law degrees with a fluent second language and international experience are becoming increasingly attractive to both commercial and nonprofit employers. In engineering schools the relatively high percentage of foreign students presents opportunities for the study of problems of environments other than that of the United States (28.8 percent of foreign students in the United States were studying engineering in 1978-79). Once again, however, the efforts of individuals are most likely to bring about any internationalizing in engineering programs.

A recent survey of international exchange programs at American business schools concluded that they are of real value and are part of a continuing trend, with increasing participation and more schools offering them in conjunction with overseas business schools (Altman and Marks 1979). The 10 schools with fully developed exchange programs as options for their MBA students are major institutions in Carnegie's first category, such as Chicago, Harvard, Cornell, and New York University. These programs are integral parts of a curriculum in business administration, which encourages one to hope that, like the AIESEC program of work internships for business students, such exchanges and programs may be increasingly valued for the international sophistication they impart. The Rand study of the marketplace for international skills found this quality to be most in demand (p. 154), rather than language fluency or sophistication in a world area. Until recently the fact that much business in the United States today has a transnational element had little effect on the way in which business administration is taught; but a 1980 addition to funding for international education under the Higher Education Act authorizes $7.5 million to foster links between universities and international business, indicating a possible change.

## 6. Continuing Education

We have thus far said little about community outreach and continuing education, but we shall return to these questions in a later chapter. Clearly, one of the most important functions of all institutions of higher education is the retraining and updating of teacher knowledge. Equally important, though relatively little exploited, is the development of effective strategies for keeping the linguistic knowledge of the community alive. Good outreach programs can give the public a reason not only to increase its knowledge of international affairs but to maintain skills learned long ago in college. (Ideally such an effort could be tied to a federal system of academic insurance, financed by a tuition surcharge, whereby colleges would guarantee to update the knowledge of their former students from time to time—but this may be too utopian an idea for our present purposes.) In any event, there is no more suitable area in which to apply such principles than that of language learning. In connection with its pioneering studies and initiatives on language attrition, the University of Pennsylvania is offering a course in French for adult students which "will systematically diagnose those areas [of the language] which have been forgotten and selectively reteach them."

## 7. Consortia

We have already noted the staffing problems faced by specialized institutions that in the past may have given little attention to international affairs. This raises the question of cooperation among institutions and the creation of consortia. Some involve links between or among institutions that complement one another. A liberal arts college might provide certain kinds of language training or instruction in social and cultural aspects of world problems for a professional or technical school. A large research university might open its courses to students from smaller colleges wishing to study uncommonly taught languages. Neighboring colleges with programs in different languages might choose to share their resources and exchange students. Several consortia across the country run study programs abroad of a scope that would be impossible for individual institutions (on consortia see Patterson 1974).

There are many consortial arrangements by which resources can be pooled for the expansion of programming for international understanding. In 1978 the University of Connecticut and the Connecticut state colleges began a program to improve instruction, cooperate with community and technical colleges to enrich international studies, and hold statewide conferences, as well as develop and share resource inventories. The Center for International Education of the Massachusetts State College System, in operation since 1972, has a wide range of similar functions, including the issuing of publications concerned with international affairs. The Pacific Northwest International/Intercultural Education Consortium is perhaps unique in having as participants public and private two- and four-year institutions, as well as a member in Canada. The achievements of this consortium in its short existence have been considerable. More specialized concerns can also be served in consortial arrangements, such as the Houston Inter-University African Studies Program, which offers study opportunities at four Houston universities. Guided by a faculty council and with no budget beyond its initial seed grants, the program develops library materials, sponsors relationships with institutions in Africa and Great Britain, and coordinates faculty and student opportunities.

Unfortunately, in the relatively change-resistant world of higher education, there is frequently little incentive, beyond a general feeling that it would be a good thing, to induce neighboring institutions to work together in imaginative ways in the international area. Such efforts require careful planning and must involve the highest levels of the institutions. Nevertheless, the effort is eminently worthwhile. By sharing resources, small colleges can operate language programs that would otherwise die. They can hire a professor on a permanent or visiting basis if they do so jointly, though they have neither the demand nor the funds to make such an arrangement alone. Because of problems of administration or accessibility, agreements to share library resources and acquisitions are often less successful, but they can work when colleges are neighbors or when planning is well organized and systematic. Small colleges as well as local school systems can also benefit from the proximity of major institutions that house NDEA (now Higher Education Act) Area Studies Centers, since the Department of Education requires that 15 percent of funds allocated for these centers be devoted to outreach. Considerable incentive thus exists for research institutions to cooperate.

## 8. Cooperation Between School and College

We have mentioned the importance of adding an international component to teacher education. Not only is it important to train teachers in international affairs; it is crucial that the international expertise concentrated in colleges and universities be available to school systems wherever possible. Creating effective cooperation between high schools and colleges is difficult, because of both bureaucratic incompatibilities and a rather ill-considered professional dignity on the part of college teachers. One obvious way in which colleges can assist schools is by offering in-service courses to teachers on world problems and other topics associated with global education. A major premise of the Consortium for Strengthening Intercultural Understanding—founded in 1972 in cooperation with the American Association of State Colleges and Universities by four historically black, developing institutions and since expanded to include four additional institutions—is to develop intercultural understanding at the elementary school level by giving local teachers the knowledge and experience to develop modules for classroom use. Activities include a six-week summer seminar for teachers in Ghana and West Africa, workshops for campus and community members, and the development and refinement of teaching materials. The Institute for Cultural Pluralism at San Diego State University has a similar, smaller scale project for the assistance of education departments in providing in-service training in cultural pluralism to teachers in local school districts.

Of course, our earlier plea for a general internationalization of college courses, even in areas outside those traditionally labeled international, is equally valid for elementary and secondary schools. Several mechanisms are available to the enterprising and imaginative teacher, some involving close cooperation with colleges and universities. Over 300 teacher centers across the United States bring together elementary and some secondary teachers for discussion, in order to enhance their skills and improve their materials. Some 97 of these centers are federally funded through NIE, through the school district in which they operate or in some cases through a university or college. Some teachers in Japan, Sweden, and Australia form a part of the network. College-based centers such as that at Hunter College, New York, can offer in-service or preservice training and can be a forum for investigating ways of bringing international perspectives to the schoolroom.

On other occasions local World Affairs Councils, sometimes in cooperation with colleges and universities, can take the lead. The World Affairs Council of Philadelphia provides a comprehensive Education in World Affairs Program to secondary schools, introducing participants to global problems while building basic skills. The council is also active in in-service programs for teachers on global interdependence and is working with the school district on the creation of an ambitious High School for International Affairs.

Since all teachers need to be sensitive to the global dimension, it is important not only to train social studies teachers in international affairs but to provide teachers in other fields with ideas and strategies for adding international elements to their teaching and to give them the experience of living in another culture. The program by which Lock Haven State College, Pennsylvania, places education students in six American schools overseas is one of the most practical methods for allowing future teachers not only to travel overseas but to gain half their teaching experience outside the United States. Over 40 students participated in fall 1980, most living with families to whom they paid room and board. The students taught only in English, which permitted the participation of those who could not otherwise hope for such an experience. Nevertheless, their language competence was greatly improved by living abroad, and they were motivated to become functional in a second language.

Small colleges in rural areas may have difficulty in maintaining an effective German, Russian, or Italian program. Indeed, some have difficulty with Spanish or French. But if their professors are willing to cooperate with local school systems, there can be courses open to high school juniors and seniors, as well as to college students, that justify their maintenance—and, incidentally, help to recruit able high school students to the college. This procedure already operates in several rural and urban institutions (including the University of Pennsylvania).

A college or university's international resources usually include not only its faculty but many foreign students, whose effect beyond the campus can be highly educational and positive if there are programs to facilitate contacts in schools, community groups, and so on. In fact, regardless of its setting and character, the university or college represents a concentration of resources of enormous importance to the community. We have already noticed how the decline in language instruction in high schools in the late sixties and early seventies was attributable at least in part to changing public attitudes to the outside world. Obliviousness to international affairs in the larger society increases the difficulty of persuading students to study international matters when they enter college. Hence a vital mission of all colleges and universities is to influence the community beyond their boundaries to learn more about world affairs.

# 4

## Putting the World in the Curriculum: Programs

# Putting the World in the Curriculum: Programs

## 1. Introduction: The Disciplines

The typical college curriculum offers numerous opportunities for learning about the world—or it should. Entire departments and major programs are focused on various aspects of international affairs. The very enterprise of academic humanities is based on the assumption that enduring values transcend national boundaries. The social sciences, though they may focus on a specific people or society, assume that the springs of human behavior can be studied in any social setting and are essentially comparable across such settings. The natural sciences have never recognized distinctions of nationality or the boundaries of states: Scientific discovery has always been international—and the law of gravity applies in Fiji as it does in France.

In practice, however, many programs, and many individual teachers, fail to give substance to the universal principles that lie at the heart of the disciplines. Some social science departments function as though their province was merely the United States, or Western society, or the industrialized world. They either ignore the rest of the world or assume that it is not different from the United States. The same is true of the humanities, where the Western tradition may flourish to the exclusion of all else. And it is a rare natural science department that attempts in any systematic fashion to come to terms with human diversity or with the specialties of a global view.

As we consider, then, the question of enhancing the international and global dimension in the curriculum, we must take all knowledge for our province. How can this sense of the universality of knowledge—a sense that antedates, but has often been suffocated by, departmental structures and course offerings and the paraphernalia of administration—be rekindled? How can we convince our colleagues to return to certain of the first principles of their calling and to remake their curricula accordingly?

Of course, some fields, principally those treating human organization in social and cultural terms, lend themselves naturally to comparative study or already have an international or comparative cast. Anthropology and history belong to this category, as does political science. The study of history has in recent years moved out from its preoccupation with American institutions and European affairs. Since the First World War and the League of Nations, the study of government and political theory in the United States, previously having focused on American institutions, has been subsumed under the discipline of political science. And in the last 20 or 30 years new patterns of thought in sociology and anthropology have also influenced the study of political institutions. While international relations may be held to constitute a separate though allied field (Palmer 1980: 345), political science departments habitually offer both optional area specializations and courses with strong comparative elements. Though they still have a long way to go, fields like economics, business administration, and finance have grown increasingly international in scope. Occasionally the more humanistic character of traditional non-Western studies has blended into modern area studies programs with their focus on the social sciences.

Most colleges have fairly extensive language offerings and some provide complete major programs in as many as half a dozen. Traditionally these programs concentrate on literary study; it is unusual to find an entire major devoted to other aspects of the society on whose language it is based. Nevertheless, programs somewhat broader (e.g., French civilization) or comparative (e.g., comparative literature) have been in operation at some colleges for many years and there is now a trend to further such options.

As we contemplate this array of "international" disciplines, we may ask whether they attract their fair share of students. The needs of the future will dictate increased awareness of the diversity of cultures, an ability to work with peoples and nations different from ours, and a sense of the interdependence of the world community. We shall need more people with these skills—perhaps more than the laws of supply and demand, as they operate in the 1980s, will naturally provide.

But two questions arise. First, are present programs equal to their stated purposes? Second, are they properly articulated with students' skills and career goals? It may be, for example, that relatively few major in languages because the programs are inadequate rather than because students lack perspective. The programs may be poorly suited to attract and hold students' interest. It may well be that Spanish majors ought to be interested in Cervantes or Calderon. But it is debatable whether an uncompromising faculty attitude on such matters truly serves the needs of the institution. Cervantes does not necessarily train students for the export-import business, and on the export-import business their sights may be set. This is not to suggest that undergraduate education should be subservient to students' career interests; but a sublime disregard for such goals may be a main reason more students do not major in languages.

More to the point, why do not the fields that are less limited substantively to international concerns attempt to face the realities that their students must, with or without assistance, eventually confront? Today's undergraduates will enter a world no longer confined by the boundaries of the United States, but, to an ever increasing degree, one in which international cooperation and understanding will be facts of life. All of us as educators must face up to the implications of this new reality and ask ourselves whether our own departments and disciplines should not be elements in a worldwide search for knowledge and understanding rather than instruments of American culture or politics. We must be willing to learn as well as teach, and understand as well as preach understanding. This, then, is the task to be faced by education.

## 2. A Prescription for Change: Launching an International Effort

Often the beginnings of an effort at internationalizing an institution will come from the president, or the trustees, or from a particularly enterprising dean. More difficult to achieve is an effort of this kind that originates with the faculty—though any such realignment of mission will depend largely on the administration's ability to work with the faculty. One needs to identify faculty members who command enough respect with their colleagues and who themselves display sufficient conviction to serve as allies in such a campaign. Perhaps the administration will establish a committee to consider adapting the academic program to suit the needs of today and tomorrow (for one such effort, at the University of Hawaii, see Heenan and Perlmutter 1980). Better still, a committee might be established by the faculty at the administration's urging and with its cooperation. (Using existing committees may reduce the visibility and effectiveness of the effort; something more dramatic is probably called for.) Perhaps this committee will draw up a statement of goals and priorities. After modification the statement could be approved by the faculty. With support from central administration its acceptance as a document of institutional policy can be achieved (Ohio's Miami University recently adopted just such a course of action).

It goes without saying that composing a statement is not easy. Differing philosophies inform the thinking of even the most enthusiastic internationalizers. Some will see the introduction of international elements into the curriculum as entirely desirable but will balk at efforts to remake the curriculum in terms of global values. Others will argue that only a global approach makes sense, that treatment of the rest of the world as an American backyard is unacceptable.

We leave these issues on one side. While we acknowledge the significant distinction between international and global studies, we are concerned here with processes of change, regardless of philosophy. Let us imagine, in short, that a statement, more or less acceptable to its drafters, has been approved by a faculty. It should of course address certain issues of educational philosophy. It should appeal to today's educational needs, and, as far as they can be defined, those of tomorrow. It should lay out certain principles of change. It will provide a firm basis for subtle intervention to examine and adapt course offerings and programs, as well as to bring about changes in personnel policy and also in noncurricular student opportunities.

In what follows we shall assume that our statement relates to a single faculty—i.e., the liberal arts faculty or division of a large university or the entire faculty of a liberal arts college. Nevertheless, our observations will also hold in some measure for other types of institutions. A universitywide effort, covering several schools, will of course be different from an effort with a single faculty, and other kinds of resources and administrative support will be deployed.

What then might be the practical outcomes of our statement? Presumably, in the course of its approval, a group of faculty has already emerged who are convinced of its importance and can articulate its advocacy. They might be drawn on (along with other more moderate but respected teachers) to form a committee charged with carrying out the statement's provisions. This committee might take as its primary mission a review of the curriculum, though other issues might fall within its responsibilities: mechanisms for the coordination of programs in international studies (area studies programs, regional studies of one kind or another, various aspects of anthropology, archaeology, languages), the counseling of foreign students and their role on the campus (including their educational role), study abroad, language study, international programming, exchange programs with foreign universities, library holdings, and so on. These responsibilities might be farmed out among a number of campuswide committees under the general supervision of what we can call the International Committee.

Our committee will review existing programs to assess their international content and direction. If it is to prove really effective in changing attitudes and convincing faculty to adjust syllabi or change courses, it must be accompanied by a support mechanism designed to help them make the changes, reward them for doing so, and otherwise make the effort more than a kind of empty stock-taking. And it will require strong and sustained leadership and support from the administration. Several measures can increase the effectiveness of the committee:

**a.** The administration might appoint one of its number to work with the committee. Institutions that already have an Office of International Programs or some other coordinating mechanism in the international field can turn to the administrator in charge. Or this person might be a specially appointed assistant dean for international affairs—or perhaps a member of the faculty seconded for the purpose and provided with an administrative stipend and staff support. Ideally this person should have a small program budget. (In fact, some funding, even a small amount, is almost essential. It should be visibly accessible to the administrator in question, since it helps enhance authority and credibility.)

**b.** When a review of a department is undertaken, a member of that department well respected by colleagues should be selected to work closely with the committee. This person, who should be knowledgeable and relatively senior, can help break down resistance to the committee and may achieve a great deal on an informal basis. In some institutions it might be advisable to reverse the machinery—that is, appoint a review committee *within* the department that includes one or two members of the campuswide International Committee. Since the aim is persuasion, obviously every effort should be made to eliminate any sense of threat or coercion posed by the committee. For example, mechanisms may already be in place to achieve the ends of the committee and it will not be necessary to create new ones. Alternatively, the entire process might be carried through not by a committee but by a faculty seminar. Or a series of symposia, perhaps with outside speakers, might be organized, with provisions for subsequent discussions among faculty.

**c.** Money should be available, perhaps necessarily in fairly small amounts, to help faculty adapt, expand, or create courses over the summer. Similar results can be achieved through released time. Faculty might also be encouraged to work together on curricular development or to call in outside consultants (academics from other institutions who have developed interesting programs, or curricular consultants of one kind or another; see, especially, Council on Learning's handbook of 62 international programs). The library should be encouraged to look with favor on requests for acquisitions relevant to this program. Special efforts might also be made, perhaps through the administrator appointed to work with the program, to acquaint faculty with reforms in other colleges or to bring particularly imaginative syllabi or course elements developed on campus to the attention of other faculty.

Ideally the International Committee or its surrogates should review not only programs and the mix of courses but the very syllabi of individual courses themselves. They should be free to recommend changes at every level—the creation of entirely new programs, the building of new programs out of existing elements, the realignment of existing programs, the creation of new courses, the adaptation of individual courses to serve new purposes, perhaps even the appointment of new faculty. While the dean will probably ask the committee not to question the competence or adaptability of individual faculty, close contact between committee and dean can help give the dean a picture of the human resources at the college's disposal. The committee should, of course, ask questions and make recommendations about requirements, prerequisites, and so on. The dean should be ready to deal sympathetically with far-reaching proposals and to align hiring priorities to bring appropriate talent to the campus. Nevertheless, the committee should be urged to make imaginative use of resources already at hand—including sharing with neighboring institutions.

The kinds of questions the committee asks will vary in scope and philosophical intensity. It is fairly easy to establish that a political science department has no courses on disarmament, or that its offerings on Latin America are deficient. A look at the catalog will show whether the department gives adequate attention to international institutions like the United Nations. A review of the vitae and qualifications of department members will indicate whether there are resources untapped by existing courses.

The committee may find (and this is the next level of complexity) that the department has an impressive array of courses on Latin America and that they might be combined with, say, an existing economics course on Latin America or courses offered in anthropology or history, to form a modest area studies program. This might in turn be tied in with instruction already offered in Spanish or Portuguese and the relevant language department might be invited to adapt its offerings to take such a program into account. Self-instruction options might also be developed. Even without a formal program, links between political science and the language programs might prove mutually beneficial. And these efforts could be reinforced by programs of study abroad, student exchange, or summer travel.

Of course, the mere existence of a substantial body of courses in a geographical area is not justification for creating a program. Such a program should probably come only after extensive dialogue among faculty sharing this interest, possibly by way of a seminar. The dialogue might also include an assessment of student interest over the long term (admissions and career placement people should be included in the conversations), consideration of seeking outside money, and discussion of how foreign students could assist the program or be served by it. Consideration must also be given to the structuring and governance of the program—and the dean must be aware that a new program, even if it cuts across departments, creates new demands for financial and professional resources.

The question of the extent and representativeness of area studies courses in the undergraduate curriculum is complicated. Should a medium-sized institution seek to cover the globe? Is it reasonable to suggest that a college that gives no attention to, say, the Indian subcontinent or North Africa or Eastern Europe is failing in its intellectual responsibilities? Such considerations expand outward all too easily into the basic philosophy of undergraduate education. Americans tend to believe that if there is no course in a subject it cannot be learned, forgetting that students are well able to acquire certain kinds of knowledge on their own. We make no attempt to solve this problem here, but clearly the answers will partially determine the committee's recommendations.

The committee may opt for depth rather than breadth, building concentrations of resources in certain geographical areas and seeking to work them into the disciplines. A set of decisions on geographical concentrations can easily be extended to more general policy areas—for example, student and faculty exchange and cultural programming. Here it is important to keep the language departments in mind. Area studies programs can go off in one direction and language programs in another, so that a college ends up with a powerful German department and no European studies, or a concentration of specialists in the Middle East and no resources for teaching Arabic. Area studies programs, or programs in culture and civilization, can be particularly good for hidebound language departments, drawing them into contact with other departments and loosening the seemingly immutable link between language and literature. Also valuable are courses linking language and society—for example, in the ethnography of language or in language policy.

If the committee makes some attempt to survey resources by geographical area, it should not neglect supportive courses of a general nature—introductory anthropology, courses in comparative religions, development economics, international education, and so on. Such courses may be needed as additional elements in new area studies programs or to give greater meaning to offerings geographically more specialized. And there is the matter of articulation: How can students be persuaded to build individual courses into clusters?

Sometimes a simple listing of these resources, with suggestions on how to group them, will help—if it is made available to students and if it is also used in advising. Scheduling is important: If sequences are recommended, the courses must be available when they are needed. It may be advisable to create an area studies committee to facilitate and coordinate such offerings across departments.

Perhaps even more important than surveying resources by geographical area is a survey of resources in terms of problem solving. Much of the rhetoric of those who maintain that we need new educational responses to the changes in the world of the past 30 or 40 years (and this book is no exception) emphasizes the emergence of some ill-defined set of "major world problems." This suggests that those problems cannot be explored, let alone solved, without a broad perspective transcending the individual disciplines, and also criticizes the departmentalization of universities as a stumbling block (see, for example, Manley 1978; Wilson 1979-80). There have been numerous attempts to lay out these world problems, sometimes in terms of some kind of overarching scheme. Even if we are skeptical about the definitiveness of any one of these lists (and our easy ability to pull a collection of phenomena together and label it a problem may only be our own culturally biased, fix-it response to a set of issues much more complicated than this), there is little harm in using it as a kind of checklist of institutional resources. If a student really wants to probe world hunger, or illiteracy, or overpopulation, are there courses available and accessible? If they are entirely missing from the curriculum, a strong case can be made for the need to remedy this deficiency. A deficiency it surely is: To have no course on a given geographical area is one thing; to be wholly deficient in thinking and teaching about a major global problem is quite another. If these courses exist but are not easily discoverable—or if experts in the institution, without actually teaching courses about hunger or overpopulation, work these subjects into their research or courses —the problem becomes more one of advising. The committee can perform a valuable service by listing these resources and giving the lists to those who need them.

In institutions with large graduate or professional programs this investigation of resources will prove more difficult but may reveal significant opportunities for a realignment of programs. It may draw new resources from graduate or professional programs into the orbit of the liberal arts or suggest new links either horizontally across schools or vertically between undergraduate and graduate programs. It may also cause these other schools to look again at their own programs and to deal with the same questions being raised in the liberal arts by the International Committee. Of course, we should ask how these resources became scattered in the first place. Merely identifying them does not create the administrative will to draw them together, and attention will have to be given to the structures within the institution that inhibit cooperation.

Certain arguments and trends within institutions can assist this internationalizing process that we have set in motion. One is the presence of foreign students in ever greater numbers on American campuses. These students are generally willing to accept American academic programs as they find them, but institutions may ask whether foreign students' needs are being well served and whether they might be better served by making curricular changes (see Baron 1979). Resistance to change may take many forms (for example, the feeling that American students should come first, or that it is precisely the Americanness of American educators that brings foreigners here), but these arguments can be countered by appeals to quality: If we listen to what our foreign students and other overseas experts say, in the future we shall be able to attract the best of the foreign students coming to the United States from certain parts of the world. A powerful program of outside speakers—from international organizations, embassies, and so on, as well as internationally minded academics, politicians, and businessmen—may also help make arguments for internationalization more convincing.

Ultimately, though, much will depend on the power of rational argument, on appeals to the need to keep pace with educational trends, to contribute to human understanding in terms compatible with the highest ideals of the college and university. Yet even here more mundane arguments may have their place: The college that looks to its international responsibilities raises itself above its rivals and becomes a leader in its community and region.

## 3. The Major

Our International Committee will undoubtedly look at the institution's major programs. Any discussion of the reform of majors immediately raises numerous questions about the nature of the major itself. There is a tendency to look on the major as somehow God-given, with little understanding of how recent a development it is (Rudolph 1977: 227-30). But even if we accept the major program as an essential vertical structure in a student's four-year program—the so-called in-depth study, set beside some kind of horizontally structured general education—what depth really means in this context is an open question. Over the years major programs have naturally become identified with the traditional disciplines, twentieth-century

by-products of the specialization of knowledge. In effect, major programs are the outcomes of a departmental structure created primarily to foster graduate study and research.

A strong case can be made for the view that this kind of traditional disciplinary major is the most effective kind, at least in institutions with extensive graduate programs. Students have a home department. They have a faculty clearly identified with them and pos-
sessing the right kinds of incentives to take an interest in their work.
There is arguably a better chance that such major programs will be
coherent and sequential and that they will instill confidence and direction. Unfortunately, however, knowledge refuses to be bound by
vertical divisions. At the most fundamental level there is even some
question as to whether knowledge, or rather the treatment and accumulation of knowledge, is divisible into a finite number of disciplines. Even if we agree that it is, we may still wonder whether the
array of disciplines in a large institution represents that division
adequately. The history of disciplinary study in this country is as
much a branch of politics as of philosophy: Certain disciplines have
won out over others, and some have created coherence for themselves that is lacking in others. Then again, several departmental divisions (for example, languages and literatures) result not so much
from methodological distinctions as from distinctions of subject matter. The practice of French literary criticism, for example, is fundamentally no different from the practice of English literary criticism
except that one is in French and the other is in English.

If we concede that the current division by discipline is at least
partially a result of historical accident, and that certain divisions
among departments have less to do with methodology than with subject matter or even with politics, it follows that there is no fundamental philosophical reason to prevent the creation of new fields to
serve new needs. The emergence of such fields as American civilization, folklore, or semiotics is evidence of just such processes. But this
should not automatically lead us to conclude that any old combination of materials and methods under any old rubric can make up a
coherent major program. The point is important because recent
years have seen the appearance of a whole range of so-called interdisciplinary and nondepartmental programs, often put together
without much sense of direction or goals. They often lack the faculty
interest or involvement to sustain them and may serve students poorly because they do not train in the basic methodologies of the disciplines on which they draw. If we accept the premise that a major
program should involve in-depth study, it must have some kind of coherent structure and should not be a mere grab bag of courses.

But many of the world's larger problems are not susceptible to disciplinary solutions. Hunger cannot be reduced to a problem of biology or botany or veterinary science. Recent experience has shown that the solution to hunger involves issues of food distribution —which in turn is a problem of management, of economics, of communications, and of the political relations among states. It is also closely related to cultural questions—those of religion, for example, which are in turn related to problems of food acceptance; or questions of child rearing, education, or social organization. It is at least arguable that many of our failures in this area are directly related to the narrowness of our approach. If improving strains of wheat only consumes more oil, or provides more for rats to eat, or dispossesses manual labor, perhaps we should not allow the botanists to dictate single-discipline answers to difficult questions. By the same token, our successes may be attributable to our ability to overcome the narrow disciplinary focus of much of education and to work together effectively to solve common problems.

Despite the utterances of modern educational reformers, this is no new problem. The great issues of human survival have never fit neatly within disciplinary boundaries. Yet our inability to handle the methodologies of the disciplines may disqualify us from confronting these issues at all. Hence we cannot ignore this question of methodology as we build major programs and as we consider the depth of undergraduate education as well as its breadth. The great problem with dividing undergraduate curricula into depth and breadth is the relationship between the two. If most human problems transcend the disciplines, we must learn how to relate these disciplines to one another and how to set them in an appropriate context. And this is the great failure of undergraduate education: We fail to teach our students how to integrate their knowledge, how to apply it to particular sets of problems.

This suggests that what matters is not so much the addition of new major programs as the creation of mechanisms to link disciplinary training with the elective system. Institutions might consider minor programs focused on world problems (food, population, armaments, and so on) and growing out of existing majors. Thus a person majoring in economics might take additional courses in other disciplines having to do with aspects of disarmament, thereby linking a disciplinary training in economics with a particular subject area. A grouping of courses in several disciplines would allow students to reach out beyond their fields. The courses could be the joint responsibility of an interdepartmental committee. The existence of several options, each treating a world problem, would also induce the major programs to include such international courses (e.g., the economics of disarmament and the arms trade, disarmament and foreign policy, power in international relations, and so on).

Since the most successful major programs are those with a firm administrative base, an institution may wish to locate a new international studies program in an existing department rather than let it float free under the auspices of a relatively toothless interdepartmental committee. Hence a major in French civilization might better be located in French or Romance languages, even though faculty have to be drawn from other fields; or a major in peace studies might do best in a political science department rather than be left to a committee drawn from a number of different fields. Obviously there are disadvantages, the main one being that such major programs will reveal a strong disciplinary bias. But there are ways to offset bias, through special funding arrangements and through carefully designed committee systems. Using existing departmental structures may also appeal to reform-minded deans anxious to convince conservative departments of the need to change.

If it is nevertheless decided to create a new major outside of departmental structures, faculty support is necessary for it to succeed; and its philosophy must be based widely enough to attract students and defined clearly enough to offer some assurance of continuity. It is always a good idea to use models from other institutions or from entire disciplines. A program in peace studies probably stands a better chance of survival than a program in arms and disarmament simply because there is a body of thought on what constitutes peace studies that transcends any one program in that subject and allows outsiders to judge the program in terms of broader criteria. A program in international relations, if it cannot be located under the umbrella of political science or government, will probably do better as a free-floating entity than a program with some more original sounding but less comprehensive title. Though experts on international relations may not always agree on the nature of their field, a definition exists, even if broadly conceived, of what that field entails (e.g., Palmer 1980). Even under the best of circumstances, such interdisciplinary majors are likely to draw fire from strict constructionists within the disciplines.

## 4. Broadening Major Offerings
In effect, broadening of the major offerings in any institution can be achieved through a number of different strategies—which are not so much neatly divisible as they are part of a continuum stretching from minimal intervention to radical realignment of patterns of con-

trol. The following are a few of the most common, arranged in terms of the degree of intervention, from minimal to radical—some already standard fare at many institutions.

a.  **The creation of new "tracks" in existing majors.** The political science department can perhaps be persuaded to develop concentrations in particular geographical or topical areas—possibly allowing collateral courses in other departments to count toward the major. Regional concentrations can be created in history, or concentrations on international or development economics created in the traditional economics department. Bringing such change about from the outside may prove difficult, though it can most easily be achieved through the judicious hiring or replacement of faculty. The basic structure of the department remains unchanged. Sometimes tracks can be created even without new courses; but in most cases some new courses will have to be developed. Where they are needed, a dean may be able to create incentives through the provision of released time for curricular development. It is important that the department appoint a committee or preferably an individual to oversee the workings of each major track, since this gives the track not only a measure of quality control but an advocate (though the latter role may easily supplant the former). Many institutions have provisions for dual majors, and special efforts might be made to allow (and encourage) students to complete major requirements in related international fields. This is a particularly fruitful approach for language departments.

b.  **The housing of new majors in departments that already have their own major programs.** The inspiration for such majors will generally originate with a faculty member or with a group in a department who share an interest. It may not be difficult to convince them to think in terms of a separate major program. Particularly if their interest overlaps with other departments, they may initially think about an interdepartmental major—which may rouse skepticism or even downright opposition among those chairing departments. Resistance may be overcome by a decision to house the major in an existing department, especially if it is accompanied by assurances that the dean will look sympathetically on proposals to hire new staff over a period of years to strengthen the new major. Obviously a solution of this kind gives the new major a strong disciplinary bias and may make it unacceptably rigid; but while the major may be subject to the priorities of some of the more rigid members of the department, it may actually loosen the priorities and reduce departmental rigidity and exclusionism. A new major may need resources from outside the department, in which event consultative mechanisms should be set up (probably in the form of a committee) or the faculty members called upon can be given secondary appointments in the major program's home department.

c. **The creation of majors in departments or well-established programs currently offering no major program.** This is most likely to occur in large universities with strong graduate programs, as for example in area studies. Such departments or programs, operating at the graduate level, may be induced to develop major programs for undergraduates and thus open themselves to undergraduate participation. Since undergraduate programs of this kind may be criticized by existing departments, they should be consulted thoroughly before the majors are launched. Of course, a program seldom begins at point zero: It is the logical result of a gradual accumulation of courses open to undergraduates.

d. **The creation of interdisciplinary majors.** This approach has been relatively common in recent years. In an effort to provide a focus on international affairs, faculty from several departments create a program essentially independent of the departmental structure. Sometimes it is a way of structuring existing courses, drawing on the services of existing departments. In other cases the program may also offer courses of its own. While this method offers excellent possibilities for the intellectual interaction of faculty and students around a set of common problems and issues, it also faces formidable obstacles. Some involve the loyalties and responsibilities of faculty; others relate to budgetary support. Interdisciplinary majors are generally supervised by interdepartmental committees whose members may feel their first loyalty is to their departments. They may be reluctant to spend adequate time advising students or teaching in the program. Particularly in large institutions, it may be no favor to untenured professors to ask that they teach outside their home departments, since this work is less visible to senior colleagues and may even be viewed as lacking in seriousness. On the other hand, if the program relies entirely on existing courses offered by the departments, strong consultative mechanisms are essential to preserve the integrity of the interdepartmental program, to maintain adequate course offerings, and to guarantee that students can be placed in the courses they need.

We emphasize these difficulties not to discourage the reader, but to stress the need for advance planning and for firm and creative leadership. Far too many programs come about simply through the energies of one or two faculty or because of frustrations or resistance within the departments. They are often set up without adequate structures in place. Particularly where staffing problems become acute, interdepartmental major committees tend to campaign for the right to hire faculty—in short, to become departments in their own right. In today's climate it is probably best to resist such approaches.

One way of doing so is to provide interdepartmental majors with strong budgets for administrative personnel (a stipend and course reduction for the person who chairs the program, for example); for programming (so that the departments actually come to the program when they need money for visiting speakers and so on); and perhaps for visiting faculty. While there are strong reasons for avoiding the hiring of permanent faculty for such programs (since they rapidly build up vested interests) visiting faculty can supplement skills already present on campus, help focus the program, and ensure renewal and change (see chapter 7). As for program money, an interdisciplinary international relations major (for example) with good resources may help induce the departments of political science or sociology or economics to schedule lectures and conferences on international topics in preference to other subjects.

Despite such problems, strong interdisciplinary majors offer significant benefits. Because they encourage interaction across disciplinary boundaries, they are good for faculty. If they are well structured, they are good for the students because they encourage integrative study. And majors located within a department—for example, a major in international relations in a department of political science—can easily become swamped, subsumed, or discarded. While there have been such failures, as well as new programs that lack adequate resources, a number of interdepartmental programs (for example, the Human Studies Program at Brown University) have flourished and endured (Kelly 1976: 145-54).

**e.  The creation of new departments.** In an era of expansion this most radical of solutions may have been practical, but it is seldom so today. There may, however, be instances where it seems advisable to divide a large department (e.g., a department of history and political science, or sociology and anthropology) into smaller units. Such subdivision can sharpen departmental goals and enhance community among faculty, though it inhibits flexibility in personnel policy and other forms of academic planning (cf. Kelly 1974). Far more common in today's straitened circumstances is to amalgamate certain smaller departments, particularly in the languages, to allow for more efficient administration and programming. While departments of foreign languages (as opposed to departments limited to single languages or groups of languages) may be somewhat unwieldy (united, the cynic might suggest, only by their inability to communicate), they can sometimes deal with the whole matter of language instruction more effectively than separate departments organized by language or language groups. A possible compromise is a department of European languages, leaving Asian or African languages with area studies or language-and-culture programs. Alternatively, language departments can be extended to include culture or area studies (e.g., a department of European studies, or of French culture, or of Spanish and Latin-American studies).

## 5. Internationalizing Existing Major Programs

We have been considering the creation of new major options in the international area. We have had little to say so far about the internationalization of existing major programs. Does the major program in political science or economics include adequate consideration of other social, cultural, and political systems? And to what extent is such consideration genuinely comparative? Does the system of requirements and prerequisites induce students to take courses with an international content? Are students encouraged to apply their knowledge of foreign cultures or languages to the material studied in the individual courses? Is a premium placed on the acquisition of such skills?

There are several ways of raising these questions within a department. Probably the most effective is to do so in the context of a general across-the-board examination of the international aspects of the curriculum. But individual departments might also be induced to appoint committees to examine their own offerings. It is, of course, helpful if there is already an internal system of departmental evaluation through which such questions can be raised. Departments generally know little about the background of their own students. Here the dean's office can be particularly helpful. What can be learned about patterns of course selection to establish whether students make the best use of courses with an international content? What knowledge of foreign languages and cultures do students already have? It may be possible to tap this knowledge in new and imaginative ways.

An investigation of a program may lead to a recommendation that some syllabi be changed; prerequisites, especially, may require modification. Or there may be a need to create new courses—though this could be difficult without dropping some already in existence. In fact, the mere addition of courses, unless students have a strong incentive to choose them over courses already in place, may have little effect. It is worth adding that many of the students taking courses in the department will not be majors. Major programs, important as they are in training specialists or in giving a special slant to general education, will inevitably touch only a limited number of students. If one of our aims is to impart that minimal global awareness alluded

to earlier, we must concentrate on smaller units than entire programs—particularly on individual courses.

## 6.  An International Dimension Throughout the Curriculum

The form of what is taught in the undergraduate curriculum, if not
the substance, dates from an earlier era, in which the imperatives of
nationhood overshadowed international concerns and national institutions were fundamentally more important than international ones.
We may ask, for example, whether American isolationism between
the two world wars was not fueled in part by too great a curricular
conservatism: A more sophisticated American awareness of the relations between nation-states might have brought about different results in the late thirties and early forties. In any case, today's needs
for a genuinely global approach to knowledge are greater than ever.

It is obviously no easy business to realign the curriculum in so fundamentally international a way. The strong market forces that bear
on the average college or university are both local and national:
There is the matter of jobs for graduating students. The vast majority, while they might benefit in the long run from an international
education, will compete for employment by local and national firms,
whose perspectives are unlikely to be wider or more cosmopolitan
than those of the universities from which they draw their staff. Professors and administrators tend to see themselves as part of a national system of higher education. Their salaries are often paid in
part by state authorities, concerned above all with local and regional needs, or by the federal government, whose concern with the
larger world is self-interested. Sponsors of research tend to be local
or national; parental horizons are unlikely to extend into international matters; boards of trustees are often drawn from the local
and regional leadership.

Given these realities and the need to service a particular constituency, few institutions are likely to have the collective will to make
themselves over into fully international institutions—ones in which
the starting point of knowledge is not local but authentically international, based not on national but on international needs. It is even
debatable whether such a total revolution in an institution is wise: It
will fall out of step with other institutions and remove itself from the
mainstream. Nevertheless, this is the direction in which, stage by
stage, we should move. Not through drastic surgery, but through
steady change. What is needed is a continuous and patient effort to
raise issues of educational policy and philosophy that are international in scope, to judge programs and courses and departments in
terms of such criteria, and to appoint appropriate faculty.

Conventional wisdom, supported by statistics, tells us that most undergraduates take no courses (beyond language) with an appreciable international content. This may be one of those areas in which statistics are of little use to us, since defining the international content of a course is well-nigh impossible. Here we skirt a deep philosophical problem that underlies this entire book. Does the internationalization of undergraduate education lift the student entirely out of his or her cultural and social nest, providing experiences fundamentally different from those associated with the United States? If so, perhaps nothing short of a study of the Tassaday or of Tibetan lamaseries is adequate; a course in Moliere or in Canadian economics may be too tame. And even if we accept that the study of the economics of Canada or the economics of developing countries is at least a contribution to the internationalization of the undergraduate, to what extent should we insist that the former consider the economic perspectives of the francophone population of Quebec (i.e., go beyond the statement that all this fuss about language is driving business out of Montreal) or the latter look with sympathy on the aspirations implied in the notion of a New International Economic Order?

There are no hard and fast answers. Nor is it possible, by waving a magic wand, to turn a palpably ethnocentric course, taught by a palpably ethnocentric professor, into a paragon of intercultural awareness. In fact, there may be many courses with less overt international content—perhaps in philosophy, English, or sociology—that are taught with awareness of cultural relativity and with a sensitivity to differences wholly absent from an offering in international finance or even comparative political systems. Ultimately it may be more important to sensitize teachers and students to questions of cultural relativity and global understanding than to load the curriculum with courses entitled international-this or international-that.

While political science or history will nonetheless yield easily to the investigations of our International Committee, since their need to give attention to international matters is hardly at issue, other fields will prove more resistant. What are the implications, for fields like biology or physics or music or the history of art, of the changes in world affairs of the past 30 years or so? And if these fields present special problems, what of, say, sociology or psychology, which are linked more closely to social concerns?

No university administrator or representative faculty committee can hope to give a definitive answer to a question as broad as this. The aid of the disciplinary societies must be sought; even they may have a hard time. At the outset, however, we should recognize that the question can be answered on several levels; the most obvious is that of subject matter itself. It is important and useful for a psychology department, for example, to look at its courses with a view to eliminating ethnocentrism and cultural bias. A course in social psychology, for example, may draw its examples and even its theory from American culture, failing to suggest that other parts of the world do things differently. The instructor can make simple changes to right the balance, perhaps by reaching out in the direction of anthropology. Readings relating to non-Western cultures may be introduced, studies by foreign scholars assigned. If, however, the very paradigms and assumptions on which the course is constructed have a cultural bias, the rethinking will be more complex and revision more difficult. The instructor might at least change the title of the course to reflect its American bias, thereby implying that its subject is relative.

Similarly, a course in the sociology of the family may stress that it is dealing with the *American* family, or it might be broadened and deepened to include material from other cultures. Greater emphasis, in fact, might be placed on comparative sociology throughout the sociology program, while courses with a narrower focus could be labeled in these terms. Needless to say, these problems arise not only from course syllabi but from the textbooks (cf. FitzGerald's study of high school history textbooks, 1979). In recent years, however, more and more textbook writers have been working to eliminate ethnocentrism from their approach.

These efforts can be extended even into fields remote from international affairs. If mathematics must use examples drawn from real life, they might as well be international ones (Schwartz 1979; Callahan 1979). Statistics can be taught with international subject matter. Even a field like physics may occasionally remind the student that the United States is not the only area in which the laws of physics operate. To an increasing degree the natural sciences, especially when taught to nonspecialists, touch on issues of public policy; courses in physics and society or chemistry and society are relatively commonplace. It requires little imagination to understand how such courses can deal with global as well as national issues and reach beyond the concerns of the United States. Many of these policy questions can come up in less socially specific contexts, too—as examples in physics or biology, for instance.

The humanities are a special case and present special problems. It has become fashionable in recent years, primarily on the part of humanists themselves, to suggest that the humanities are in disarray. Certainly the humanistic disciplines have become fragmented, losing something of their common purpose and direction. Now that we need them most, they seem disinclined to formulate values or offer even the most tentative of prescriptions. Perhaps the whole concept of the humanities is essentially Western, based on a specific definition of culture and a particular sense of the structure of society. This was one of the criticisms leveled at the field by participants in an international conference sponsored by the Rockefeller Foundation some years ago. The challenging report of the conference (Rockefeller 1976) contrasts sharply with a recent report sponsored by the same organization (Commission on the Humanities 1980), which largely ignores the international dimension of humanistic study and assumes that the humanities can be defined in American terms.

Of course, our society is part of the Western world and the courses we teach are grounded in Western cultural traditions. This is as it should be: An understanding and appreciation of Mozart or Michelangelo or Shakespeare is essential to an adequate education in our society. But with an understanding of the major phenomena of a great tradition can come an understanding that this is *a* tradition, not *the* tradition: that the expressive forms of China or Benin, India or Samoa, also have value. The question, of course, is what value? How do we relate these products of other cultures to the value system of our own—or, more to the point, how do we transcend our own value system to touch on the universals and contradictions implied in Terence's famous phrase, aptly quoted at the Rockefeller conference, *Homo sum et nihil humani a me alienum puto* (I am a human being, and nothing human do I consider alien to me)? What makes the problem particularly difficult is the corollary to a statement in the Commission on the Humanities report (page 10): "No society can flourish if its citizens deny the possibility of a common culture that unites all despite differences in origin, education, and outlook." And no society can see itself as separate if it does not regard its own culture as in some sense unique.

The philosophical problems here are real and they must be faced. At the very least we need a three-tier structure for education in the humanities, consisting of a knowledge of this country, of the roots of this country in Europe, and of the world in general. It is possible that without a sense of his or her uniqueness and difference, a person cannot come to terms with what is universal about humankind (Tonkin 1979).

This does not mean—and the point needs emphasizing—that all things are relative. The cultural values of the West have sustained a civilization of astounding complexity and accomplishment. Many of these values offer hope for peoples who do not yet share them. But they also carry their tribute of human suffering, of opportunities lost, of roads not taken. For the professor educated in a particular tradition, it may take an effort of will to understand this, but the effort should be made. Certainly our students must learn where they came from. If we do not know our own origins we cannot appreciate why others' origins are important to them. We should be constantly aware that our origins are not everyone's, and that Western tradition has no monopoly on sagacity.

Efforts such as these will meet resistance, and there is certainly a limit to how far a good program can deviate from orthodoxy and maintain its standing. But a general pushing at assumptions and a constant refusal to accept narrow definitions is especially important in the changing priorities of our perplexing age. Much can be achieved by a kind of quiet subversion—organizing symposia on the state of the discipline or its relationship to other disciplines, for example, and persuading faculty to participate; or bringing in speakers with challenging and unconventional views. In fact, our present agenda is to create situations and structures in which the new realities of world affairs are forced into confrontation with the methodologies, philosophies, and programs of the disciplines, and their practitioners are obliged to come to terms with them. This will not be easy, since the disciplines are built on a sense of objectivity suspicious of these pressures.

How can students be induced to take a full range of courses, including those that extend beyond the customary European frame of reference? We shall discuss inducement and motivation in later chapters. But as long as general education requirements exist, they should include some international and global dimension. We refer not to the language requirement, which may be essential in undergraduate liberal arts education, but to courses that challenge the student with problems of cultural difference and with what might be called major world problems. The two are not entirely the same: One is associated with anthropology, the other with such fields as political science, sociology, and economics. The first instills an understanding of cultures and values; the second asks us, given such differences of cultures, to analyze and understand problems of global magnitude which may be value based but that have also a purely practical dimension. Both merit a place in a basic general education.

Whether any random course in anthropology or any random course in international aspects of the social sciences can perform these functions adequately is questionable. It would seem unlikely. Ideally faculty with such perspectives should be identified and induced to design and teach courses for nonspecialists that confront these issues directly. They might be seminars for freshmen or larger general courses offered under the auspices of departments and designed for freshmen and sophomores. While general education courses seldom live up to the expectations we thrust on them, a constantly changing program of strong offerings, perhaps under the direction of an imaginative and highly touted interdepartmental committee, offers the best hope. If general education courses are not always as successful as we would like, distributional requirements may be even less useful, though the ease with which they can be administered is confused with educational efficacy.

Far more difficult to administer than general education courses are thematic programs or clusters of courses. We have referred to minor programs in world problems growing out of disciplines. Where thematic programs have been tried they have generally run up against scheduling difficulties and their unconventional nature has tended to discourage students. But in principle such programs afford real opportunities to study world problems in depth and from several different perspectives.

### 7. The Configuration of the Disciplines

Subject matter is only one level on which the question of internationalizing the disciplines needs to be addressed. There is also the research on which this subject matter is based. One of the saddest aspects particularly of study in the social sciences is the extent to which readings and textbooks are drawn from American research described by American researchers. The problem cannot be eliminated by simply adding a few books from France or Japan to the reading list (though that might help), since the tradition of certain disciplines is rooted in American assumptions about the scope of the discipline and the nature of its method. Nevertheless, this bias should be addressed more frequently by teachers and students, and greater efforts should be made to explain that there are other lines of approach. The main limiting factor here is the barrier of language, which may have helped create these divisions in the first place and which is a problem not only for the student but often for the teacher (who may be as ignorant of other languages as the students). Yet simply seeing texts in foreign languages on reading lists or reserve shelves, or reading translations of them, will help convince students that there is an inevitable ethnocentricity in their training and that they must be aware of it. While professors may not want to require their students to read texts in other languages, they can certainly encourage it and can provide references in other languages for those capable of reading them. At the least, translations might be used so that the views of scholars of other nationalities are taken into account.

But ultimately the problem goes deeper than this. The configuration of disciplines in American intellectual life and in the academy is a result of many forces, not all—maybe not most—intellectual. Unfortunately, the departmental structure, reinforced by budgets and professional organizations and the full panoply of journals and certification and self-definition, has been distinguished over the years by a sharp delineation of turf and territoriality. The disciplines have learned to avoid poaching on one another's land. The emphasis on boundaries and exclusivity has had an inhibiting effect on the definition of the context of individual disciplines: They are seldom required to account for themselves, to explain why they approach phenomena as they do and how they fit into the larger pattern of the pursuit of knowledge. Like so many nation-states, they have created customs barriers and passport systems. While their domestic policies are crystal clear, they lack a coherent foreign policy, a set of cooperative attitudes toward other departments and disciplines that would encourage cross-fertilization or the joining of forces around common problems.

There are many exceptions to this rule, and we could all cite a few. But the premise remains: As Altbach (1979) puts it, "Academic departments tend to inhibit change not only for organizational reasons but also because they reflect particular conceptions of knowledge" (page 83). While our present concern is only with the effect of these traditional structures on rapidly changing world affairs, it is precisely the international area that highlights the need to address such issues. We are not asking for the dismantling of the disciplinary structures. They have served us well and will continue to do so. We do, however, insist on constant self-criticism and self-examination. We must continually ask if our department, our program, our discipline is properly organized to instill in students a sense of the global dimensions of world problems. And students must be taught enough about the context of a particular discipline to ask this question for themselves.

If fields like physics or biology must ask such questions, the need is even more acute in the humanities. For the most part the humanities have abdicated their role as the conscience keepers, the moralists, of the academic enterprise. Seduced by the scientific method into a sterile objectivity, they have lost their hold on values. While the development of methodology in the humanities in the twenties and thirties—spurred by the natural sciences—has had enormous benefits, it has, as we have noted, led to a trivialization of the enterprise. It is bad enough that humanists recoil from value judgments about the phenomena they study, but it is reprehensible that they will not act as their own apologists in the larger arena. This unwillingness probably springs from their sense of their own vulnerability. Yet it is surely not unreasonable to raise questions about the usefulness of German or the study of Chinese art, provided the questions are couched in the broadest terms. Above all, the answers should be honed and ready.

Teachers of language and literature are as much to blame as teachers of other aspects of the humanities, but they tend, like other humanists, to retreat behind their departmental ramparts and reduce all intellectual questions to matters of credit hours and teaching assignments. It is not enough to argue that the study of a topic is important just because (as was said of Mount Everest) the phenomenon is there. The point about Mount Everest is that it is higher than all others and that there is only one such mountain. Yet our academics go triumphantly planting their flags on molehills and in the depths of valleys, declaring all who dare to challenge their activities philistines. Importance is a legitimate criterion in the evaluation of scholarly work and it is relevant to the question of what should be taught (and sold, nine times out of ten) to students. If it were left to us, we would restore philosophy to its central place in the humanities, not as an adjunct to physics or linguistics but as a custodian of moral and ethical questions. We emphasize questions rather than answers: A strong philosophy department might constantly raise just the questions about departments and disciplines and programs that their practitioners lack the courage or ability to see.

In the meantime we have only an International Committee asking timebound questions about courses on Latin America, but even that is a beginning. It is clear that the problem of ethnocentrism in the academy—the tendency to look at the world from an American point of view—is not only a matter of subject but of style and intellectual approach. This ethnocentrism is paralleled in a curious way by the rigidity of the structure of disciplines. The removal of what we might call disciplinary chauvinism can aid in an important way the removal of national ethnocentrism.

If the disciplines do not look often enough beyond their own boundaries to define their usefulness in relation to the common intellectual enterprise, they are also reluctant to face the consequences of the use to which their products are put when exported. The Vietnam War brought this problem into focus. Social scientists, bound to objectivity with a Hippocratic self-confidence, saw their products used politically and their objective methods serving a kind of political social engineering. "Instead of acknowledging that ethical or moral preferences play a vital—indeed inescapable—role in defining issues and in measuring progress toward or away from the resolution of issues," writes Burns Weston (1979: 70), "the overwhelming tendency is to insist upon empirical (or 'scientific') quantification and description as the only proper concern of education, and to dismiss as ideological or unprofessional almost anything that is consciously prescriptive." Weston goes on to point out that "this dismissal often is made through appeals to the *values* of academic freedom and professionalism." The problem is as old as the atomic bomb, or dynamite, or gunpowder, or Prometheus. We are not, as some have done, arguing for the abandonment of objectivity; it is a necessity for the proper weighing of certain evidence. We are suggesting that all knowledge has a context, that the context is not and cannot be value-free, and that the context must always be studied along with the knowledge itself. Thus it is essential to raise questions about the larger cultural effects of economic development, to ask what is being lost as well as what is being gained by the expansion of education or literacy or public health services.

Hence we are confronted with a paradox. Scientific objectivity is, as we know (though we do not always face the consequences), an ideal, a myth rather than a reality. We should ask ourselves more frequently how near or how far we are from that objectivity, how hidebound by disciplinary, social, or national loyalties. Hence we need to draw questions of value closer to the realm of scientific objectivity. On the other hand, when we look at the context of our research we must broaden and objectify our visions to take account of other people's values and views. If philosophy is central to the humanities, anthropology is or should be central to the social sciences.

By the same token, biology, the science of life, lies at the heart (literally and figuratively) of the natural sciences. With our new concern for the environment and for problems of industrial waste, we have become more aware of this. It is not illegitimate to ask how philosophy, anthropology, and biology can help us establish criteria for setting up programs in international studies and for judging the usefulness of topics and approaches.

It is becoming harder to prevent our International Committee from turning into a disciplinary Trojan horse, raising questions that extend far beyond international studies. The admonition "Beware of Greeks bearing gifts" may be more than a lesson in the difficulties of cross-cultural understanding. But even the achievement of our own restricted purposes calls for a measure of destabilization, of questioning the underpinnings of the disciplines and departments. Again, we cannot emphasize too strongly the necessity of doing this in an unthreatening fashion. Departments and individual faculty must be assured that they have a contribution to make to a general dialogue. If it is done carefully, this is not difficult. Though their behavior as sociologists or French professors or physicists may be disconcertingly predictable, faculty as individuals are (need we say it?) considerably more intellectually courageous and inquiring than some jaded administrators or skeptical students tend to think.

The translation of self-questioning into the specifics of academic programs leads us back to general education. As we have noticed, the problem with general education programs is that they rapidly become routine, losing the excitement and challenge that only the accomplished teacher can convey. Partly because they touch every student in an institution at some time or another, and hence are a concern to every faculty member, they often suffer from rigid structural constraints and an inability to adapt to changing circumstances. Above all, they need a constant philosophical renewal, best achieved through the guidance of an individual or a group willing to raise fundamental questions and having the political and academic authority to see that they are addressed. Giving students an early taste of the relations among the disciplines, their limitations, and the ethical implications of their work and methodology is arguably essential to a liberalizing education. And it will help them come to terms with their role in a world that extends beyond the comfortingly American. Appointment even on a temporary and rotating basis of a professor or two willing to raise such issues—especially from an anthropological or philosophical (or biological) point of view —could have a significant impact on students' ability to deal with world problems. (And we reiterate that in the Council on Learning student survey it was precisely on world problems that respondents proved weakest.)

## 8. Curricular Design and Development

Our excursion into the heart of the academic ideal should not distract us from matters of housekeeping. The more departments and faculty are obliged to deal with issues of philosophy, the more their questioning will translate into courses and programs—and not only at the level of general education. It is vital that faculty have support from colleagues and the means to bring about changes they feel essential. Some institutions, notably community colleges, have brought faculty together to revise syllabi or develop new units or modules for existing courses. Hence a course in accounting might include an international module, or a course in sociology might have an element dealing with comparative issues. Modules can take several forms. They may be a set of notes or a text, with appropriate references and readings, developed by a faculty member for the use of those in charge of a course. Approximately 20 such modules have been developed by the Consortium for International Studies Education (CISE). In this case the faculty member plays the role of consultant. Alternatively, the module may include the faculty member: A professor is brought in to teach part of a course in which he or she has expertise. Here the professor in charge of the course may or may not participate in the module, depending on whether the aim is to team teach or simply to impart an area of knowledge that would otherwise be missing.

This cooperation is, of course, easiest in institutions where syllabi are subject to evaluation by an instructor's peers or where faculty routinely sit in on one another's courses. In other institutions, faculty will be reluctant to tell one another what to do. In institutions where cooperation is not the norm, administrators will probably achieve greatest success by a piecemeal approach, rather than issuing blanket invitations to cooperate. They can convince one or two influential faculty to lead the way, publicizing the results and persuading others to follow. As soon as some momentum is achieved, cooperation can be institutionalized—for example, by making small grants for the development of units or modules and by appointing a committee to oversee their administration. The process is much easier in institutions with offices to assist in the improvement of instruction, since it may be possible to incorporate such efforts into their programs.

Instructors who resist the importation of entire and alien units into their courses may be persuaded to use new materials if they are made available. An imaginative assistant dean or department chairman could help by identifying materials likely to be useful to faculty and seeing that the materials are received—or by approaching a teacher with a request for advice; "We need help in improving our library holdings in international economics" may help convince Professor X to introduce international elements into his or her economics courses.

Some faculty may suggest launching team-taught courses. This is not the place to give detailed consideration to the merits and limitations of team teaching. Much depends on faculty personalities and the administrative structure of the institution. In general, it is important that any teaching team have a clearly recognized leader with formal responsibility for the course. Continuity is also important: Discrete lectures with no attempt at links confuse students. Ideally the team leader should work closely with members to shape their contributions to a common goal—and the goal must be clearly articulated (preferably in written form). The leader should attend all lectures and sessions of the course and provide, at the very least, some commentary after each contribution by a member. Team teaching, of course, also raises problems of administration—especially with respect to teaching load and (if the course is interdepartmental) distributional and major credit. It is advisable to address these issues squarely before the course begins and to set up procedures for further such proposals.

From the design of modules or team-taught courses it is only one step up to the compilation of materials, de novo, for an entire course. One of the main reasons more courses on international topics do not turn up in college catalogs is the unavailability of textbooks, collections of readings, and so on. While the situation is improving, thanks to such organizations as CISE and a few enterprising publishers, the need remains acute. Deans who encourage faculty to compile their own materials and who provide duplication resources are performing a service beyond the courses in question if these faculty then publish their compilations or share them with colleagues elsewhere.

Curricular planning is not only a matter of content but of process and form. International studies, especially if they are focused on a global problem or issue, are particularly well suited to the small discussion group or seminar, perhaps designed as part of a freshman or sophomore seminar program or built into the options available to juniors or seniors. Such courses may be avowedly cross-disciplinary—for example, bringing economics, political science, and anthropology to bear on the problem of hunger—or they may originate in a single discipline, with references toward others.

At the other end of the scale, large lecture courses concentrating on some aspect of international studies might form an ingredient in a general education program. In fact, global problems or international politics or the history of a world region are topics that, if presented right, lend themselves to imaginative and stimulating popularization. In his recent Ford Foundation study, McCaughey (1979: 42) mourns the passing of the courses "that once packed them in on Morningside Heights or in Cambridge." His observation that large courses help pay for small ones should not be dismissed as academic time serving. Large courses can bring international studies to an audience otherwise unreached, and they need not be pitched at a low intellectual level.

As changes occur at various levels with departments and programs, we must continually ask about their larger educational impact. Can students steer themselves easily to the new offerings? Can they combine them with other components in their education? Are there problems of articulation between courses? In a larger context, what effect do they have on the processes of credentialing and on job opportunities? Devising routine ways of raising these questions is very important, not only for international studies but for undergraduate education in general. Sometimes students build qualifications almost without our noticing it. A group of courses (to go back to our old example) in Spanish and Latin-American studies may pass unnoticed on a transcript. There may be some way to recognize this as a minor or special concentration on the transcript so that it takes on salability in the eyes of the placement office and the student is able to turn accumulated knowledge to good account.

We may also ask whether our new courses and programs in international studies have a bearing on programs in graduate and professional schools. There may be ways of convincing graduate and professional schools to accord them special recognition—or programs developed at the undergraduate level may prove exportable, after modification, to graduate programs. We shall say more about these possibilities in the following chapter.

### 9.   "International" Colleges

We began this chapter with an allusion to the average college curriculum. Before closing this rather cursory discussion of programmatic changes, we should point out that there are a few institutions whose programs are anything but average as far as international activities are concerned. Some colleges' entire focus has been international, or even internationalist, from the beginning. The tiny Friends World College, based on Long Island, is one. Founded in 1965, it has a chain of study centers across the world (Kenya, England, Guatemala, India, and Japan) at which students follow programs they have designed and executed themselves, ranging from conventional college study to experiential and cooperative projects. Dag Hammarskjold College, founded in the late sixties, very much in the Peace Corps spirit, was another—but that faded with the return of student conservatism and fiscal hard times.

In a separate category are institutions specifically designed to provide training in international studies. The School for International Training, for example, was established in Brattleboro, Vermont, in 1964 by the Experiment in International Living. In addition to its language programs and various short-term training sessions, it offers a two-year World Issues Program leading to the bachelor of international studies degree. California's Monterey Institute of Foreign Studies provides upper-level instruction in languages and area studies and in such fields as international relations and international economics. Florida International University, which opened in the early 1970s for upper-level undergraduates and graduate students, espouses an internationalist philosophy but has been expanding in more conventional directions. Another specialized school for international training is the American Graduate School of International Management in Glendale, Arizona, which is affiliated with the American Management Association. Offering a Master of International Management, the school primarily trains corporate managers for service abroad.

More interesting from a practical point of view as an example of a conventional four-year college with an international focus is Lock Haven State College. One of the few Pennsylvania state colleges to take the Commonwealth's Master Plan seriously, it pursues its specialization with enthusiasm and imagination. A few institutions have built on a historical interest in international studies to create unusually extensive options—Earlham College, for example (Gumperz 1970). Others have had such a focus from the start. When Eckerd College was founded as Florida Presbyterian College in 1958, it was given a specific internationalist and intercultural thrust, with strong language offerings and a range of programs in history and cultures (Williamsen and Morehouse 1977). Middlebury College in Vermont has become nationally known for its language programs, its summer institutes in language, and its study-abroad programs. Other institutions, both private and those that are part of a state system, have put special emphasis on study abroad—among them such major institutions as Stanford, Michigan State University, and the University of Massachusetts at Amherst. The last has some 40 study-abroad programs, 22 of which are reciprocal.*

We have discussed in this chapter a number of aspects of the international dimension that can be injected into the undergraduate curriculum. We have, however, barely touched on one of the most central and difficult areas, one which merits a separate chapter: the study of language.

---

*For an excellent compilation and description of effective international education programs at the campus and consortium levels, see Education for a Global Century: Handbook of Exemplary International Programs, Change Magazine Press, 271 North Avenue, New Rochelle, N.Y. 10801; $7.95.

# 5

# Communicating With the World: Language

# Communicating With the World: Language

## 1. The Situation of Language in the World

**D**evoting a separate chapter to language study is a measure of the importance we attach to the subject rather than an indication of how we think the curriculum should be organized. We strongly believe that language and language differences should be fundamental elements in every phase and aspect of undergraduate study—indeed, of study in general. Far more arresting than the fact that 300 million people speak English as their first language is the fact that an overwhelmingly greater number do not—and that the sum of knowledge in the world is conveyed (or would be, if we could understand) in a myriad of tongues. Language study and the study of other subjects should be as closely integrated as possible.

There are those who argue (even some experts in international studies) that the study of language is of little importance. The counterarguments are well known and it is not necessary to repeat them here. But one argument persists and we shall discuss it before proceeding: that English is already the world's lingua franca and it is only a matter of time before everyone speaks it. If English is a lingua franca, it is because the United States has power in the world—particularly technological and economic power—and because the U.S. has in part succeeded another great world power, the British Empire, whose language was the same, and from which our nation was to a degree derived. Today the dominance of the United States, and of the industrialized world, is being challenged. New nations understand, for example, that one of the factors contributing to the imbalance of the international flow of information is the international status of the former colonial languages: The British, Americans, and French enjoy marked linguistic advantages over the developing world. The native languages of the developing countries enjoy little or no status internationally. Often these countries are also hampered by wide linguistic diversity within their own boundaries—in fact, many must deal with huge expenditures for language instruction in the schools. In this as in so many other areas, the onus is on the poor and the weak to conform to the practices of the rich and the dominant.

Some of these linguistic disadvantages are shared by the industrialized nations. When an international conference is held on, say, deep-sea mining, Britain selects delegates on the basis of their knowledge of the topic, but Indonesia chooses people also on the basis of their ability to communicate in one of the official conference languages. When a Japanese scientist attends an international conference, he must struggle to deliver his paper in English and may have great difficulty engaging in dialogue with his colleagues. And when these fellow scientists nominate experts to UNESCO or some other international organization, they pass over the Japanese, who may be much the better scientist, in favor of an American who has intervened with great facility in this or that debate in this or that conference. At the United Nations, Japan, Brazil, and Indonesia pay their contributions to the language services like everyone else, even though they are paying for translations out of one language foreign to them into another language equally foreign.

The list of examples of language discrimination is almost endless. And its victims by definition cannot communicate their frustrations. There is a tendency to minimize or ignore these problems, and it is sometimes abetted even by those whose languages are discriminated against: The fluent speaker of English from a country where English is normally not used may occupy a position of authority in international life for linguistic rather than intellectual reasons. Americans tend to assume that "everyone speaks English" across the world, failing to realize that the people they are likely to meet are precisely those whose knowledge of English is best. Even the informal networks of scientists and intellectuals have their linguistic norms, and those who lack linguistic knowledge simply get excluded. (See Guerard 1941, Tonkin 1977: 4, Tonkin 1979.)

Figures about the spread of English are impressive: According to Fishman (page 16), for example, 76 percent of all secondary school students in the non-English-speaking world (excluding China) are studying English—a vast increase over just a few years ago. And there are more native speakers of English across the globe (about one in twelve of the entire world population) than of any other language except Chinese (Fishman, Cooper, and Conrad 1977). Ken Burgin, writing in the *Times Higher Education Supplement* (London), points out that 98 percent of those learning a second language in West Germany are learning English. In the Netherlands that figure is 90 percent, in France 81 percent. Even in Italy, where French continues to hold a strong position, English represents the second language for 56 percent of foreign language learners.

Advances in the computer sciences and in the mechanical handling of language (including everything from simulated speech to the compilation and manipulation of thesauri) may seem to point the way to mechanical solutions to language differences. This would obviate the need to learn and use foreign languages for the great majority of those having to communicate with speakers of other languages in other countries.

In light of these facts, optimists might conclude that language problems are already solved, or at least on the way to solution. But other points should give us pause. First, it has frequently been pointed out that the strength of a language is associated with the economic and political strength of its speakers. In a widely quoted article describing the possible decline of English, Frederick Starr (1978) notes that of the 10 nations that send the greatest number of travelers abroad, three are English speaking. Hence it is hardly surprising that the tourist industry, the airlines, and the hotels make widespread use of English. As long as the United States and other English-speaking countries have something to offer buyers, they will be able to deal with foreigners in English. But as America's share in world markets declines and as its dominance in basic research and development weakens, its long-range ability to determine the linguistic terms of global communications also decline (cf. Knepler 1980).

Even if we acknowledge that the use of English internationally is on the increase (though whether it is growing in proportion to the total increase in international contacts is less clear), more and more languages in the Third World are gaining in importance as languages of government and culture. Between 1970 and 1979, for example, two major countries have shifted their official language from English to a local tongue—Pakistan to Urdu and Kenya to Swahili —and several others have added native, indigenous languages to English as coequal official languages. Spurred above all by the work of UNESCO in the 1950s and 1960s, and by such organizations as the Ford Foundation, many Third World countries have shifted from colonial languages for instruction in the schools to the native tongues of the pupils themselves (Fox 1953). We are witnessing, in short, a diversification of language use at various levels. The lead of English is thus by no means clear or permanent. We should remember that the great increase in the use of English internationally is a phenomenon of the nineteenth and twentieth centuries, the period of the flowering of the British Empire and the growth of American economic and military power. In the world of tomorrow these conditions may no longer hold. What looks like the permanent dominance of English may turn out to be but one historic phase.

Recognizing the connection between language and power, some

advocate the spread of English for reasons of self-interest. English, states a British Council Annual Report, "carries the odium of being the language of the haves, of former Colonial masters," but "it is also the language of those who want to have—of those who may acquire influence and power, as well as of those who possess them already.... There is a hidden sales element in every English teacher, book, magazine, film-strip, and television programme sent overseas." William Benton, writing in 1967, is at pains to emphasize that his is no mere self-interest:

> I propose...that the United States enlist the cooperation of private organizations and foundations to underwrite special research to determine the most effective methods for teaching English as a foreign language and for promoting such teaching.... I emphasize again that this is not because of any special pride of ours in the English language—but as a humanistic effort to spread knowledge and advance communication among men. (Page 23.)

Randolph Quirk, writing in the London *Observer* (1978) is less of an idealist:

> When we're thinking of the wealthier countries of the world, the export of English is just as much big business as the export of manufactured goods. British Leyland may excite little enthusiasm in Japan, but British English sells like hot Suzukis.

But these statements make more sense in a seller's than a buyer's market. As soon as American or British goods must compete with the homegrown article, English is less likely to succeed in Japan, Korea, or Spain. A good knowledge of Japanese, Korean, or Spanish may prove necessary to make a sale. Is it better, then, to go for broke—to continue to set our own terms of discourse in the hope no one will notice our hand has weakened—or should we acknowledge a reciprocity of interests with foreign peoples and deal with them on a more equal basis? It is our contention that, in the long run, the second is the only practical way.

And what applies to business applies to diplomacy. The enormous increase in the number of students from abroad studying here over the last 20 years has created a large cadre of English speakers across the world. These are primarily people with a commitment to the new technology: They have learned their skills in the United States and many apply them in their home countries in the employ of American corporations, or in a Westernized educational system, or in a centralized government modeled after bureaucratic patterns derived from the industrialized countries. These people, with their commitment to or at least comprehension of Western ideas and ways, often serve as middlemen between monoglot American diplomats and the people at large. These diplomats hear what their Westernized contacts want them to hear; their perceptions are filtered through the contacts' Western lenses. But a wise foreign policy should be based not just on the talk in Hilton bars but on the talk in the bazaars; not just on the life of the shopping streets of capital cities, but on the life of the villages. The bazaars and the villages are largely closed to Americans, not so much because of restrictions on their movement but because they cannot understand the languages used there. And if any country has taught us in recent years the importance of such understanding, it must surely be Iran.

As for machine translation, the optimism of the 1950s and early 1960s has been largely replaced with a more sober assessment of the applicability of computers to the processes of translation. As early as 1946 the possibility of using computers to assist in translation was broached in a conversation between A. D. Booth of the University of London and Warren Weaver of the Rockefeller Foundation. Experiments in the late forties and early fifties led to increasing interest in the idea, but the problems proved not so much mechanical as linguistic: Efforts to build a model of language accessible to machines proved more difficult than many experts had imagined in the heady early days of transformational grammar, and by the midsixties interest in the idea declined sharply. While there are useful ways of employing computers as dictionaries and thesauri (especially in helping translators deal with technical terms), the hope that machines might one day render texts or speech from one language to another, unaided by human intervention, has proved largely a chimera (cf. Kay 1974).

In a recent speech to the British Overseas Trade Board, the Duke of Kent, a member of Britain's royal family (normally staunch supporters of the Queen's English), suggested that the widespread use of English abroad might even be a hindrance to Britain's effort to increase exports:

> Britain's major customers give preference to firms who take the trouble to approach them in their own language. They are likely to react unfavourably to an approach made in English.... Fifty percent of French firms give preference to foreign firms speaking French. Fifty percent of German and Austrian firms require correspondence in German. British firms cannot expect their products to speak for themselves.

But there is another kind of self-interest, what one might describe as a moral self-interest, in the use of foreign languages overseas. "Ich bin ein Berliner," said John F. Kennedy in a famous speech, and the inhabitants of that city took him to their hearts. Pope John Paul II spoke to the French, the Americans, and the Brazilians in languages they understood, with electrifying effect. Acts of linguistic generosity, in a world otherwise characterized by linguistic chauvinism, may do more for the American abroad than any amount of crusading zeal for the civilizing power of English.

## 2. The Situation in the United States

There are both national and international reasons for learning languages. And there are practical and moral reasons as well. We stress this point only because these principles frequently are but dimly understood by language teachers themselves and often ignored completely by specialists in other fields. This is not to say that there is a dearth of eloquent statements on the importance of language learning. In fact, one of the more depressing aspects of the entire field is the sheer quantity of such statements and the lack of progress they have produced. Whole portions of William Riley Parker's *The National Interest and Foreign Languages* (1954) are as current now as the day they were written, and most of the statistics on language learning or the lack of it either remain the same or are worse than they were then.

Amid the apocalyptic rhetoric of the advocates of language learning, it may be worthwhile to reflect that statistical declines in numbers of learners may have had little effect on the national capability in foreign languages. Recent improvements in language pedagogy, coupled with increases in student study and travel abroad, may well have offset the declines in total numbers (Barrows, Clark, and Klein 1980). Studies suggest that only a small percentage of those studying languages in high school and college end up capable of using them (Burn 1980b: 50).

The recent Council on Learning survey would seem to bear out this last observation. One of its sections had to do with knowledge of foreign languages. While a majority of college seniors (almost 90 percent) indicated that they had learned or studied a language, only a third of these felt they could "order a simple meal in a restaurant" without difficulty, and less than a third could "with some difficulty...understand news broadcasts on the radio." The vast majority began language study before college, generally in high school. But high school students who do not go to college, along with many of those who do, frequently fail to cross the threshold at which they have accumulated sufficient knowledge of the language they studied for it to become functional. In 1976, for example (Simon 1978), only 4 percent of all high school graduates had studied a foreign language for more than two years. Most colleges in this country offer degrees for which no language requirement exists at all.

The brevity of language instruction—the fact that students fail to study a language long enough for it to come alive—is one of the fundamental hindrances to making Americans able to communicate in anything other than English. In most countries children begin to learn languages at an early age, but this has not been the pattern in American education. A few school systems have, over the years, offered language instruction in elementary school. The first major system to do so was probably Cleveland, which established such a program in 1922 (Levenson and Kendrick 1967: v). But in most systems language learning begins in high school if at all (and for 85 percent of all high school students it does not).

In a much publicized 1952 speech to the Central States Modern Language Teachers' Association, Earl J. McGrath, then U.S. Commissioner of Education, called for language programs in elementary schools on a much broader basis. He emphasized, in the words of a Modern Language Association statement in 1956 (Levenson & Kendrick: 10), that "real proficiency in the use of a foreign language requires progressive learning over an extended period," and that only by starting early could students cross the functional threshold. By the midsixties the so-called FLES (Foreign Languages for the Elementary School) movement was in full spate, with programs in numerous school systems across the country. More and more teachers were hired to offer language instruction to younger students, conferences were held, publications on the virtues and methods of early language learning appeared in great quantity, and school boards raced to keep pace.

For numerous reasons FLES declined even more rapidly than it grew. There were problems with federal funding in the late sixties and with changing attitudes among parents and school boards. But probably more decisive were two other factors: an overextension of resources (many of the teachers hired were not competent to do the job), and an inability to work out problems of articulation between elementary and secondary schools. There was little point in learning Spanish in elementary school if the student would move to a secondary school offering only French—and the lack of a standard curriculum, coupled with the mobility of adults in their late twenties and early thirties (the pupils' parents) made this a frequent problem. With the nation's turning away from international entanglements in the late sixties and early seventies, and the dropping of college language requirements under the pressure of the student rebellions of those years, FLES largely disappeared. Today only a very small percentage of elementary schools offer language instruction.

Unfortunately, the rise and fall of FLES was no isolated phenomenon, but part of a nationwide decline in language learning even at the secondary school level. Of 22,737 secondary schools in the United States, almost a fifth, or 4,344, have no foreign language programs at all. As for overall enrollments, they show a steady decline from the midsixties to the late seventies (President's Commission 1979: 6; Burn 1980a: 49; Brod 1980: 20; Starr 1979: 10). Though this erosion has now been largely halted, the ground lost over that period has still to be regained.

The situation in other countries is drastically different. In most nations with comparable levels of education, foreign language is a requirement at the secondary level for all or most students, and in many countries (China, for example) it is required or strongly encouraged at the elementary level. Even among English-speaking countries the United States lags (Simon 1980): Australia's average enrollment figures are about double ours, and in the United Kingdom 85 percent of secondary school students study a language for three or more years. Of course, these figures tell us little about the actual accomplishment of the students. One study showed that the vast majority of Japanese students of English never acquire even an elementary proficiency (see Brownell 1967), and even in countries where English is widely taught in the schools it is unusual to find among the population anything but the most rudimentary ability to use English (there are, of course, exceptions, but these are largely confined to parts of Europe).

## 3. The Language Requirement in Its Present Form

If we accept that knowledge of a language should be part of a general education, we must ask how it can best be obtained. Traditionally we have relied on the requirement, generally for graduation, that a student study a language during a certain amount of time and receive a passing grade. We are unusual in our emphasis on elementary language at the college level. According to Lambert (1973: 180), "Of the language-related courses, two thirds of the undergraduate and about one quarter of graduate enrollment is at the level of basic skill acquisition of the first three years." In most countries it is assumed that students will acquire this elementary knowledge at an earlier stage and that language will be required for entrance to college rather than for graduation. Though some American colleges do have a language requirement for entrance (not always strictly enforced: Schulz 1979: 2), it is generally argued that the extreme diversity of our educational system dictates a reliance on graduation requirements. Yet this creates a situation symptomatic of the entire problem: Elementary language learning at the college level is deemed impossible for students unless they offer for-credit courses.

Whereas in most countries people pick up language skills as they need them (though not, of course, effortlessly; that is another myth), here they are built in as special fields of study. They are not organic, not a fact of life, but a sometime piece of the curriculum.

We are not convinced that this need be so. Much of the difficulty lies in our failure to work on establishing national norms and to decide exactly what we would like the schools to do. In language learning, perhaps more than in other areas, there is a need to coordinate and articulate the efforts in the schools with those in the colleges. Just as steps have been taken to set national standards in the sciences, we need to take such steps in languages. If there is a difficulty, it may lie with the colleges rather than the schools. The colleges compete for students. If a college established a stiff entrance requirement in languages, it would lose out (or at least fear that it would) over the others, especially since many colleges have no language requirement at all.

Fundamental to the present college language requirement is an assumption about the relation of time to proficiency. It is assumed that a certain quantity of class time spent learning a language, especially if it is divided into portions labeled First Year Spanish, Second Year Spanish, and so on, will result in a certain level of competence. In reality, the grading system is such that even students with a very low level of attainment are certified to move on to the next stage, though they may not be ready. While students may be tested when they enter college, most institutions have no final proficiency test, so that passing is a matter of endurance rather than skill. Very few fail completely; it is almost unknown for a student to be denied a diploma for want of language proficiency, or even for failing language grades. Since the system is not set up to deal with failures, procedures are conveniently adapted to change the definition of success.

The very terminology of American education reveals the premises on which it is based: In our discussion of general education we refer constantly to the need to give students *exposure* to a discipline or area. Students must be exposed to natural sciences or international studies, or exposed to a language. There is no suggestion that natural sciences or languages must be exposed to the students and that until that exposition is complete and the student understands, credentials should not be awarded.

In many respects the system works well. Students learn something of the methodology of the fields they study, even if their knowledge remains sketchy and imprecise. But language is different. Acquiring a foreign language is a cumulative process, in which prior knowledge must be assimilated and stored at every stage and each new piece of information set in a context. It is not well suited to a system based on exposure rather than mastery (unless that exposure includes total immersion), or on endurance rather than proficiency.

Most language requirements call for completion of one, two, or three years of a language. They stop short of the threshold at which a language becomes genuinely useful. Of all fields language perhaps requires the most up-front investment. Students must spend a good deal of time on straight memorization before the language begins to be useful. But most never experience an appreciable yield on the investment. They become discouraged and demoralized. Of course, it can be argued that the language requirement has aims other than fluency. It is designed to show students how languages work and to acquaint them with a linguistic system different from their own. They learn linguistic relativity. In this sense, to be sure, they benefit from the very beginning. But while this is important, it is precisely at the stage of using a language that the student becomes fully conscious of the relativity. Frederick Starr's description (1979) of the situation in high schools is apt:

> Attrition is enormous. The most common experience for American students of modern foreign languages is to endure the most difficult and least rewarding phase of a program without gaining access to the natural rewards that make such study tolerable. Most American students don't learn enough to build upon later and in fact do not build upon what they learn. Quitting after a year or two, their experience with modern foreign languages is marked by understandable bitterness and frustration. Later, when such students find themselves on local school boards, they act upon this unsuccessful...experience, to the detriment of language programs (page 11).

At most, then, the language requirement brings the student to a level at which authentic college study, using a language as it ought to be used in college, might begin. Colleges do not insist that students continue study or use of the language, nor do they do much to facilitate its practical application. Though students may elect to continue using the language they have begun to learn, for many it represents a distraction from their main interests. Why must we insist that if a student is to continue with Spanish, he or she has to take courses in literature? The economics student is unlikely to do so. Yet the economics student might gladly take a course relating economics to Spanish. The biology major might well be willing to continue with Spanish in a context related to biology.

Because of the nature of language requirements where they exist and the relatively low level of competence achieved by most high school students who do study a language, beginning classes at college can pose particular challenges to teachers. They can demoralize instructors, since classes tend to be populated by students who have avoided languages or who have learned very little in the classes they have taken. Though many colleges have dropped the language requirement for the wrong reasons, their sense that this way of doing things is a poor investment for all concerned is understandable. The language requirement would have survived in more institutions if the results had been demonstrably beneficial. In fact, we might ask whether the astronomical expenditure on language instruction is worthwhile. Results must be improved if we are ever to justify language learning on intellectual grounds.

## 4. Quality of Instruction

Quality of language instruction, which Starr (1979) notes as a problem in high school, is a problem throughout the educational system. It is not because language teachers are less competent than others, but because so much depends on the teacher in a language class. While from time to time this or that method of instruction is introduced as the answer to all our problems, method is considerably less important than a teacher's power of personality, and only a limited number have that power. Much can be done to improve instructional quality by giving teachers suggestions on how to teach and how to define objectives, and by identifying the approaches that work well for them (interesting efforts have been made along these lines in several graduate departments in recent years), as well as by pointing out their shortcomings. But relatively few professors now teaching languages have ever had formal instruction in teaching methods. There is much resistance to such instruction in PhD programs, though the realities of the job market are changing this. (Both Harvard and the University of Illinois, for example, require their graduate teaching assistants to complete an accredited course in language teaching.) We might add that many language professors have never had instruction in linguistics, either—and frequently not in the history of their language. They were trained as literary scholars and critics.

An additional problem is a phenomenon we might call the language loop. It manifests itself in large research universities. The hierarchy of values in such institutions (where language professors are trained) places literature at the top, elementary language at the bottom. This means that the graduate and upper-level undergraduate courses, most of them in literature, are accepted as the most desirable. These are taught by the senior professors (language departments tend in any case to be conservative on questions of hierarchy and seniority). Graduate assistants teach the elementary language courses. There is little scope for teaching by graduate assistants at higher levels because those courses are small and do not require section or recitation leaders.

It is generally believed that graduate students should teach only the lowest level of courses unless they are directly supervised by a faculty member. This convention holds not only for language but for other fields. This view is probably mistaken, incidentally, since graduate students, who are working on the specificities of graduate courses and dissertations, are better acquainted with the materials of some upper-level courses than with the basics of elementary courses. Be that as it may, the result of this principle in language departments is that graduate assistants teach the basic courses —those whose clientele is particularly problematic and in which adaptability and ingenuity of approach (the qualities that come with experience) are at a premium.

This situation suits the economy of language departments. Senior professors prefer not to teach elementary language; they have served their apprenticeship and feel that they can devote themselves to more "serious" scholarly pursuits. Accordingly they need a certain number of graduate and upper-level courses to sustain them. If they were to begin teaching elementary language, they would reduce the necessity of employing large numbers of graduate assistants. The dean would stop giving them teaching fellowships; they would lose the graduate students supported on the fellowships and would have no graduate students to teach. They then would have to teach elementary language and stop teaching advanced literature. Thus, in this department-that-Jack-built, all the elements are symbiotically related. The only element essentially outside the system is the student in elementary language who is taught by the least experienced teachers in the least prestigious courses.

It is no wonder that language teachers are demoralized. The teaching they are asked to do is among the least stimulating in the academy (this, we hasten to add, is not a comment on the teachers but on the nature of the material and its setting), and many have lost a sense of the purpose of what they are doing. The demand for their field, despite occasional upturns, has been dropping for decades. The problem is especially great in two-year colleges (Schulz 1979: 57), where languages are distinctly peripheral. Students here often lack linguistic experience, and there is no scope to teach the literature for which the teachers were trained. But personal observations suggest that the problem is more general. Again, while many language teachers have boundless ingenuity and energy, this buffeting over the years has created a sense of defeat that manifests itself as dog-in-the-manger attitudes even toward deans anxious to breathe life into language instruction and thereby improve the lot of foreign language faculties. There is no area more in need of funds for curricular development, opportunities for faculty to travel and retrain and rethink their priorities, and activities to expand their horizons so they can take advantage of the new opportunities for language study that increasingly present themselves.

### 5. Proficiency-Based Instruction and the Language Requirement

We can draw two conclusions from this melancholy recitation. First, it is arguable that we should institute a language requirement at the college level if we regard language as important to all areas of study. In this best of all possible worlds everyone in a college would study languages for, say, two years, regardless of level of proficiency. Advanced students might select from several subjects in which courses would be taught in the language in question. They might be general education courses. Why not learn about hunger or literacy or world health in a language other than English—perhaps drawing on the publications of the United Nations and UNESCO in French or Spanish? Economics, sociology, or the history of art might be taught in French or German or Italian. Such courses are offered in more enterprising institutions, among them the University of Wisconsin (Conner 1977).

Other students could fulfill their requirement with two years of elementary language, perhaps adding beginning Chinese or Arabic to Spanish or French already studied in high school, or beginning their language study at the college level. Such an arrangement would encourage students to learn the less commonly taught tongues rather than feel they must continue with European languages begun in high school.

Our second conclusion relates to the nature of language instruction on a course basis. Though there is formidable resistance to this, we are convinced that language programs at the high school and college level must shift to a proficiency-based system. The weight of informed opinion is behind this idea. Three principal problems, and possibly a fourth, prevent its immediate realization. The first involves the lack of uniform standards. Addressing this matter in its final report (Brod 1980), the Modern Language Association Task Force on the Commonly Taught Languages called on the MLA and the American Council on the Teaching of Foreign Languages, in association with other organizations, to develop an outline of realistic proficiency goals by stage of achievement. Language associations, the Task Force suggested (page 20), "should develop handbooks that provide a variety of specific curricular models to enable teachers to achieve the proficiency goals for the various stages." At present, it was pointed out, "it is usually impossible to interpret with any accuracy the level of achievement after 'first-year French' or 'third-year Russian,' given the wide range of courses taught under such headings." A parallel Task Force on Institutional Language Policy supported these recommendations and went on to propose that other problems of articulation and standardization also be addressed in due time.

In developing universal standards of proficiency, education will inevitably be faced with the fact that language can be used, and taught, for different purposes. But whether universal standards can or cannot be established, nothing prevents an institution from setting its own or borrowing them, and developing a program based on their achievement. They can be modified later if need be.

In the course of clarifying its recommendation on proficiency goals, the Task Force on the Commonly Taught Languages points out that "it is assumed that courses offered at the various levels (ranging from the elementary and secondary schools to the colleges and universities) will require different lengths of time to reach the established goals." Here lies our second problem. Programs based on proficiency are not time dependent, but a system based on courses and credits is. Currently a student who enters an institution with his or her language requirement unfulfilled takes courses in a language and these credits count toward graduation. A student who has met the requirement receives no credit. But what of the student who begins college with no language, spends the summer following the freshman year in Madrid and continues to study Spanish alone in the fall, and who then passes a proficiency test equivalent to two years of Spanish? Should he or she receive credit toward graduation equivalent to four courses?

Perhaps we should conclude that learning a language outside the classroom does not entitle a student to credit, though it does exempt him or her from taking courses to fulfill the requirement; but even then issues of equity, not to say common sense, remain unresolved. This is especially so since new formats are being developed for language teaching—intensive courses, individualized instruction, self-instruction, and so on—that blur the distinction between classroom learning and what might be called experiential language learning. The Task Force on Institutional Language Policy specifically called for the extension of such options (Brod 1980: 12). Conner (1977) has reported on some of the intensive programs developed in recent years, Phillips (1974) has reviewed individualized programs, and Boyd-Bowman (1973) reported on his efforts to develop self-instructional programs and offered advice on setting them up (on Ohio State's initatives in this area see Scully 1980).

A third problem is less clear but may be more essential. A proficiency system exposes faculty to external evaluation. The late sixties and early seventies saw the demise of most comprehensive examinations in undergraduate major programs. With their disappearance went the last remaining opportunity for disinterested assessment of the quality of instruction in the fields within a department, at least at the undergraduate level. Today teaching and the evaluation of students are usually handled by the same person, without external intervention. A proficiency-based system reintroduces external review. What of the professor whose students all fail or barely pass the proficiency test? Or, to put the matter in a more operational frame, how do we deal with the fear of a professor that this will happen? Or the fear of a department chairman that he or she will have to account to the dean for such a failure? If this delicate and complex set of issues can be resolved, it will be only by systematic efforts to involve all the teachers in a department in the planning and establishment of goals and in the administration of the system. They should be encouraged to look at systems already in operation (travel money might be provided for some department members) and themselves to make decisions on their applicability. And everything should be done to reassure them (indirectly, no doubt) that they will be protected against the consequences of personal failure with the new system. The primary aim, after all, is to teach the student, not penalize the instructor.

Language instruction is a domain in which students can and should be involved in curricular reform. In most language departments there is a significant gap between the aims and expectations of students taking courses and the orientation of the faculty. This gap needs to be closed before student and teacher frustration can give way to something more positive. Surveying language students, and perhaps including them in a task force, would help implant the notion that change is needed and set the scene for reevaluation of course offerings and teacher competence. If the whole department is brought to a point of reorientation, it may be easier for individual faculty to agree that they need help in becoming effective teachers of courses that stress functional competence and oral proficiency.

While no college seems to have moved entirely to a proficiency-based system of language instruction and certification, several —among them the University of Southern California and the University of Pennsylvania—are experimenting with the idea. Tulane has probably gone furthest: It has such a requirement for all undergraduates except those majoring in engineering and architecture. Proficiency in a second language is assessed for all freshmen on the basis of test scores and foreign language placement questionnaires. Some place out of further language instruction; others are required to attain, by whatever means they choose, a similar level of proficiency before graduation. For students wishing to be tested in uncommonly taught languages, ad hoc measures are being developed.

One organization that has been working with proficiency testing for over 20 years is the Foreign Service Institute (FSI). Its spoken language test is standard procedure in the establishment of language proficiency levels in the Foreign Service. Recent experiments suggest that the FSI test might be applicable to more conventional academic situations (Frith 1979), perhaps as one element in a set of proficiency standards also covering writing and comprehension.

An additional problem is the fact that since most college language teachers are not trained as teachers of language, they know little or nothing about learning theory and seldom stop to consider *how* students learn. The question is not high in their priorities (Brod 1980: 16). In this regard teachers of English as a second language (ESL) are considerably ahead of most teachers in conventional language departments. This may be because many ESL teachers come out of such fields as linguistics, whereas most teachers of French, Spanish, or German come to language teaching by way of literary criticism. It is hard to convince this latter group of the importance of assessing achievement and looking at the process in terms of its efficiency in producing measurable results. There is even some question as to whether results can be measured. Teachers of ESL are also blessed with a specific and easily verifiable goal—to teach their students to function effectively in an English-speaking environment. Foreign language teachers are often confused about goals and uncertain about the principal purpose of their enterprise.

In proficiency testing, and in determining how students' attitudes influence their ability to learn languages, work is being done under the auspices of the National Association for Self-Instructional Language Programs (NASILP). Self-instructional language learning is quite different from self-paced or individualized learning, which is essentially the tailoring of conventional student-teacher relationships to the student's needs. It is most useful where a strongly motivated student does not find on campus a course in a language he or she wishes to learn. The method involves texts, tapes, and sessions with a native speaker (who does not act as a teacher, but provides corrections and an opportunity for practice). A study guide accompanying the tape addresses typical questions and is designed to prepare the student for the whole experience of language learning. Students are tested on oral proficiency; and testing methods and standards are reaching an impressive level of sophistication. Self-instructional programs are likely to be particularly useful for the less commonly taught languages (as in the Critical Language Program at Temple University) and for students majoring in unrelated fields who need basic oral competence in a foreign language.

Ultimately the humanization of the language requirement can probably best be achieved by tying it to proficiency. How can we convince the faculty as a whole to accept proficiency-based requirements? Perhaps this will become one of the concerns of the International Committee we recommended in chapter 4. Whether this broader committee has responsibility for language or not, it is probably a good idea to establish a campuswide standing committee on languages. It would be responsible for advising on language needs across the campus, language instruction and its coordination, and support mechanisms for language instruction (Brod 1980: 13). This committee might consist of representatives of the language departments plus a few faculty from other fields. It should have strong administrative and staff support, to provide follow-up and coordination. Since the departments will probably appoint people with an active interest in language instruction, the chances are that this committee will be considerably more forward-looking than the average language faculty member. It may therefore be the right place to float the idea of proficiency-based instruction. The language departments can then be brought into the process gradually and specifically charged, department by department, with the development of standards and procedures. While some coordination across departments may prove necessary, variations in arrangements from department to department should probably be ignored in the early stages and can be ironed out after a year or two of operation. The matter of credit would also have to be addressed, perhaps through other existing mechanisms and committees.

Maintaining language skills is another important issue. Although some institutions are better than others in this regard, most students who fulfill their language requirements move out of the classroom into a totally monoglot world, with few opportunities to put foreign language to practical use. Of course, with a proficiency system in place, an institution is better able to gauge the size of its competent population in the various languages and create an appropriate maintenance program. But in any case there should be abundant opportunities to speak foreign languages outside the classroom, read foreign books and periodicals, and participate in foreign language events. Some of the most enthusiastic students might be reached by language houses or special classrooms set aside for immersion (Conner 1977: 98) and with magazines, newspapers, and records. But it may be even more important to create an atmosphere in which *all* students feel that linguistic diversity is a fact of life and that knowing and using a second language is a useful advantage. In a later chapter we shall examine ways in which the campus environment can better reflect those desirable conditions of linguistic diversity and how language programming can reinforce language learning.

Ideally a college should continue to take an interest in the maintenance of language skills after a student leaves, perhaps through alumni refresher courses or special foreign language publications. We shall return to this idea in our chapter on people.

### 6. Articulation and Integration

We have been considering institutions which now have a language requirement. But many have none. According to Brod and Meyerson (1975: 43-8), between 1966 and 1974 colleges with language requirements for admission dropped from 33.6 to 18.6 percent of the total, and those with requirements for graduation dropped from 89 to 53 percent. This plunge (to which should be added reductions in the requirements in many institutions) reduced the strength of language departments in many colleges (Schulz 1979: 2). It did, however, have one advantage: It eliminated the captive audience of students obliged to satisfy the requirement and placed language teachers on a par with professors in other departments, for whom it is a daily necessity to make courses interesting to students. While we are not suggesting that the unregulated market economy is an appropriate model for institutions of higher learning, neither are systems of monopoly, which can lead to inefficiency and conservatism. In many colleges and universities without language requirements, language teachers, and indeed entire departments, work hard at making language learning interesting and appealing. At these institutions and in others, numerous new approaches have been introduced over the past few years, some with considerable success (Schulz 1979: 8-9, 54-5; Conner 1977). Referring to the abolition of requirements, Schulz comments as follows concerning the survey of language teaching reported in her volume (1979: 10):

> A few departments claim that, while they initially lost some enrollments, they have actually benefited from the elimination of require-

ments in terms of higher quality students, heightened achievement among students, more positive attitudes among students and instructors, more enjoyable working conditions, and improved instructional quality from teachers who realize that special efforts must be made to hold "volunteers." In the words of one chairperson, "Without the prop of an externally imposed curricular subsidy, our teaching must be imaginative and sophisticated, and all our students are in our language courses because they wish to be."

Numerous descriptions of "nontraditional" approaches to language learning have been presented in publications of the American Council on the Teaching of Foreign Languages, the Modern Language Association, and other organizations, and we shall not repeat them here. Suffice it to say that there appear to be three hurdles to expanded enrollments: articulation, faculty flexibility, and public attitudes toward languages.

Articulation (linking programs at one level with programs at the next) is a problem throughout the system. As we have seen, the difficulty of linking language learning in the elementary school with language learning in the secondary school was one of the factors contributing to the disappearance of FLES (Foreign Languages in the Elementary School) programs. Articulation between secondary school and college adds a further dimension. The choice of languages in secondary school tends to be small; instruction is of varying quality. Making an easy transition from secondary learning to college learning should be one of the main planning priorities of the language-teaching community.

One of the areas most directly affected by this problem is that of the less commonly taught languages. They are not usually available in high schools. In recent years magnet schools in some cities (specialized high schools drawing their students from an entire school district) have made some of these languages accessible, but much more could be done. Teaching materials are needed, particularly for students learning one of the less commonly taught languages as a first foreign language. Above all, school systems and colleges need to work together to develop programs straddling high school and college and work with admissions officers on a system of preferred admission for students who enter such programs.

Even within the college setting there exist difficulties of articulation. The discrete hour-long class, meeting three times a week or so, is not the ideal setting for language learning. But other, more intensive, patterns are hard to integrate into a student's schedule. Above all, what is learned in the language classroom has so little to do with what a student is studying in other fields. Renate Schulz's survey (1979: 3) suggests that many disciplines regard language learning as essential or helpful to their work. But it has proved difficult to meet these disciplines halfway—to present French, German, or Russian in terms of music, history, or chemistry.

Here we raise our second problem—that of faculty flexibility. There is an almost limitless range of possibilities for joining language study to other disciplines. But the vast majority of language teachers, trained as teachers of literature, have difficulty reaching out to other disciplines since they do not have the disciplinary competence required. Furthermore, they do so with mixed emotions. They are anxious to preserve and strengthen their upper-level literature courses. Directing their attention away reduces their ability to offer a full literature program, and it may cause students to study, say, political science in French rather than Balzac in French. Yet if they do not respond to pressures to offer nonliterary courses, perhaps faculty in other fields will be asked to do so, and they will lose their Balzac students anyway.

We have no universal prescription. As literary scholars point out, literature and literary study have their methodologies and special characteristics. But, fundamentally, literature is about human interrelationships and human efforts to define a moral basis for action. It thus reflects the processes out of which the social sciences and the humanities are made and is not so much a discipline as the raw material of many disciplines. But the turn that so much of literary study made under the New Criticism was away from this interdisciplinarity and toward its establishment as a separate and distinct pursuit with its own methodology and modes of procedure. We make no general judgment on this disciplinary separatism, but in this specific case—the teaching of languages to students of all persuasions—the effect has proven, on balance, negative. It has made the language and literature teacher a kind of disciplinary schizophrenic, shuttling between verbs and isolated literary texts. The training of many, if not all, of our language teachers simply has very little bearing on much of what they do, and the processes of professional socialization they passed through in graduate school and as young professors have actually created barriers between their sense of their professional selves and the larger task before them.

This is not only a matter of professional socialization but of ethnic socialization. Language and literature teachers often identify strongly with the cultures whose works they teach. This is not in itself a bad thing, except that they often adopt the prejudices of those cultures—a tendency to look askance at the Spanish of Latin America, or to concentrate on Paris to the exclusion of Brussels, Montreal, and Brazzaville. It may be shocking to suggest, but in the long run

Canada and Mexico may be as important to our cultural survival as France and Spain.

This is not to say that teachers have made no attempt to overcome these barriers. There are many whose courses in literature are imaginative, broad-gauged, and responsive to the inquiry and aptitude of their students (cf. Dathorne 1974). We need to encourage these tendencies by supporting skilled teachers, especially those whose approach to their materials extends outward to the concerns of other disciplines and aspires to a world view. There are real issues here—of priorities and, indeed, of the future of general education. A dean who denies research funds for a literary project and grants funds to a professor who wants a broader grasp of neighboring disciplines is open to accusations of philistinism and support for dilettantism. But it is important that a dean take such a stand, particularly if it can be done without fueling the fires of disciplinary defensiveness. We strongly suggest that, at the very least, funding be made available for curricular development in upper-level courses in language departments. And certain other moves might be contemplated as ways of encouraging language departments into fruitful relationships with other disciplines:

a.   Teachers in language departments who have some expertise in other fields might be offered secondary appointments in other departments (perhaps without voting rights, and on a term appointment). A professor of Italian with knowledge of Italian art might be given a secondary appointment in art history, for example. Not only would this produce new opportunities for language teachers; it would create a voice of advocacy for languages in other departments and might encourage faculty to seek a more integrative role for language instruction in their disciplines and to use foreign language texts in their own teaching. This advocacy could be made more or less explicit, depending on the political and social circumstances of the faculty.

b.   Departments might be encouraged to cross-list courses taught by language departments whose subject matter intersects with theirs. In fact, certain grants for curricular development could be assigned to language departments on condition that the course be cross-listed.

c.   Faculty might be encouraged to work with members of language departments on joint courses. A German-speaking biology professor, say, might develop with the German department a course jointly taught by the two. The biologist's lectures would be linguistically directed by the German professor, who would advise on range and vocabulary, the introduction of new concepts, and so on. Credit might be given either for German or for biology. The formal lectures could be reinforced by additional language instruction and by work with the language laboratory. Alternatively, a course might be given in two languages, with general lectures in English and reinforcing modules in a second language. Or the process might be reversed (lectures in a second language, with English-language recitations to clear up problems of comprehension and to review, in English, particularly difficult concepts). Many variants of these procedures are described in the literature on new curricula and teaching methods.

**d.** There is, of course, a difference between linking language with the disciplines and uniting language with preprofessional training. Again, there are numerous examples of courses along these lines offered at the college level (see, for example, Born and Buck 1978). Particularly among business educators there is a rising sense of the importance of language training (Nehrt 1977; President's Commission 1979), though converting this into curricular terms is problematic (for one imaginative approach see Kuhne and Jordan 1980). Probably several of the ideas already mentioned could be applied to undergraduate schools of business, particularly the integration of faculty and the team teaching of courses. But just as we must create among arts and sciences faculty a sense of the international nature of the curriculum, we must do the same in business. Until this comes about, business education cannot revise its curricular priorities to give an adequate role to language.

In all these efforts to link fields and tie language to its practical application, we should remember that students taking these offerings are still very much *learners* of the language: They require a great deal of support. Teaching language under any circumstances is expensive: The nature of the field dictates small classes and much practice. But interdisciplinary study is particularly costly. Above all, we should consider the need for top-level instruction. Kelly (1974: 155-6) speaks eloquently to the matter:

> Probably the most serious threat to continued growth of interdisciplinary studies is the mounting cry of amateurism being directed, quite justifiably in some instances, at curricular innovations employing interdisciplinary titles in one form or another. True interdisciplinarity is motivated by curiosity and the desire to explore new questions rather than trying to answer old ones. The exploration must proceed, however, from a base of competence informed by hard knowledge. Students still feel more secure working with interdisciplinary teachers who have had formal training in the fields under study in a given course.

## 7.  Reintroducing a Language Requirement

Changes in teachers' and students' attitudes toward the curriculum have made it realistic to talk about reintroducing a language requirement in institutions that dropped it a few years ago, or about raising its level. Obviously we have mixed feelings about this. A simple reintroduction of the old requirement would probably be counterproductive, for the reasons we have cited. We do not agree with the recommendation to that effect by the President's Commission. As it stands, their bald statement, "Schools, colleges, and universities should reinstate foreign language requirements," smacks of a certain special-interest mentality. We strongly agree with the spirit of the recommendation, but only if it can be shown that the new requirements can do a better job than the old. Any institution interested in bringing the requirement back would do well to ask itself precisely what it wants to achieve, and try to build a program based on that aim.

When we speak of achievement, we are referring not to procedures but to outcomes. The aim of a history major is not to have students take 12 courses in history but to teach them certain methods and facts about history. Listing these methods and facts will determine the procedures required to teach them. If the aim of a language requirement is to bring students to a certain level of proficiency, we should identify the best set of procedures to (a) bring them to that point with as few failures as possible, (b) ascertain that they have in fact reached that point, and (c) generate in them the enthusiasm and interest required to move beyond that point and assist them as they do. Only if agreement can be reached on these questions, and procedures set, is it worth moving ahead with a requirement.

On the other hand, many educators, perhaps more than would be willing to vote for the requirements we now have in most colleges, believe in the intellectual value of language study. How can we make it work? Frederick Starr speaks of massive attrition. There are few things more depressing for the teacher of language than the progressive falling away in the size of a class in the first week or two of a semester (in institutions where there is a requirement and students cannot vote with their feet, they simply vote with their brains, quietly turning them off). Perhaps students should be introduced to linguistics—to how languages work—in a realistic and sympathetic way at the college level or at the beginning of high school.

In this regard remarkable success has been achieved with Esperanto as an introduction to language study. Language teachers tend to underestimate the achievements and potential of Esperanto as an aid to language learning and as a functional means of international communication in its own right. It merits serious investigation. The simplicity and regularity of its structure make it relatively easy for the new language learner, and this helps keep interest high.

Furthermore, students rapidly pass the threshold at which the language becomes practical. It is not unusual for a class in Esperanto to be corresponding with students in other countries well before the first semester is over and visiting other countries before the year is out. With this self-confidence firmly in place, they can move on to an ethnic language with less fear and with greater sensitivity to the complexities of language. Esperanto, in short, can be a powerful ally of the language teacher (Goodman 1976). It might also provide one way of introducing a language requirement in institutions that presently do not have one: A year of Esperanto might be required, and students might then be encouraged to move on to other languages. Language professors could add Esperanto to their repertoire with relative ease, given time and support. Several institutions, including Southern Illinois University, Wesleyan University, and Principia College, have experimented with the teaching of the language (Wood 1975). San Francisco State University offers courses for teachers. Since such courses are frequently not offered by language departments, they seldom turn up in statistics on language study. The principal organizations working in this field are the Esperanto Studies Association of America, the Esperanto League for North America, and the Esperantic Studies Foundation.

Other possible approaches include working into an introductory language class elements from other languages or special exercises designed to develop a student's linguistic sense. Emphasis should fall on confidence-building exercises. Students need a good deal of individual attention, at least in the first few months, and, if possible, they should have more than one person to call on for help. Social events (and not always foreign language ones) should be held to draw students into a state in which they are sufficiently open to communicate their problems to their teachers. Ideally the introductory class should be taught by an experienced professor, with help from graduate assistants.

As soon as students are ready, they might be introduced not only to literature but to texts in other fields as well. They might choose the kinds of texts they work with and read. Other faculty could be invited into class to give short talks in the foreign language on topics related to their fields. Foreign students could be involved in this same way. All in all, we should do everything we can to demonstrate that languages are alive and full of meaning and useful.

One further element to consider as institutions contemplate reintroduction of a language requirement is the learning environment. In
a later chapter we shall discuss the creation of a campus environment conducive to a sense of the international and global. We remind our readers of that International Committee we called for as
the central mechanism for a campuswide effort. A language requirement should ideally be just one element in a total campaign to internationalize every facet of the institution. Let it not be one more burden in Dotheboys U. but one more opportunity to teach and to learn,
and to apply knowledge to an understanding of the world.

## 8.   Overcoming Public Resistance to Language Study

In his comments on high schools Starr suggested that the bad experiences of school board members in their younger days can turn them
against language teaching in the schools. The whole question of public attitudes on language merits greater investigation. On this subject, a great degree of irrationality can be generated by otherwise
reasonable people. Consider, for example, the debate over bilingual
education, or the resistance to the use of other languages in the law
courts or on ballot papers. In these latter instances we are dealing
primarily with Spanish. Millions of Spanish speakers in this country
were born here, as were their parents; their ancestors lived on the
same plot of land, Spanish then, U.S. territory now. Yet in a recent
court case in New York, where a Spanish speaker was tried for mur-
der and testified in Spanish, all Spanish speakers were barred from
the jury on the ground that they would have an advantage because
they could understand the defendant without having to rely on interpretation (Tuchman 1979).

Though we have millions of native speakers of other languages
within our borders, it is hardly noticeable from the mass media or
from public attitudes (Keller and Roel 1980). We cannot escape the
feeling that one reason people resist recognizing the existence of
other languages is a deep-seated anxiety about our own national
identity and place in the world. If language is power, and the use of
English is a sign of power in the world, using foreign languages appears to some as a confession of weakness, a deliberate giving away
of our sense of superiority.

We are equally unrealistic about the beauties of English, the sub-
tleties of language. Languages (we quail at the comparison) are like
computers: If they are badly programmed, they do not do what we
want them to. If they are well programmed, they are at most mirrors
of our thoughts. It is we who are subtle or crude, not the languages
we use. And how often, in our dealings with one another, are we mis-

understood, or half understood! As for English, we are told that its vast vocabulary gives it a certain superiority to other languages. But most of that vocabulary sits between the covers of the Oxford English Dictionary, unknown and unused. The actual working vocabulary of an English speaker is not significantly different from that of a French or an Arabic speaker. Besides, other languages have other qualities, some lacking in English. All in all, we need to demystify the matter of language and deal with languages as they are: remarkable creations of human ingenuity and repositories of the history of peoples and nations.

Steven Grant has pointed out (1980) that the United States has never actually declared that English is its official language. Shirley Heath (1977) has shown that for a considerable part of our history we were essentially a bilingual or multilingual country. But as Paul Simon suggests, speaking another language has more often been a source of shame than of pride (Simon 1980a: 12). To counteract this negative aspect of Americanization, we should learn more about our linguistic past and present.

Colleges share a particular responsibility in this regard. Although much of this chapter has been devoted to curricular options and related questions, we should take a leaf from a later chapter and point out that in many respects the secret to successful college language programs is heightened public awareness about the role and importance of language in everyday life. This requires a systematic attempt to reach out to the community, deal with school boards and administrators, offer special courses and information to the public, and, above all, to try to make language useful and effective. We must remember the principle of investment: Learning a language must be worthwhile, the decision to learn it must offer a reasonable expectation of success, and the making of the decision must be based on a realistic assessment. At the moment language teachers regularly make exaggerated claims about their wares, students have exaggerated expectations about the ease with which they will learn, and all of us have exaggerated beliefs about the efficacy of sitting students in a foreign language classroom whether they learn anything or not.

The best hope students have of acquiring functional competence in a language is to spend a period in a country where that language is spoken. This is only one of the advantages of study abroad, which, even for students who choose English-speaking countries, provides an immediate broadening of horizons. No institution with a commitment to internationalization can afford to neglect the possibilities opened when students—and, indeed, faculty—spend time overseas, and it is these possibilities that we will consider next.

# 6

## Meeting the World Halfway: Study Abroad and International Exchanges

# Meeting the World Halfway: Study Abroad and International Exchanges

## 1. Study Abroad: Its Forms and Its Potential

In 1977-78 some 120,000 American students went abroad to study in U.S.-sponsored programs. Others enrolled independently in foreign institutions. All told there are 10 times as many American students overseas as there were 15 years ago (Burn 1980b: 70). There are now some 1,800 college programs offering academic-year study abroad and no less than 900 summer programs. The number of American students visiting foreign countries for other purposes has also increased enormously: 133,150 passports were issued to students in 1963; by 1978 this figure was up to 596,660.

Most American students go abroad for a full academic year (generally their junior year) or for a single semester, or else in one of a number of summer programs sponsored by American or foreign institutions. If they go during the academic year, it is usually in one of the following ways:

**a.** As a regular or special student, admitted directly by the foreign institution for a semester or a year.

**b.** Under special auspices, such as a formal agreement between the foreign institution and the student's home institution giving preferential admission to those from the American college.

**c.** As a member of a program sponsored by an American institution at a foreign university. Such programs generally offer special facilities overseas for the participating students, such as help with housing or registration, orientation, possibly special tutorials. A program in this category may be run by an individual American college (generally, but not necessarily, the student's home institution), a consortium, or an American organization created to offer study abroad.

**d.** As a member of a special program for foreign students sponsored by a foreign university. Occasionally programs ostensibly in the third category may turn out to have this character (i.e., students are not integrated into the regular programs of the university but are separated out into special classes). But the system is especially used by universities in countries whose languages are not widely known in the United States, such as Japan (e.g., Sophia University, Kansai

University), where integration would be particularly diffi-
cult. Among other countries with programs of this type are
Italy, Holland, Denmark, Norway, and Sweden (Garraty,
Klemperer, and Taylor 1978: 132).

**e.** As a member of a freestanding program primarily or exclusively for American students, generally located close to a
university and drawing on its facilities or faculty. Many of
these programs also seem to belong in the third category, but
students enrolled in them are not regarded as students of the
foreign university near which the program is located.

**f.** As a participant in a work-study or cooperative education program. These are becoming increasingly popular.
Some are run by American colleges (such as the Lincoln University program in Nigeria or the extensive cooperative education program provided by Antioch College). Others are arranged by international coordinating organizations. The International Association of Students in Economics and Business (AIESEC), for example, offers practical experience in
these fields to American students through placements in
over 50 countries. The International Association for the Exchange of Students for Technical Experience (IAESTE) provides placements, during the academic year and in the summer, for students in engineering and technology and some
other fields. Former AIESEC and IAESTE students are particularly sought by American business.

Summer programs, as might be expected, vary enormously. Some
are organized by foreign universities anxious to keep their facilities
occupied during the summer months. They range from carefully
planned and high-quality offerings to fly-by-night programs of little
academic merit. Others are sponsored by American institutions,
sometimes as adjuncts of academic-year programs. This category
shades off into various practical activities, placements, field work,
or just glorified vacations. IAESTE has a particularly active summer
program. Others provide intensive study or training in the fine arts
or languages or international institutions or any of a number of
other subjects.

Students choose to study abroad for many reasons. Some wish to
improve their language skills, and many of the older and well-established programs (such as Sweet Briar's program in France, New
York University's program in Spain, Smith's program in Italy) were
created to meet this need. Students benefit enormously not only from
their exposure to languages but from the cultural immersion.

A second category of students travels abroad in search of the special facilities offered by foreign universities or cities. A few (a dimin-

ishing breed, alas) go to study with famous scholars. Others, following in the footsteps of generations of American expatriates, gravitate to major centers of art—Florence, Rome, Athens—or enroll in specialized programs provided by foreign universities in numerous fields in the humanities and social sciences. Some of these, and others, engage in various types of field work, perhaps preparing for senior projects on their home campuses. Several of the better American programs offer facilities for such students with special interests and help to link them with local scholars or institutions.

The third and largest category travels abroad for less specific or premeditated reasons. They go because their colleges offer the chance or encourage them to seek such opportunities. They go because they are anxious for the experience of living and studying in another country: not so much to acquire some specific piece of knowledge or expertise as to keep up their studies while experiencing a different environment and possibly a different approach to study. Above all, they are anxious to see and feel what they have read about and researched, heirs to that fine American virtue (and, occasionally, vice) of curiosity, of wanting to see for oneself. Most go to Europe, many to Israel—in numbers sometimes overwhelming, in fact; and they represent not only a wonderful opportunity for American higher education but a lucrative and eminently exploitable market, largely unregulated and subject to all kinds of abuse.

It is this last fact that creates skepticism in some quarters regarding the value of foreign study—or fuels a skepticism already present. Some colleges go out of their way to encourage students to study abroad. Foreign study has traditionally been an important feature of small liberal arts colleges, partly because of the emphasis on the European roots of American culture engendered by their curricula, partly also because of the socioeconomic background of their clientele. Many have their own well-respected and long-established programs abroad and others are served by well-organized consortia (e.g., the Great Lakes Colleges Association). In some colleges a very high percentage of students take these opportunities (though despite the aggregate numbers, the overall percentage of American students studying abroad is relatively very small).

Many faculty wonder about the quality of the programs their students clamor to participate in. Are they as strong as programs at home? Do students spend enough time studying? Even if American puritan images of a degenerate and decaying Europe remain far from these faculty members' heads, they worry about the extent to which their students' minds are on their studies. And appeals to the value of experience may work with some faculties but are unlikely to do so with others: Attitudes toward experiential learning, at least for credit, are ambivalent at best.

Some of these fears are far from groundless, since there exist in fact many poor programs. Even those run by a student's home institution may not be subject to the close scrutiny and quality control applied by the faculty to programs nearer home. And this can be a circular problem: Faculty neglect weakens programs, which in turn become less willing to submit themselves to scrutiny. In fact, the question of quality control in study-abroad programs is becoming increasingly pressing as programs and numbers expand from year to year, frequently at the lower end of the quality scale. For the most part, American accrediting associations make no attempt to evaluate study abroad, though the Council on International Educational Exchange (CIEE) does so for its members (a total of 170 colleges and organizations) and there is a fairly well-established informal network of study-abroad administrators and advisors who can provide reliable judgments—supported also by such organizations as the Institute for International Education.

Added to the problem of accreditation is the difficulty of evaluating students' performance abroad. American academics are used to a system of credit hours and grading wholly alien to many of the countries in which their students study. Not only do many higher education systems in Europe and elsewhere provide no grades but some do not even offer courses in the traditional American sense. This exacerbates the problem of equivalency. Is the student's work in chemistry at London University really equivalent to Chemistry 101 at home? Is an Oxford tutorial really the same as a course in the history of English literature? With the best will in the world, the American professor or registrar cannot figure out what to enter on a student's transcript—and these technical problems of transcripts and credit and grades tend to overshadow the validity of the educational experience itself. Faced with inadequate or incomprehensible data, the American professor, especially with no experience of foreign universities, is apt to become impatient—or to harbor the suspicion that someone, somewhere, is hiding something. This problem is particularly difficult in fields where the United States can claim to be a world leader—the natural sciences, to some degree, but particularly engineering and business administration. Can a course in business at the University of Mexico really compare with one at a U.S. institution? If it cannot, perhaps business students should not be allowed credit for work abroad. So goes the argument.

Some faculties are actively resistant to foreign study. Administrators of study-abroad programs soon learn which departments on the home campus are sympathetic and which are not. The reasons for resistance are sometimes understandable (some foreign universities simply do not offer the quality instruction available at some American institutions), though they are often reinforced by ignorance or suspicion. Others are less obvious. A language department fighting to maintain its upper-level courses and to attract majors may have mixed feelings about shipping off its best students to Madrid or Paris; given that so selfish a motive cannot be acceptably articulated, the department raises all kinds of technical problems, in a kind of psychological displacement, to render a program inoperable. A college trying hard to increase enrollment may be reluctant to let students take off for other countries if it must fill their places from a dwindling pool of eligible candidates.

On the other hand, study-abroad programs can help in the recruitment and retention of students. As more colleges become aware of this, resistance to programs is much reduced. Some institutions (Kalamazoo College, for example) regard foreign study as a routine part of their undergraduate programs and regularly plan to enroll more students than they can accommodate at one time on campus.

The fact is that study abroad, under the right conditions, can be immensely rewarding for the student ready to undertake it. Some of the reasons are obvious. Many students speak of the need to stand on their own feet, to cope with an alien environment, to make the most out of new surroundings: Study abroad helps students to mature, to handle their own lives. Others who have passed through the experience years before note that it gives one a certain critical distance with respect to American society and has what the President's Commission called "a lifelong impact on values." Cultural relativity, a healthy skepticism, objectivity, distance—we need to cultivate these qualities in America. Being obliged to defend one's country's record in foreign parts may also help one establish what is valuable about the United States and its traditions. And study abroad brings tolerance and an awareness that there are other ways of doing things (Sanders and Ward 1970: 91) and that this country has no monopoly on common sense or sanity.

There has been relatively little research on the impact of study abroad. Barbara Burn (1980b: 133) points out, however, that the research done "suggests that it may be most important in terms of the personal experience of living in another culture and interacting with the nationals of another country." Nevertheless, it can have a more directly intellectual impact, too. The American student may be surprised to discover that there are other ways of organizing a curriculum than through discrete courses, and that even in the same academic field different countries have their own sets of gods and wise men. Even in English literature the American student discovers that the British admire a set of critics quite different from the Americans and that they are willing to raise questions (about the social function of literature, for example) virtually never encountered in the American classroom.

Finally, there is the indirect, the multiplier, effect of foreign study. If 100,000 Americans go abroad to study each year, 100,000 return. Most resume their studies at American colleges. Their social and intellectual contribution to the widening of the horizons of students and faculty with whom they came into contact is immeasurably important; it may ultimately be the most important contribution, from an institutional point of view, that foreign study can provide.

## 2. Making Study Abroad More Accessible

If we accept that study abroad, for any or all of these reasons, is valuable and that more students should participate, what can the administrator or teacher do to make it easier? The following points are at least a beginning.

a. **We can remove obstacles to credit**. Many institutions are extremely ambivalent about the award of credit for foreign study. Lacking the will or the expertise to distinguish between good programs and bad, they tend to drag their feet on all of them without forbidding the transfer of credit entirely. They may be nervous about equivalencies in their own programs as well.

Two steps seem essential here. First, there must be someone on campus with a good knowledge of study abroad or the resources to acquire it—perhaps the administrator charged with the technicalities of credit transfer from other institutions (i.e., U.S. as well as foreign) or the study-abroad advisor. This person might be assisted by a committee or board consisting of faculty with experience of foreign institutions.

Second, we can establish guidelines on the transfer of credit from foreign universities and U.S.-sponsored programs. This is probably best carried out by a faculty committee, which should be charged with producing a general statement on the value of foreign study to which the guidelines can be appended. The statement can be used for catalogs and the like; also, its composition will predispose the committee to come up with practical proposals in the guidelines section of their report. If the committee takes the stance of an adversary to the entire concept of foreign study, the result will prove extremely restrictive—though it may be better to have strict guidelines than no guidelines at all, since the latter situation leads to squabbles after the fact. The committee should include the administrator who evaluates foreign credit and anyone else directly involved with study abroad—as consultants, if not as voting members.

The guidelines should be widely discussed and finally approved by the faculty. They then become part of the institution's academic regulations. Ideally, they should define as clearly as possible the types of programs and institutions for which credit will be awarded, so that students and advisors can determine whether a program is eligible. While students should be encouraged to obtain advance approval for the course of study they wish to pursue at a foreign institution or in a U.S.-sponsored program, this may occasionally prove unnecessarily restrictive and may be academically counterproductive. Many foreign universities do not publish comprehensive (or annual) catalogs. We all know how hard it is to make wise choices on the basis of catalog descriptions even at American universities; it is clearly far more difficult with foreign institutions. It is much better to be able to say to a student, "We regard the University of X or the program run by College X as inferior and not worthy of credit, but we will give credit for the University of A or the program run by College B." This system may occasionally lead to inequities or soft options, but it is far more practical than advance approval of individual courses. Why should a student going to the London School of Economics or the University of Geneva be committed in advance to a specific selection of courses?

Obviously, this is only part of the problem. Giving credit for a course or program is one thing. Giving major credit or distributional credit is quite another. Again, flexibility is important. Nothing is more maddening to the student than having to establish the precise equivalency of a course abroad with one at home. It is best if the major department can be persuaded to give the student a set of criteria *in advance* and in writing to apply in selecting major-related courses at the foreign institution. This correspondence then becomes part of the student's file and can be included in the assessment and certification of his or her record (provided, of course, that a notation can be made—a matter not always easy in this computer age).

Once clear guidelines have been established, certain patterns of behavior follow. Those in charge of study abroad, or anxious to create links with particular programs, strive to select options that fulfill the academic criteria laid down by the guidelines. Hence the problem of quality control is reduced. There are fewer individual problems with credit after the fact. Students learn what is possible and what is not. The whole process becomes easier to administer. And this brings us to the second point...

**b. We can provide students with advice on study abroad.** Every institution should have an individual or an office expressly charged with advising on study abroad. There are other reasons, too, for a college to have current information on foreign institutions. The admissions office, for example, needs data to evaluate foreign transcripts. It is advisable to build a library of basic materials—standard reference works on foreign universities (*The World of Learning*, the *Commonwealth Universities Yearbook*, and so on), catalogs from the more important institutions, publications on higher education in other countries (these are often issued by the governments concerned, by the U.S. government, or by such organizations as AACRAO and NAFSA), and the standard handbooks on U.S.-sponsored programs in other countries. The Institute for International Education publishes guides and handbooks on foreign study, the Council on International Educational Exchange specializes in student travel, and organizations such as UNESCO publish guides to work opportunities in other countries.

If the college in question has no study-abroad programs, the person charged with this responsibility should build personal contacts (perhaps in consultation with relevant on-campus departments) with good programs at other institutions. General contact with the study-abroad community—through the National Association for Foreign Student Affairs, for example—is extremely important.

It is vital that the study-abroad advisor be able to act as advocate for students in their dealings with academic offices and with the faculty. Hence the advisor should be a faculty member or someone with good access to friendly and supportive teachers. Nothing is more deadening to students' initiative than having to plead their cases before their major departments—very possibly before people unsympathetic to foreign study and unlikely to excuse student ignorance of the workings of foreign institutions. The advisor should also have good links with faculty who have studied abroad, with foreign nationals on the faculty, with foreign students who can advise Americans contemplating study abroad, and with foreign embassies. And we cannot overstress the importance of maintaining good links with returned American students. No one can better advise the sophomore considering study in Paris than the senior just returned.

Whether the person who advises on foreign study should also be the one who assesses credit for it depends on the size of the institution and the qualifications of the individual. Combining the functions is convenient, but it can lead to a conflict of interest. Linking this person with the office that handles foreign students is, however, extremely important. It is a good idea to put foreign study and foreign students under the same administrative roof.

Since much faculty resistance to the accreditation of foreign study springs from ignorance of foreign conditions, a modest public relations effort should be included in the mandate of the foreign study advisor. It is a good idea to put foreign visitors to the campus in touch with relevant departments, to tell faculty about particularly interesting programs overseas, and to see that interesting foreign projects undertaken by students receive maximum publicity on campus. Faculty traveling abroad could be encouraged to contact students from their institutions and to see better programs firsthand. If their visits can be subsidized, so much the better.

Such visits are also useful for establishing personal contacts with foreign institutions. More and more countries (Britain is a recent addition to the list) are establishing quotas on the number of foreign students admitted to their universities. Contacts can help overcome these obstacles and gain admission for students. For similar reasons contacts with the directors of U.S.-sponsored programs can help place students in them.

It is advisable to establish a faculty committee on foreign study to oversee programs the home institution might run and to help in the administration of guidelines, the solution of special problems, and so on. The committee might be charged with selecting students or awarding scholarships. It can help maintain dialogue with departments about the facilitation and smooth administration of foreign study and the development of special programs. It can also serve as an advocate for the study-abroad advisor.

Finally, we must emphasize the importance of personal and direct advice to individual students. Going abroad is more than selecting an academic program: It is a decision to change one's life, for a shorter or longer period, more or less totally. The more students know about what to expect in the program or institution they have chosen, the better. Students also need reassurance—that they will not fall behind in their studies, that their grade point averages will not collapse (possibly time abroad should, as a matter of policy, not be calculated in GPAs) and so on. Obviously an advisor should not give false assurances, but it is a measure of the success of the operation that such assurances can be obtained from the faculty and passed on to students. Those unsuited for study abroad, academically or emotionally, should be discouraged. Others should be made aware of the risks involved and also of the special opportunities and advantages. And if their peers who have already studied abroad can be brought into the dialogue, this will help.

**c. We can provide financial assistance**. Perhaps the biggest obstacle to foreign study is the cost. Although limited federal funds are available for graduate study abroad (through the Fulbright program, for example) there is no generally accessible source for undergraduates. Regulations regarding the use of state scholarships for foreign study vary. In some cases they may not be taken outside the United States, though even in these instances it may be possible to use them —if such an arrangement has the approval of the donor—by regarding students studying abroad as technically in residence on their home campus, and by arranging for tuition payments to be funneled through a student's home institution.

While most institutions let students use financial aid to participate in study-abroad programs they run, these students may get into difficulty if they take leaves of absence to enroll directly in foreign institutions on an independent basis. Federal aid such as Pell grants can be used for this purpose, however. Financial aid officers may also resist study-abroad programs because of the complications they entail and because they may represent a net loss in tuition unless a fee-paying student can be found to fill the vacated place.

An effective study-abroad administrator on campus can do much to create a friendly relationship with the financial aid office and eliminate administrative problems confronting the student seeking to go abroad. But a more fundamental problem concerns the identification of scholarship money specifically to assist students with travel or other expenses who wish to study in other countries. Traditionally such assistance has been low on the list of priorities of the average American college, perhaps because the investment brings few tangible results on the home campus. It is vital that such money become available; this should receive primary attention in any effort to internationalize the institution. In some countries tuition differentials for foreign students have recently been introduced, making study in Britain, for example, very expensive for foreigners. However, tuition costs in most countries compare favorably with those in the United States, making study abroad at least a possibility for almost any American student.

One way in which some of the burden can be reduced is by direct exchange of students with a foreign university, on a bed-for-bed basis. We shall have more to say about exchanges in a later section of this chapter.

**d. We can give students good preliminary training**. One of the biggest problems faced by students wishing to study abroad is the language problem. Though an art history student might benefit enormously from time in Italy, or a student in economics from learning in

Japan, or an anthropology student from a stay in India, they seldom have the language skill to move beyond special programs for foreigners in the countries in question. And without adequate language skill, the entire experience is devalued. A systematic attempt should be made specifically to train students for stays abroad, especially for countries whose languages are not widely taught.

Among the possibilities colleges might examine are intensive language courses the summer before departure (Middlebury College does this), especially if money can be found to aid students who would otherwise spend the summer working. Year-long programs might also be designed for students outside the arts and sciences who plan to spend a year at a technical or business school in another country. The latter activities require that students know well in advance that they are going abroad, and may also require the participation of a minimum number. But imaginatively planned programs can do double duty as training programs for students going abroad and as elements in an international studies program or the offerings of a language department.

At issue here is not only the desirability of serving student needs but the importance of convincing nonlanguage majors to acquire language as a tool and to use it to break out of the English-speaking world in pursuit of their academic interests. Such experiments would be good for language departments, too. Because of the link between literature and language, there is a tendency to equate skill in a language with an interest in the humanities; we must break down this false perception.

What is true of language is true of other topics and skills as well. A systematic attempt to prepare students academically for foreign study will enrich the entire experience and, incidentally, make the fact of foreign study more central to the regular curriculum. Good publicity and strong administrative support are crucial here. Many students will be chary of committing themselves to a semester or a year abroad, concerned about the academic risks. They will need good advice, reassurance, and strong support programs. In this and other respects (including, on occasion, language training), foreign students from the target country, students returning to the U.S., and faculty with foreign experience can be very helpful.

We might add that the growth in the number of students going abroad has been accompanied by certain disturbing trends: (1) an increase in English-language programs in non-English-speaking areas of the world, (2) a general turning away from programs in the developing world toward programs in Europe, and (3) an overwhelming concentration of American students in certain key European cities (London, Paris, and Madrid especially). This lack of adventurousness, this movement toward the conventional, may reflect a shift in the political and social interests of students; but it probably also signifies the colleges' inability to devise sufficiently imaginative mechanisms to encourage students making unconventional choices, or to steer them into such paths.

Study abroad remains something of a stepchild of the undergraduate curriculum. Changing this situation may ultimately require a national effort, primarily to make sufficient funding available to democratize the process. But if numbers increase, overcrowding, primarily in Europe, also increases—and hence greater efforts will also be required to disperse the students over a larger area. This, in turn, will be possible only when academic programs at home channel students to unconventional options. The fundamental problem confronting our efforts to promote foreign study may relate less to the quality of the overseas experience (though these shortcomings should not be underestimated) than to the matter of articulation—meshing overseas experience with the remainder of the student's academic program. And this is a double problem. Not only must we remove technical obstacles to foreign study but we must adapt our domestic programs to fit its imperatives and exploit its advantages.

Bringing about such a change will require special effort, especially (paradoxically) at large institutions. Since smaller liberal arts colleges send a larger percentage of their students abroad, their faculties tend to be more involved in the process than those at large institutions, and the larger percentages make special arrangements more feasible. At larger institutions, students with some interest in going abroad are scattered across numerous programs, often with few common denominators. It is necessary to reach beyond the language major, the international relations major, and so on, to students in other programs. Perhaps special arrangements can be made with foreign institutions for students in highly structured programs like engineering, the natural sciences, and business—since these students, too, can derive enormous benefit from contact with another culture. Then again, for students in major programs with an obvious international dimension, study abroad should come to be regarded as a matter of course. In short, we should place a high priority on developing curricular options on *the home campus* for students intending to study abroad.

### 3. Establishing A Study-Abroad Program

Thus far we have made certain assumptions about the nature and problems of study abroad. We have concentrated above all on how foreign study can be integrated smoothly into the programs of the average college. Apart from our closing observations, we have confined ourselves largely to a reactive strategy, simply clearing away problems rather than taking new initiatives. We have also assumed that study abroad comes midway through undergraduate study. We have not considered the possibility of going abroad before the freshman year or after graduation. While these options obviously exist and might be encouraged, they lie outside the immediate scope of this volume.

We have also given little attention to the question of initiating and administering a study-abroad program primarily or exclusively for one's own students. Before launching a program, one should survey the options and assess the pros and cons very carefully. Good study-abroad programs can be expensive, particularly at first. And if they do not respond closely to curricular needs they may become a liability, and a limit to flexibility, rather than an asset.

If, then, we identify a need—let us say (to take two conventional examples), opportunities for German majors to study in Germany or for international relations majors to learn about development processes in the Third World—we should first ask whether there are already programs that could fill it. A review of programs in Germany or in developing countries might turn up suitable options. In fact, by using other people's programs a campus might be able to offer its students a wider choice of programs. Assessing the quality of existing programs can be difficult. Ideally a college representative should visit some of them and talk with their staffs, but if that is impossible such organizations as the IIE can be useful and much can be achieved through personal contacts.

While using other programs involves little financial risk and few administrative headaches, the client institution can exercise little or no influence over them and students have no guarantee of admission. However, some of these conditions can be changed by signing a contract with an existing program. Many need students, not least because the incremental cost per student is quite low while the fixed costs are high, and they are very willing to consider preferential admissions for institutions that can guarantee a regular supply of qualified participants. They may even consider changes in the programs, special arrangements for visiting faculty, and so on. Even a simple promise to steer one's students toward a program—or make it a preferred option, to which students will be initially referred

—may bring assurances of special treatment or other advantages.

Many study-abroad programs do not turn up in handbooks and catalogs because they are intended exclusively for the students of a particular college or group of colleges. It may be possible to enter into a cost-sharing agreement with a college that has such a program, or buy into an existing consortium.

If these options are not available, an institution can talk with other colleges interested in sharing the costs of establishing a program. The major higher education organizations (ACE, AASCU, and so on) may help identify them (working through one's own president is a good idea) or regional councils for international studies or other bodies may help find interested colleges nearby (proximity eases planning and cooperation). The administration of a cooperative effort will depend on the nature of the program and on local factors, but it will probably be easiest to concentrate most of it in a single location at one of the participating colleges and to work out financial contributions accordingly.

While launching one's own program carries considerable financial liability, this can, of course, be converted to an asset if the program is opened to students from other colleges. If recruitment is good and students can be brought in quickly, it may prove possible to recoup the initial investment and reinvest in improving the quality of the program, making financial aid available or increasing faculty participation. The study-abroad landscape is dotted with profit-making programs—often at the expense of academic quality and sometimes under conditions that border on exploitation. If the new program is a success, it may prove hard to hold the financial officers on the home campus at bay; but it is very important to invest in good programs rather than skim profits off the top.

Let us suppose that we are considering our own study-abroad program. What conditions should be fulfilled before a decision is made to go ahead? The list will vary depending on local circumstances, but we can single out these important points:

    a.   We should know clearly what we want to achieve. Generally the initiative for a program comes from a single faculty member or group of faculty. The initiators should be encouraged to prepare a statement of objectives. This should be reviewed, at least by an appropriate faculty committee and possibly by the entire faculty, and any modifications made. The objectives of the proposed program should be examined to see whether they are compatible with, and an enhancement to, existing undergraduate programs, especially those from which participants would be drawn.

**b.** There should be adequate financial resources available for the program, and in sufficiently flexible form. Foreign study programs are expensive to staff and often never pay for themselves. The financial officers on the home campus should understand this. They should be willing to invest money not only in on-site facilities and staff (though *not* real estate if it can possibly be avoided, at least initially) but in recruitment and in faculty and staff travel. Too many initial restrictions can condemn a promising program to failure.

**c.** We should have good affiliation arrangements with the host institution. It is impossible to generalize about the precise nature of such arrangements, since they will obviously vary from country to country and program to program. The arrangements may simply consist of guaranteed admission to certain types of courses, library privileges, and so on. Other factors to consider, either as items in an agreement or as matters that the program itself will have to deal with, include housing, health insurance, access to facilities, and special arrangements for faculty attached to the program. In any event, the agreement should be in writing and should involve contact between the two institutions at the highest possible level. At the same time we should be satisfied that the middle-level administrators charged with carrying out the agreement are competent and cooperative. Unforeseen technical problems will surely arise and we must be prepared to deal with them expeditiously.

**d.** There should be strong support for the program on the home campus from faculty and departments most likely to be involved in its execution. They should be willing to cooperate in committee work, recruitment, admissions, and so on. Faculty should feel that they have a stake in the success of the program and that it involves tangible advantages for them. Program plans might include some faculty travel and perhaps residence of a faculty member or graduate student at the host institution on a rotating basis. There should also be adequate administrative support for the program on the home campus, including time and resources for recruitment of students.

**e.** There should be plenty of student interest, either potential or already manifested. Students should also be willing and able to pay the fees. The better the financial and academic arrangements, the higher the interest; therefore, efforts should be made, in line with our earlier observations, to remove technical obstacles in the award of credit, adapt academic programs as needed, advise interested students, and (if possible) make financial aid available.

We should now turn our attention to the structure of our program. Certain basic principles of organization are applicable fairly universally. First, the site of the program itself. In our earlier reference to the nature of the agreement with the host institution, we alluded to arrangements for participation in that institution's academic programs. In principle, American students should be among students of the host country as much as possible. Unless they are needed for compelling reasons (e.g., language or lack of academic preparation), it is better to avoid special programs for foreigners organized by the host institution and to avoid setting up one's own such arrangements. If the American students are to derive maximum benefit from their stay abroad, integration into the life of the host institution and its academic programs is always better than the ghettoizing induced by special programs, extensive extracurricular activities for the Americans, and so on. Isolation may actually heighten prejudice rather than eliminate it. In cities with large populations of U.S. students it may be necessary to create subterfuges and strategies to discourage too much socializing among the Americans—and this is a strong reason for picking a provincial university as the site rather than one in a major city that already has numerous links with American institutions.

Though integration is desirable, there may be good reasons for providing supplementary programs to help students find their way around the academic opportunities of the host institution or to coordinate their studies with their programs back home. Some colleges offer seminars for their own students, sometimes taught by a member of the college faculty in residence abroad. In any case it is important to have someone on the spot who can deal with administrators in the host institution (in their language); help students with registration, housing, and so on; and serve as a link with the U.S. campus. Ideally this person should be a permanent or semipermanent program director—a member of the U.S. faculty assigned to this position for three or four years or a local person thoroughly familiar with the U.S. campus and American students and academic life in general. The director might be assisted by a local person (if he or she is American) or by a faculty member visiting from the U.S. campus (if he or she is local). There should be an office and common room, at the very least, to serve as headquarters for the programs, located on or near the campus of the host institution.

Some U.S. programs provide special housing for their students. Local conditions may make this a necessity, but in principle it is better to place American students either in regular university residences or with host families. The latter arrangement is better in that students must deal with local people daily, thus gaining more insight into the culture than they might otherwise. But a host family program requires good supervision by a program director on the spot. And a decision to provide special housing for the Americans may entail heavy investment in renting or buying property, administering it, and maintaining it. If numbers fluctuate from year to year, the problem is compounded.

The program director should be well known on the home campus. There should be ample opportunity for regular visits to the U.S. for consultation, perhaps timed to coincide with the admissions process so that the director can be involved. The director should cultivate good ties with the host institution, encouraging U.S. faculty to meet those at the host institution with similar interests and facilitating such contact. Foreign faculty might be encouraged to visit the home campus when in the United States, and efforts might be made to arrange meetings between the chief academic officers of the two institutions from time to time. The director may also find it useful to create an advisory committee, consisting of members of the host institution and local citizens, to help plan the program and to provide liaison with the community.

Sound administration abroad should be matched by sound administration at home. On the home campus a single individual should have general responsibility for the administration of the program. This person might be a member of the dean's staff or of the international programs office or possibly a faculty member. It is best to entrust the administration to a professional administrator, who works closely with faculty responsible for advising and for helping with admissions and recruitment. The faculty member should receive adequate compensation (a stipend or released time or both) and be well respected by his or her colleagues. There are many reasons for this dual administrative arrangement. While the intricacies of the program require the attention of a professional, without good links with faculty, teachers may doubt the importance or academic standing of the program.

The on-campus administration should be supplemented with a faculty committee that sets general policy and handles admissions. Even if the program is intended primarily for students from the sponsoring institution, admission should not be automatic or pro forma. As we have already noticed, though students will sometimes blossom when away from home, it is never prudent to send high-risk or problem students abroad. They will lower the standing of the program with the host institution and may create administrative woes.

One of the main questions to consider in planning the program is the length of time to be spent abroad. Much will depend on the compatibility of calendars between the United States and the host institution, but in principle a full academic year is much superior to a semester or trimester. Students need time to get settled, to find their way around, to make ties. A large part of the first four months or so will be consumed by this process of acclimatization, especially if there are significant cultural or linguistic differences between the host country and the United States. On the other hand, it may be better to compromise for certain kinds of students, such as those in business or engineering, rather than deny them the opportunity to participate. It may also prove desirable to run not only year-long programs but summer plans for undergraduate or continuing education students, depending on the site of the program and the facilities.

Almost as important as the quality of the program itself is the quality of the procedures at either end: predeparture orientation and debriefing upon return. Predeparture programs take many forms, ranging from special courses or tutorials in the academic year before departure, through summer courses or programs, to seminars of a few days' duration at the end of the previous academic year. Some kind of orientation program after arrival is also a necessity. In a non-English-speaking country this might include an intensive language program, or a summer-long program for those whose mastery of the language is weak and for other students wishing to spend just a summer abroad.

Returning students will have much to tell the program director in the host country or the administrator in the U.S. about the running of the program and ways to improve it. They should also have ample opportunities to share their experiences with students back in the U.S.—through campus newspapers, language classes, and so on, and perhaps as recruiters for future years.

### 4. Exchanges
While most study-abroad programs involve the movement of students in only one direction—from the United States to the foreign country—a few are based on exchange arrangements between two institutions that may include, besides students, American and foreign faculty. This may be the direction in which study abroad for Americans will have to go, as the dollar fluctuates and tuition and living costs in other countries rise. One indication of this trend is the formation of the International Student Exchange Program (ISEP) based at Georgetown University. Funded by the International Com-

munication Agency, the scheme involves a growing number of American higher education institutions entering into arrangements for sending Americans students and receiving foreign students through ISEP, each student paying tuition and fees and a set amount for living costs to the home institution. The plan is particularly advantageous for colleges with limited experience with study abroad and for those with low tuition.

ISEP is a new program. Until now truly reciprocal arrangements have been limited to institutions that have established personal ties with overseas counterparts. Exchanges often originate with individual faculty who have spent time at the other institution or have special contacts with it. Occasionally student exchange may be just one element in a comprehensive agreement also involving faculty exchanges, collaborative research, and other elements. Because of the diversity of these arrangements it is impossible to generalize beyond a few observations regarding ways in which various exchanges can be facilitated.

The advantage of student exchange is that it can be based on parity between the two institutions, in terms of numbers of students or the amount of money involved, and hence obviate the need for the transfer of large sums. For foreign institutions with bureaucratic constraints or countries with currency restrictions it may represent the only way to send appreciable numbers of students here for temporary study. There is no need to exchange the same types of students; it may be mutually advantageous to send advanced students in one direction and undergraduates or their equivalent in the other.

Though exchanges may be financially easier than one-way movement and carry many other advantages, they may not be entirely without costs. Travel is one expense; then there may be differences in living standards that make it necessary to supplement the funds of the foreign students while they are here (or of American students abroad). Such programs are also difficult to administer, and travel funds for occasional administrative visits to the other institution may prove desirable.

Faculty exchanges can also be based on parity, even to the extent of exchanging houses, but again there may be a need to supplement the salaries or at least provide funds for travel. It is better to begin comprehensive exchange programs with faculty rather than students. Faculty build contacts and become advocates for the new program on their own campus, so that when student exchanges begin there is already a reserve of goodwill at both institutions. Programs that begin with student exchanges are likely to run into technical and administrative, and sometimes intellectual, problems because of faculty ignorance, suspicion, or indifference. This is particularly so if the institutions guarantee admission to one another's students.

Though it is tempting to greet plans for comprehensive exchanges with much fanfare and signing of protocols, it may be better to begin at a modest level with a limited understanding before moving to a full-scale agreement. The best exchanges have a firm sense of reciprocity; grow in response to a felt need, especially on the part of faculty; and carry mutual advantages (cf. Heenan and Perlmutter 1980: 159). Faculty on research leave from the foreign university may be glad of a base in the United States that offers general hospitality, access to a library, and so on, even if such services are limited. Faculty here may welcome these facilities there. Modest inducements can encourage contact at this fairly rudimentary level—in the form of travel grants to U.S. faculty to visit the sister university abroad, entertainment money for visitors, or small grants to encourage joint research or consultation on common interests. It is important that faculty at each university know the extent of the resources and the interests of the faculty at the other. Special efforts must be made to acquaint them with these matters.

Such relatively informal contact may well be accompanied by the first teaching exchanges, or the exchange of teaching faculty may grow out of other types of contacts. Out of faculty contact will grow student exchanges, and, stage by stage, a full-blown program of cooperation can emerge. At this point—probably several years into the reciprocal contacts—a comprehensive formal agreement can be signed. Exchange programs require care and imagination—and generosity—on both sides and a willingness to work hard to make them function. We cannot emphasize enough that without a sense of common purpose and need exchanges cannot succeed in the long run. As far as their administration is concerned, most of the principles that we have discussed in connection with other programs hold true here: strong faculty involvement, well-coordinated administration, adequate funding, and attention to public relations.

Any of a number of outside agencies may be willing to lend assistance in comprehensive exchanges. Depending on the countries involved, the State Department and USICA—particularly the latter —may have an interest. There may be funding available for faculty exchange through the Fulbright program. If Eastern Europe is involved, funding for certain activities will probably be available through the International Research and Exchange Board (IREX). It may be possible to tap U.S. aid moneys, particularly if developing countries are involved, or funds may be obtainable at either end of the exchange through existing cultural agreements between the foreign country and the United States. In short, the program may rest on an intricate network of arrangements involving university money and funds from both governments. If the program is worked out with imagination and skill, it can do much to open the U.S. institution to international currents and connections.

Of course, the vast majority of exchanges and reciprocal contacts abroad that most institutions generate never turn into comprehensive exchange agreements, nor should they. These frequently remain at the level of individual faculty or departments and are based on some community of interest that cannot be generalized to the institution as a whole. There are ways of fostering and promoting even these kinds of contacts: through the provision of travel money, the facilitation of reciprocal visits, help with language training or translation, and assistance in seeking outside funding. A policy of looking sympathetically on such contacts can bring important dividends, not least in persuading faculty to meet foreign scholars, to travel, and to break out of the confining assumptions of the American academy.

# 7

# Living in the Academy and Living in the World: Actors and Constituencies

# Living in the Academy and Living in the World: Actors and Constituencies

## 1. People

Hardly a book or an article on internationalizing the curriculum fails to mention the importance of people. "In the last analysis," Saunders and Ward remark (1970: 230), "a college or university will make real progress in broadening the international component of its educational effort only to the extent that a substantial number of individual faculty members feel a responsibility to do so and are prepared to act upon it." Barbara Burn (1980b), discussing faculty exchange, refers to the need for "local entrepreneurs at the campus level." On reform of the undergraduate curriculum in general Levine and Weingart (1973: 140) stress the importance of enlightened administrative leadership. While structures can inhibit or stimulate change, without people the structures are powerless.

In this chapter we shall look at people—in fact, at a number of groups, each with its special concerns and priorities. Who are the principal actors we must persuade to cooperate in making the institution more responsive to international needs? Who will be most affected by such changes? Inevitably much of our attention will fall on the role of the faculty, but we shall look also at the function of administrators, the role of students, and the influence of such indirect agents as trustees, legislators, and parents. All these groups are both agents of change and obstacles to it, and changes in one part of the system will affect people in other parts: Everyone acts and is acted upon. Furthermore, while it would be oversimplifying to suggest that resistance to change springs invariably from a feeling that one has not been consulted, or that one has somehow been excluded from dialogue, consultation with all affected groups is extremely important. If they still resist, there might be good intellectual reasons; these should be listened to and taken into account. Alternatively, the reasons may be structural, in which case structures should be altered to encourage the shifts of objectives and behavior that seem to be needed.

## 2.  The Faculty

We shall begin with the faculty because they are the central element in the teaching process. Clearly their professional interest and involvement in international matters will depend a great deal on their fields. Faculty in such fields as languages and international relations deal daily with the realities of international contacts and communication. For some others such international matters are significant but essentially peripheral to the generally perceived theoretical base of their disciplines (e.g., economics, sociology, management, education). A third group normally has no reason even to reflect on international aspects of their disciplines: fields like mathematics or chemistry, of course, do not deal with such issues.

These three levels of disciplinary involvement will affect the ways in which faculty respond to a pressure group within the institution seeking to increase their consciousness of international affairs. At the very least there will be no peer pressure to resist such overtures on the part of international relations faculty—though language may be a special case, since language teachers are not always internationalists in any comprehensive sense. Too great a preoccupation with international aspects of economics or sociology may seem a little odd to traditionalists in those disciplines; they may need more than a gentle nudge to resist the subtle mainstreaming that is so essential a part of the disciplinary psychology. In fields like mathematics, chemistry, physics, or accounting, appeals to the importance of teaching their international aspects will have little or no effect: The person making the appeal will probably be dismissed as ignorant or eccentric. It will be more fruitful to approach these professors in terms of changing the entire focus of undergraduate education to take realities of interdependence and globalization into account. In any event, they will win no points from their peers through such enlightenment, and we must be aware of that.

The varying pressures to conform are not merely a matter of disciplinary loyalty. They are reinforced by departmental constraints. As we have noted, departments have grown up over the years as budgetary units as well as intellectual colleges. Their main purpose, at least in large universities, is to train specialists in the disciplines they represent—and this leads to a measure of functional conformism. But there is even more to it: They do indeed represent disciplines. The history department on a large campus is as much a chapter of the American Historical Association as it is a functioning unit dedicated to one element in a comprehensive education. The loyalty of an English department may be more tied up with the Modern Language Association than with the freshman English program. This fact—and we do not pass judgment on its merits or limitations—means that a professor's contribution to the institution is typically filtered through his or her contribution to the discipline and its representative, the department.

We must take these realities into account if we are to influence the thinking and behavior of faculty. It may be more important to convince a department chairman to look favorably on internationalization than to convince an individual faculty member to become involved in, let us say, a general education course outside the responsibility of the department. In many institutions department chairmen play a key role in determining salary levels, assigning courses, and so on. Their actions help set not only the reward system but the value system that flows out of it. In the long run we are more likely to affect the overall complexion of the undergraduate curriculum by working with such constraints and turning them to good account. Of course, it can be argued that trying to change attitudes from within simply reinforces, or at most renders slightly more responsive, a system fundamentally out of tune with the needs of the undergraduate curriculum. We do not take that view—and in any case we believe it is crucial to change value patterns *within* the disciplines as well as outside them.

One of the groups most likely to support internationalizing efforts is the younger faculty. They have come to political and social consciousness in a world far different from that of their seniors; certain realities of international communication are taken for granted. These younger faculty, because of the intense competition for jobs, tend to be genuinely accomplished teachers and skilled researchers (others fail to find jobs at all)—and are ideal candidates for special programs outside the departmental structure. But taking them out of their departments may be the worst thing to do in terms of their careers: Reappointment and promotion begin with departments and they need to remain visible contributors to departmental work. They are therefore best reached *within* the departmental structure. Younger faculty may be best employed to shift the focus of a department's offerings, while their older colleagues can be called on to teach in interdepartmental programs, general education programs, and the like.

There is often a direct connection between the kinds of research and writing faculty do and the subjects they teach. Some try out ideas in class and go on to publish them. Others publish and teach courses out of their publications. We should therefore try to influence their research priorities. The most obvious way is through allocation of research funding, to encourage faculty to embark on projects with an international dimension, and particularly on curricular development. We can also ask the administrative office in charge of grants and contracts, if the institution has one, to pay particular attention to federal and foundation programs in the international area. Through the services of this office, and perhaps the office of international programs, we can promise help with grant proposals and other assistance. Looking at matters from the opposite perspective, we can encourage faculty to seek outside help in the form of grants for curricular planning.

Somewhere out beyond direct institutional concerns lies the discipline itself, with its priorities and customs and traditional ways of doing things. Here, too, we may have an impact by encouraging our own faculty to raise certain questions in disciplinary forums. We can offer support for travel to conferences, especially those with an international focus, and for the preparation of papers on matters international. If a fund of this kind is available through, say, the office of international programs or through an administrator particularly charged with the supervision of international affairs, departments and individual faculty will be inclined to change their behavior to draw on it, especially if travel money is tight (as it is these days). We are concerned here not so much with international travel as with travel to regional and national conferences, though some money might be made available for international travel too, perhaps as partial grants.

It may seem that we are falling into the error, too common among administrators, of regarding faculty as highly manipulable. While certainly patterns of organization and overt reward systems affect faculty behavior, other kinds of motive also operate. High idealism is more prevalent on campuses than in other settings. Faculty rise to challenges, often teach as they do out of passionately held beliefs, and are capable of immense dedication to a cause. These qualities can have a decisive effect on a new or struggling program and can make the least promising material shine. And, in the long run, appeals to the better nature of faculty will, we believe, bring better results than administrative sanctions or crude manipulation of the reward system.

One of the aspects of that better nature is concern for the relevance of material to students. Many faculty have foreign students in their classes—in fact, they are often particularly numerous in fields with no special international content, such as mathematics and physics. The foreign students provide an excuse for reaching these faculty and drawing them into a dialogue, but they are in any case a constant reminder that education is not a purely local or national affair but involves the world.

Some faculty know this at first hand because they were foreign students overseas. Many members of the average faculty have degrees from foreign universities or have spent a year or more abroad in active study or in connection with their dissertations. Others have taught in foreign institutions. Still others are engaged in research or consultation that requires extensive contact with colleagues in other countries and may involve foreign travel. Not only are such faculty predisposed to an appreciation of the importance of international contacts, but they are an important repository of information and can be valuable allies in advising students traveling abroad, counseling foreign students, and devising special cooperative arrangements with foreign universities.

For other faculty the importance of the international dimension may be more a matter of belief than practice. They may follow international events closely (in which case they can be drawn into international programming on campus) or have a special interest in some part of the world. Even the most conservative professors (indeed, they more than others) may be touched by appeals to the universality of knowledge, the international character of great institutions of learning, and the need to promote the free flow of ideas and individuals regardless of frontiers. At least in major institutions, parochial faculty are rare. But finding the particular interest that will trigger a response may be difficult.

This is not to suggest that isolationism is unknown. Departments are not only havens for disciplinary isolationism but are convenient shields against a wider involvement in matters in which the teacher is not expert. One of the principal assets enjoyed by the "internationalizers" is the fact that international matters carry a certain cachet, a measure of status. A cosmopolitan ease, familiarity with the capital cities of the world—these qualities are as desirable to professors as they are to any other impressionable group. On the other hand, these superficial qualities in others tend to drive some faculty, perhaps those with more honesty or less confidence, into domestic hibernation. They may feel ill at ease in the flashy environment of development types and jet-set consultants. They worry about their ignorance of languages, or their inability to tell the difference between La Paz and Lima, and prefer simply to ignore the whole agenda. Perhaps our picture of the hounded and beaten down faculty member is exaggerated, but it carries at least a germ of truth. This attitude needs to be taken into consideration and careful and cautious address is required if it is to be overcome.

The picture of the jet-set faculty member may be only a slight exaggeration, too. While it is not our purpose in this book to delve too deeply into what constitutes "true" internationalism, we must point out again that mere international involvement does not guarantee a lively awareness of the complexity of international relations. Consulting for Pepsi-Cola or AID or the United Nations out of Hilton hotels in 20 countries may fill a passport with exotic stamps but will not necessarily lead to an understanding of the cultural trade-offs and sacrifices involved in the workings of the international economy. In fact, it may not lead even to an understanding of that economy. Critical attentiveness on the part of the coordinators of our internationalizing effort may prevent this kind of superficiality from being taken for the real thing. This is not to say that the jet-set faculty member has nothing to offer, only that he or she may need change as much as those who have never left their figurative backyards.

We should add that international experience and its transferability are elusive things. International experience is not necessarily broadening: A year's residence in Japan may not improve a professor's perceptions of the larger world to the level achieved by a more observant and empathizing soul living out a life in Ohio. Sometimes the best traveled faculty member, who moves around the world with bewildering frequency, will teach the same old course he has always taught, as though his international experience has nothing to do with the knowledge he should convey to his students. Richard Lambert (1980: 157) makes a similar observation: "Faculty travel abroad has become part of professional and research activities, yet has little to do with their teaching. For the past decade we have witnessed the diaspora of the overseas experience; linking it to the education of students calls for a considerable effort." The curriculum, in short, lags far behind the actual experience of those responsible for teaching it. Even before we think of increasing faculty experience, we must work out ways to use the experience they already have—to bring it into the classroom and make it teachable.

### 3. Getting Faculty Members Involved

What devices are available to inspire faculty discussion of, and involvement in, international issues? We have suggested that we should stimulate debate at every level on internationalizing the curriculum. Many faculty can be drawn in as members of review committees at the college or department level, raising questions about the international content of the curriculum and suggesting ways to make changes. Others might serve as consultants on curricular matters because of particular skills or expertise. Faculty might be asked to participate in meetings or symposia on the internationalizing of certain fields, especially if they can bring to these discussions a point of view derived from special experience. Since so many faculty have international links of one kind or another—a point substantiated by, among others, Norman Palmer (1977) in his survey of University of Pennsylvania faculty—they can be shown that they have a special contribution to make to the debate and can enlighten and instruct their colleagues. As soon as they are convinced on this point, they are already partly won over.

There are numerous ways to involve faculty in the normal international activities of a college. It is a good idea to convene a college's experts on some geographical area or world problem from time to time, to discuss institutional support for their work (Is it adequate? Should its form be altered?) and to talk about courses, curricula, and programming. Faculty can help host foreign guests or counsel and look after newly arrived foreign students. They can be asked to serve on admissions committees for study programs abroad, advise students considering foreign study, or help with the administrative committees involved in such programs.

While asking people to contribute is often the best way to win their loyalty and support, it is still important to demonstrate the usefulness of an interest in international affairs and to give faculty suggestions on how they might involve themselves more. There should be good lines of communication between the administrative structures created or coopted to help internationalize the college (e.g., the office of international programs, the assistant dean for international affairs) and the faculty. Professors should regularly receive information on foreign developments in their fields; new foreign contacts of the college from which they might benefit; opportunities for teaching, research, and study overseas; and anything else that encourages them to broaden their interest and to regard as a matter of course the fact that the college is interested in international affairs.

As for their courses, we have mentioned the importance of making money available for curricular planning and revision of existing courses. This might come in the form of grants for work over the summer, supplementary grants to cover materials and other incidental costs, or travel grants. Money should also be available to compensate departments so that faculty can be given released time or leaves to work on projects. This compensation is very important: Departments should be glad to have their members engaged in such activities and should not feel that if they contribute to the internationalizing effort they will be financially penalized. In fact, deans might consider looking with special favor on departments that strive to internationalize their curricula, giving them particularly generous allotments for salary increases, providing them with program money, assigning them graduate assistantships, and so on.

In the context of their efforts to revise and revitalize the international aspects of the curriculum, faculty might be particularly encouraged, through the incentives we have mentioned, to work together on curricular projects—within disciplines and departments, and across departmental lines. In this connection we should not forget the value of collaborative research. Several institutions have been successful in mobilizing their faculties to cooperate in a range of research projects with a foreign institution, or in assisting a foreign institution to establish itself. Recent planners of higher education in the developing countries have been looking to new models for the organization of colleges and universities. Increasingly they turn to the community college. A comprehensive link between a community college in this country and an institution with similar aspirations in the developing world seems a natural fit. The better established institutions in the developing countries look to the U.S. not so much for help as for equal partnership; but here, too, there are many opportunities for comprehensive ties—which can in turn serve as a mobilizing force for an American faculty. International development efforts, such as the United Nations University, may also offer suitable links for a large-scale research effort. At a less ambitious level faculty can be encouraged to work together on projects with institutions overseas, or with international organizations—especially those based in this country, such as the United Nations, the World Bank, and the Organization of American States. This kind of action-oriented research has numerous payoffs in the classroom, not only in terms of subject matter and faculty revitalization but through new contacts that can lead to placement and internships for students and links with foreign governments and universities.

When considering the value of links with large international governmental organizations, we should not neglect the many nongovernmental organizations that operate in the international arena. Some, like Amnesty International or (in a quite different sphere) the International Standards Organization, carry on or promote an extensive program of research, and they may help provide the college with productive overseas links. Occasionally the college might be a meeting place for the governing bodies of such organizations. There are also numerous national organizations interested in international affairs or in the promotion of international or global education—such as the Institute for World Order or the U.S. United Nations Association. These groups are actively interested in studies of world problems, the development of curricular materials, and so on. In fact, faculty should be encouraged to share their curricular successes with organizations such as these, as well as working with them in other ways.

### 4.  Hiring: The International Quotient

One other area in which deans can influence the priorities of departments is through hiring and decisions on promotion and tenure. There are many reasons, in today's tight financial situation, for institutions to look for faculty who have demonstrated their versatility and adaptability, or at least have the potential to change and adapt. Unless the budgetary system in an institution is such that departmental moneys are tied to enrollments (and sometimes even then), departments often look for people who show excellence in a specialty or set of specialties sometimes rather narrowly defined. The question, "What else can this teacher do?" seems legitimate for a dean under any circumstances. Faculty with broad interests are simply a better long-term investment than narrow specialists—philistine though that conclusion may sound. Hence building a versatility quotient into appointment decisions (always taking into consideration the dangers of superficiality) makes good sense.

Though it might be difficult to prove, international experience and versatility probably correlate well. A foreign education or prolonged stays abroad, a knowledge of languages, a familiarity with world affairs—these qualities indicate people whose horizons extend beyond their immediate surroundings, perhaps intellectual as well as geographical. A professor with international contacts and familiarity with the larger world is also an asset to an institution anxious to make its way internationally, since he or she can help link the institution with an international network of scholars and experts, as well as help organize study programs abroad, coordinate research, and so on. One way of applying the versatility quotient is through the application of an "international quotient": An institution might try specifically in all disciplines to hire only faculty with some kind of international experience. While exceptions would have to be made, there could be no clearer signal to departments and faculty that the effort to internationalize the institution is serious. Of course, a sudden decision to introduce the international quotient would be a questionable move, more likely to antagonize than to reform. But a gradual and steady bias in that direction could be introduced, especially if it is accompanied by ample opportunity for faculty to improve their international skills, change their curricula, and involve themselves in international activities.

We stress that this kind of effort is more than defensible on intellectual and academic grounds. Just as personnel committees favor editors of scholarly journals ("By hiring Professor X, we shall bring to our institution the Journal of Thus and So"), they should consider the international contacts that a potential faculty member may have built. In a larger sense it is not only defensible but imperative to understand that the future priorities of any self-respecting American institution must include a leap in its international involvement.

Not only might these criteria be used in hiring faculty (and they apply equally to the reappointment or promotion of existing faculty), but departments that have made a special effort to internationalize might be regarded with special favor in decisions to fill vacancies. It could be made clear that, at least in appropriate fields, proposals for new appointments should be directed in the first instance to strengthening the institution's international dimension. Not only would this encourage departments to fill vacancies in areas already recognized as international but it would inspire them to formulate their needs in terms of an international bias. It would probably also encourage a certain productive subterfuge—that is, attempts to fill specialties by no stretch of the imagination international with individuals who also have international experience and hence can be presented to the dean as specialists also in international studies.

In many institutions personnel decisions involve three criteria above all: quality of teaching, publication of research, and service to the institution and the scholarly community. We have noted that the first two have an obvious international dimension. It is important that in the third area as well, that of general "citizenship," attention be given to a faculty member's international and internationalist service. This might take many forms, among them serving on college committees devoted to international affairs, assisting with foreign students at the college, advising students going abroad, and serving in study programs abroad (e.g., accompanying students on study trips or at overseas study centers). Outside contacts should also be noted—service with local councils for international visitors, UN Association branches, and so on; contributions to national organizations in the international field; or service overseas.

Of course, it is one thing to decree that all this happen, but quite another to bring it about. While deans may have a great deal to say about personnel criteria, they are not omnipotent. In the absence of a campuswide effort to internationalize the institution, recognized as beneficial and having the blessing of the faculty, resistance to the international quotient might prove severe. Using personnel decisions as a device for bringing about internationalization is potent and important, but it should not be done in isolation, and only in the context of a much larger network of decisions.

## 5.   Teachers as Learners

In our discussion of curricular change and related matters we have avoided the term "faculty development," partly because of its negative connotations—as though the faculty is something to be made over and recycled. Nevertheless, there should be some provision even in so-called elite institutions for faculty, particularly those with tenure, to deepen and broaden their knowledge. This is especially so of international affairs, where change is particularly rapid and the need especially great. Faculty should be allowed the time and facilities they need to acquire a greater knowledge of the larger world. Among the numerous possibilities are summer institutes for the study of regions or languages—perhaps specially set up for faculty in one college but available also to faculty and others from outside institutions. External funding may be available for such an effort; but expenses would probably be modest, even if faculty were paid for their participation (on the ground that this constitutes time lost from their other pursuits). Funding might also be offered for attendance at summer institutes on other campuses or for similar programs in other countries. Language-study grants might be available for overseas travel, perhaps in conjunction with an on-campus program (faculty might study a language during the year and, if they complete the course, be funded for attendance at a summer program overseas). These activities may not be labeled "faculty development" any more than research leaves or curriculum development grants fall into the category, but they actually serve this function.

Faculty development efforts should be closely linked with the overall goals of the institution. In fact, applying "institutional" criteria to the entire range of special opportunities for faculty is probably good, as we have been suggesting. But this needs to be done humanely and with flexibility. It may turn out, however, that the best kind of faculty development is not special programs for learning particular skills but new challenges and new goals. In short, faculty development will occur most effectively through the self-examination we have described, aimed at challenging professors to change curricular priorities and reshape courses and programs. Cynics may claim that this is impossible, dreamers that it is unnecessary; but a carefully coordinated program of consultation and action can achieve results and eliminate what Rosabeth Moss Kanter, in an interesting paper on academic reform (1979), has termed "stuckness." Kanter, we might add, calls not simply for consultation but actually for internal competition. She suggests "systems of 'internal proposals' in which 'requests for proposals' on relevant, pressing problem areas go out from top leaders to all organization members, who can then form a team to bid on the job, with release time appropriately negotiated if needed." Some may feel that such competition would harm our larger goals, but no one can deny that there is a need to create in most institutions a new sense of challenge and achievement. So internationalization is both an end and a means to an end.

## 6.  Foreign Faculty Members

To some the subject of foreign faculty will conjure visions of Nabokov's Professor Pnin, stumbling hopelessly over English idioms and laughing uproariously at incomprehensible Russian jokes far beyond the capacity of his students. Others will imagine dashing cosmopolitans, capable of moving a college into the international mainstream by their very presence. The truth, as always, lies somewhere between. In principle, a leavening of foreign faculty helps open an institution to broader influences and has a positive effect on both students and other faculty.

With the tightening in recent years of Justice Department and Labor Department regulations, it has become far more difficult, though not impossible, to hire permanent faculty from other countries. Because of the difficult job market, particularly for college teachers, the onus is normally on an institution to prove that there is no American candidate for the position with credentials equal to those of the foreign candidate and that a thorough search for American candidates has been made. This search must be carefully organized, in conformity with all government stipulations. It follows, then, that even if a college wishes to hire a foreigner to fill a vacant position and knows that there is no one as well qualified as the person in question, it must conduct a proper search—for that position and no other—before offering the job to the foreign candidate. While there may be absurdity in such backhanded procedures, and while they certainly contradict the whole idea of a university as an international center of learning, administrations that have dealt for years with still more complex affirmative action procedures will have little difficulty handling them adequately.

Faculty and department chairmen are notorious for their refusal to submit to procedures that they regard as foolish, demeaning, or incomprehensible. A few failures with the Immigration and Natural- ization Service may lead them to conclude that hiring foreigners on a permanent basis is essentially impossible. Some will even doubt, un- necessarily, the desirabilty of hiring Permanent Resident Aliens. It is vital to prevent such negative attitudes from prevailing, even though they are understandable. From the point of view of the gov- ernment departments in question, keeping jobs for Americans may make good sense; from the point of view of the pursuit of knowledge and the exchange of ideas, it makes no sense whatsoever. So depart- ments must be convinced both that they must follow procedures me- ticulously and that if they do so, hiring foreign faculty is perfectly practicable.

Because of the complexity of the procedures and because making it appreciably more difficult for departments to look beyond the bor- ders of the United States is inadvisable, the paperwork in these cases is best put in the hands of a competent administrator, such as someone in the office of international programs. While the services of an immigration lawyer may be needed at some point, turning the entire matter over to one is needlessly costly (and therefore another deterrent...), and much can be achieved simply by maintaining good contact with local INS officials and seeking their advice.

Though foreign teachers may add diversity to the faculty, it will not happen automatically. The informal style of American colleges and universities can be very different from what they are familiar with and they may take time to adapt. On the other hand, most for- eign faculty who gravitate to permanent positions in the U.S. know the system from earlier visits or from study in this country.

One of the most fruitful ways to use foreign faculty is through sys- tems of visiting professorships or exchange programs, whereby the visitors come to the college for perhaps a year. As colleges become more and more strapped for funds, visiting professorships are hard to preserve and are apt to disappear or to revert to the standing fac- ulty. Yet in times of fiscal difficulty this cross-fertilization is espe- cially important, since the normal mobility of professors among insti- tutions largely disappears, there is little movement from one college to another, and the faculty soon becomes frozen and immobilized. Vi- siting professorships specially reserved for foreign scholars may be easier to defend and preserve than other kinds.

## 7.   Administrators and Their Commitment to International Affairs
Much of our discussion of the role of faculty in a college has involved

consideration of the role of administrators. They are crucial. The current structure of the academy is in many respects inimical to educational and intellectual change because it fosters conservatism and isolationism in the faculty (some people, of course, may even argue that this is a good thing). At the same time, financial and demographic imperatives make administrators reluctant to take risks and nervous about investing in such areas as language instruction, which will always be expensive and will never turn an impressive profit. If the faculty in a college can resist pressure from an enlightened administration, a benighted administration can equally well resist pressure from an enlightened faculty.

It may be possible to convince an administration on its own terms —to point out that a revitalized language faculty will at the very least be less expensive than an unregenerate one, or that international studies and the international dimension can only become more important, and hence more in demand, in tomorrow's marketplace. There is a good deal of evidence, if somewhat ambiguous, to support such a contention. Certainly the internationalization of the curriculum can help move a college into higher prominence and give it a greater sense of its intellectual and educational worth—and that esprit de corps and sense of movement can generate better students, attract more funding, and bring attention to the campus.

It would be an exaggeration to suggest that any idea initiated by the faculty cannot succeed without the support of the administration. Everything depends on the nature of the idea, the strength of the faculty support, and the attitudes of individual administrators. Nevertheless, a proposal to move toward the comprehensive internationalization of an institution cannot proceed far without strong support by senior administrators. Heenan and Perlmutter's comments (1980: 145ff) on efforts at internationalization at the University of Hawaii bear this out graphically. In fact, given the fragmentary nature of faculty, it is more likely the idea will originate with the administration (Levine and Weingart, in their book on undergraduate education [1974], suggest that only the administration can effectively move an institution into reform), or at least that the two will hatch the idea simultaneously through good lines of communication.

The best condition, then, for beginning to strengthen the international dimension of a college, is one in which there are already good lines of communication between administration and faculty and an idea originating with one can easily be espoused and advocated by the other. Dialogue and discussion are essential. This is not to suggest, however, that the administration should act only on the basis of consensus. There may be some holdouts among the faculty, or some problem areas. Administrators must judge how important those areas are and possibly proceed without them if another course would involve compromising the original idea out of focus or out of existence. Good leaders try to achieve consensus but are willing to take risks when general agreement cannot be reached.

Leadership, however, is not only a matter of decisiveness or of articulating a coherent educational philosophy, but a matter of style and personal involvement. Senior administrators who naturally involve themselves in international activities, or have contacts abroad, or move freely in an international environment of colleagues and fellow educators, demonstrate by their very conduct their commitment to international matters. This question of style is crucial —in fact, it could be the decisive factor in certain environments. Presidents, too, must have their international quotient. The people they surround themselves with must reflect their values.

We can imagine, then, a situation in which the idea of internationalizing the curriculum and the college originates with the senior administrators. They select certain key faculty known for their international interests, their response to new ideas, and the respect they enjoy with their colleagues. We have discussed how they go about convincing the remainder of the faculty and persuading them to work together. But what of the middle-level administration, whose cooperation is so essential?

College administrators, in the present climate, are generally of three types. Some have reached their positions from the faculty. A few of these will probably remain permanently in some branch of the administration while continuing to hold a faculty appointment and perhaps teaching part time. Most of the others will revert to full-time faculty status after their stint in the administration is over. It has often been pointed out that administrators are chosen from a group of individuals, namely the faculty, who have shown distinction in a set of skills having more or less nothing to do with administration. The point is partly correct. Particularly in their dealings with people—making decisions about other people's lives, managing a staff, and so on—faculty newly translated to administration often prove inadequte. But a college administrator is constantly called upon not only to run offices but to execute, interpret, and often determine policy. In this regard faculty status is crucial since it allows an easy relationship with faculty colleagues, who must be persuaded to follow a course of action and who like to feel that they participate in major decisions. Thus a knowledge of the ways faculty conduct their affairs and reach decisions is an essential qualification for many administrative posts. The career administrator lacks the day-to-day familiarity with the tribulations and successes of faculty life that helps lend credibility when decisions are made.

A second category is the career administrator—those who occupy middle-level positions as, for example, admissions officers, student affairs officers, administrators of residences, or librarians. Just as faculty mobility among institutions has declined, movement among administrative positions has dropped, so that today many administrators at this level seem set for a long tenure in the position and have limited prospects for advancement. Where advancement does come, it is increasingly to those who demonstrate a fiscal efficiency that is in many respects inimical to the broader academic ideals of the institution. There is a constant tension between academic and intellectual priorities on the one hand and financial priorities on the other—and this reflects a structural dysfunctionalism that is in urgent need of address. In this book we can deal only with existing structures, since our purpose is to show how to achieve certain goals within them. But the larger question—the need to create approaches that reinforce goals and goals that are not merely the product of existing and sometimes unresponsive systems—should be high on the agenda of those concerned about the future of American higher education.

Our third category is somewhat expressive of this dysfunctionalism. It is a growing and increasingly important group whose potential is still underutilized and underesteemed. These are individuals who have entered academic administration by a kind of lateral transfer, after completing all or part of the PhD. Reasons for such a career change are varied, but they often have skills and talents that do not fit easily into conventional academic molds; they choose to remain in the academic setting but reject the struggle for teaching positions in an ever-tightening market. Not infrequently their skills may be in social sciences or the humanities, may be interdisciplinary, and may include an international dimension. The relationship between these administrators and the faculty tends to be uneasy, partly because of faculty attitudes toward such career moves and partly because of the complexity of their own feelings about the academic establishment and their place in it. While those in this group face difficulties within the administrative structure, they are often natural allies of curricular reform and may have talents and energy that, together with their familiarity with the academic enterprise from several angles, make them effective administrators.

Administrators in the second and third categories are likely to find themselves second-class citizens in the academic environment. There is a problem of major proportions here, one that frequently creates distrust and sometimes disdain between faculty and administration, even where individuals may be qualified and respected academically as well as gifted administrators. The whole system is difficult to work with; but a frontal attack aimed at developing the international focus of the institution in an attempt to change the value system is likely to achieve little. In any case, a refusal to write off professional administrators simply on the ground that they are not faculty should be a principle of action from the beginning.

Advancement in administration, particularly for those in the third category, represents a general problem. The lack of obvious avenues for promotion, especially for those in student services or advising, can lead to an unwillingness to accept new ideas or elaborate changes. But much can be done by creating structures for consultation and collective decisions and by giving careful consideration to the use of the skills and interests of the individual.

Though the fact that the administration constitutes a hierarchy, with clear lines of responsibility and accountability, does make shifts in the reward system somewhat easier than they might be with faculty, it is important to draw administrators at all levels into consultation, as fully and as early as possible, on internationalization plans. They should feel they have a stake in the process and they should be encouraged to come up with ideas. A certain amount of funding, even if it is small, should be identified centrally to help underwrite worthy initiatives. Directors of administrative offices, especially those having to do with students (admissions, financial aid, athletics, and so on), should draw plans, in consultation with their staffs, for programming and other activities relevant to the overall internationalizing effort. Thus the admissions office might choose to strengthen its program for the recruitment and admission of foreign students, or to give greater emphasis, in recruiting American students, to the college's international resources. The financial aid office might be willing to set aside money for study-abroad fellowships. The athletics office might be interested in sending teams overseas or hosting them at the college. All these moves would strengthen the college's international dimension, but would involve significant changes in priorities. Hence having some funding available, even if only for marginal adjustments, seems essential.

Changes in curricula, as opposed to adding new nonacademic programs or changing admissions procedures or financial aid, would have less direct effect on the administrative staff; but even here shifts of focus and priorities would affect the advising and counseling staff, the admissions office, and numerous others. At the very least they would have to understand and in a measure support the reasons for the changes. If the faculty is relatively well traveled and cosmopolitan, one cannot make the same generalizations about the administrative staff. So a special effort is needed to make them aware of the significance of international affairs in relation to higher education. Administrators might be included in faculty discussions on these matters, and it might also be advisable to organize administrators' seminars from time to time, to be addressed by faculty engaged in the internationalizing effort or by outside speakers. These might deal with world problems or with geographical areas. They might be organized as luncheons or at the end of the day. Consideration might also be given to special incentives not only for faculty but for administrators, to improve their knowledge of international affairs by taking courses, traveling, or learning languages. This might prove particularly attractive to the third group, the "PhD administrators."

Above all, it is imperative to instill in middle-level administrators a sense of the importance of international affairs and an awareness that the college is trying to cultivate in its students a new broadness of vision. They should be constantly reminded of this fact, through the setting of planning goals, in staff meetings, through memoranda —in fact, in every aspect of their professional lives. The more they share such views intellectually, the easier the progress will be. Administrators who are also faculty members obviously occupy a key position in the educational effort, by carrying over into the faculty the aims of the senior administration and by bringing into the administration the knowledge and expertise of the faculty—particularly if they are associated with internationally focused departments.

### 8. The Trustees

Before turning to the role of students in the internationalization of the curriculum, we should consider a group often forgotten by curricular planners—the trustees. The level of trustee involvement in the life of the institution varies from college to college (and from trustee to trustee), but in matters of broad policy they are likely to be consulted. Furthermore, they are often in a position to exercise firm and imaginative leadership. Hence they must be regarded as one of the decision-making elements in our campaign to internationalize the college. But they can also be regarded as an important resource —for funding special programs or activities and, more important, for providing numerous contacts with the larger world and perhaps a measure of expertise.

They should be drawn into the internationalizing effort from the very beginning. They might, for example, issue a policy statement emphasizing the need to adjust higher education to fit the new priorities of an interdependent world and to prepare for the increasingly globalized economy of the future. The statement might request the president to keep the board informed about progress and it might establish a committee on international programs to examine the president's reports and to help secure funds for international programs.

Some of the trustees, at least at major institutions, will probably have extensive international business connections or belong to institutions with international links. They can be valuable in bringing key elements within the college into contact with international resources. Trustees who travel extensively can also serve as contacts with foreign alumni and perhaps assist in the recruitment and selection of foreign students. As the membership of the board changes, efforts can be made to recruit new trustees with extensive international experience or relevant contacts—not only ex-ambassadors or corporation presidents but people who have experienced the problems of developing countries at first hand or worked to solve global problems.

Some enlightened boards may take to this ordering of priorities very easily—especially if they are chaired by people who share our views. But others may have to be persuaded. Administrators responsible for contacts with the trustees can influence agenda settings and perhaps give special emphasis to international programs, foreign study, and the like. They can do their best to identify the international interests of individual trustees and ask for their help or keep them informed about developments on campus relevant to their interests. They can see that good and frequent information goes to the trustees about international studies on campus and their importance nationally. They can point out how international involvement reflects well on the college and gives it special prominence.

The trustees confer honorary degrees. Efforts can be made, at this level and below (since generally there is a role for faculty and students as well), to make sure degrees go to important international figures, especially people connected with international organizations or those who have contributed to public understanding of international issues. The same is particularly true of commencement speakers.

Finally, and more important, the board selects the major academic officers. It is vital that they choose people convinced of the importance of international affairs and of education for an interdependent world. This will happen only if the board regards it as important. It is in part the task of the senior administrators to convey this sense to the trustees, so that search committees are charged accordingly, suitable candidates are chosen, and the selections go to people who can carry the internationalizing mission forward.

## 9. Students and Their Goals

We have emphasized that in the processes of change each participant acts and is acted upon. Students are in no sense exclusively passive participants, and their attitudes can make a crucial difference to the success or failure of our efforts. If, for example, the faculty emphasizes to administrators that an increase in the international component will not cause financial strain, the faculty will be proven right only when students enroll in the new courses in reasonable numbers and adapt their programs to take advantage of additional offerings. Furthermore, it is important to sound out students' feelings, not simply in order to follow their wishes (legitimate though that may often be), but so as to build on their interests and channel them in fruitful directions.

Over the years there has been a good deal of misunderstanding about student attitudes, brought on particularly by the events of the late sixties and early seventies. We are all capable of applying our own brand of pop psychology to these events. But we will resist that temptation here. It does seem, however, that much of the students' motivation, then as now, concerned their attitudes toward the future: They feared the assembly-line structures of college that seemed designed to move them uncomplainingly forward to a future they had no wish to collaborate in. Students today are still fixed on the future, but now it contains the imperatives of qualifications, career choices, and getting a head start in the difficult task of gaining entry to a profession (perhaps by way of graduate school) or finding a satisfying job.

The emphasis of this generation of students on goals raises barriers to their acceptance of what may be perceived as extraneous or useless international elements. Unless these can be brought to them as a matter of course, or in combination with what they perceive as functionally necessary causes, they may pass this crucial point without key exposure to the international. But even though students today appear exceptionally resistant to change and innovation, they are at a point in their lives when, perhaps for the last time, they routinely expect every day to encounter concepts fundamentally strange to them and they are attuned to confronting intellectual novelty. The secret to successful curricular planning, therefore, seems to lie in the twin elements of career goals and intellectual challenge. There is an institutional responsibility at stake here as well as an issue of philosophy and, in the largest sense, political will. How, for example, should we respond to the news that 80 percent of the students in French language at Penn State are participating in that department's joint program in French and business? Is this the right balance between career and challenge? Perhaps so, especially if the alternative is foreign language illiteracy.

Faculty tend to see students in terms of one-year or four-year trajectories, ending in graduation. While they certainly understand that students go on to make careers, operationally they are apt to see graduation as the end of the line. Given the conflict between one group that thinks of nothing so much as the implications of life after graduation, and another that concentrates resolutely on the present, it is no wonder that so much of curricular planning is a dialogue of the deaf. But this difference does account for many of the problems and misunderstandings we experience in coming to terms with the nature of undergraduate education. We stress that the problem is, above all, operational. It may translate itself into philosophical terms, but the difficulty arises because one group sees undergraduate education as a way station while for others it is an end in itself.

This gap should be taken into consideration in planning. Some institutions, for financial reasons, have accepted the entire set of student perceptions and plan their programs strictly to qualify students for careers. Higher education is at least in part a commodity, to be bought and sold like any other. But the opposite view—that we should set up roadblocks to career objectives and emphasize the value of undergraduate study for its own sake—is at least latent in the minds of many faculty, who consequently feel no pressure to explain or justify their subjects. This attitude is linked with some we have already observed, particularly the unwillingness to cross or even examine disciplinary boundaries. Being obliged to justify one's discipline is regarded by many as a breach of academic freedom.

On balance it seems better to meet students where they are and to build a curriculum that will help them prepare for a career while broadening their horizons and showing them how their career choice (if they have made it) relates to the universe of knowledge. Opinions differ on the extent to which students are inherently interested in world problems, though the Council on Learning survey suggests a relatively high level of concern. This sense of the supranational nature of problems of human existence—that they transcend cultures and regions—should be impressed on students from the very beginning, through general education programs, freshman seminars, special courses for freshmen, and so on. It should be built into requirements and core curricula, emphasized in catalogs, repeated by the faculty, and reinforced in the campus environment. Freshmen should be shown how a knowledge of the world will help their careers and prepare them for tomorrow's world. And this proof should take the form not only of grand statements but of concrete examples—from the placement office and from outside agencies. We may feel inhibited about making exaggerated claims on this last point, but we can at least acquaint students better with existing opportunities and with the likelihood that international affairs will increase in importance.

Since most undergraduates' only introduction to international affairs is through foreign languages, it is doubly important to change their attitudes toward language study while trying to draw them into other types of international studies. Many language departments and faculty are disinclined to justify themselves. But they should be able to defend the study of language—even if that means setting it in a context, showing students how it interrelates with other fields, and, above all, creating specific curricular opportunities for such interrelationship. Since for many students the only justification for language study is its utility, courses oriented toward the rapid achievement of functional competence, perhaps in relation to business studies, nursing, or engineering, are particularly important. Another practical consideration, aside from careers, is the more immediate prospect of study abroad.

We cannot stress enough the importance of giving students adequate justification for international studies from the very beginning. Our efforts should also include advisors, publications, and anything else that influences student choices. A really effective campaign will also help create peer pressure, as students convince one another and as they observe how their more advanced fellows have used the institution's international programs to enrich their studies. And as this interest grows, it can be used as justification for additional curricular change.

We should never forget that, like faculty or administrators, students have their own reward system. Their priorities can be changed by changing the system—that is, giving them a stake in change. Students tend toward conservatism, especially under today's pressure for credentials and career choices and jobs. Just as the bait of discussion about liberal education may draw a faculty member out of his disciplinary lair, the promise of something we call "excitement," but which might be labeled "challenge," may cause the student to drop momentarily the grade-point-average shield and turn aside from the quest for graduate school or a large salary. But that is not enough. We must reduce the student's risk in reaching out to new options in the international field.

Unfortunately, the present reality of student behavior is that challenge—what some of the more starry-eyed among us always imagined to be the essence of undergraduate education—is fraught with frequently unacceptable risks. It is better to play for safety. So we must make it easier (even in terms of such crude yet vital measures as grade point average) for students to study abroad, explore new majors, or engage in various kinds of thematic study.

And we must increase the international element in the conventional, the bread-and-butter courses. Our most radical intervention in the reward system is traditionally the graduation requirement: We simply oblige students to behave in a certain way by telling them that if they do not they will not graduate. Here, too, as we have noted, much can be done to build the international component into the undergraduate core, whatever form the core may take. On the other side of the scale, we can offer financial inducements (or at least remove financial obstacles) to help students study abroad.

Even here, though, we tend to forget the importance of persuasion. Ten years ago, when requirements were under attack and freedom to do what one liked was the battle cry, many people argued (correctly) that it is up to the faculty to persuade students to do things the faculty regards as important. If professors do not really believe in them or cannot come up with reasons, the arguments went, students should not be obliged to do them. But, countered traditionalists, if the faculty spends all its time in persuasion there will be no time for classes. One needs requirements because they avoid the necessity of constantly going back to first principles.

Both sides had validity. If indeed we were forever arguing about what students ought to do, we might never get around to having these things happen. On the other hand, teaching and persuasion may be far more akin than we think. It might be good if we had to justify our subjects before the jury of the students more frequently. Requirements (and this is the other side of the coin) may mask an abdication of faculty responsibility—a refusal to engage in dialogue, to ask about priorities. Without calling into question the system of graduation requirements, we emphasize that much more needs to be done to engage students in dialogue about the nature of their education—not by asking what they want us to do, but by continually raising questions about what it means to live in the world of today and tomorrow and how the accumulated wisdom of higher learning can be brought to bear on these realities. Students are, or ought to be, partners in change.

Indeed, it is frequently argued, with some justification, that students should determine the principal priorities of their education. Many imaginative educators have proposed ways to do this. We agree that frequent consultation with students on such matters is vital. Putting students on curriculum committees and the like is helpful, but may not be enough. There should be other, more general, occasions for listening to students. It may also be valuable to graft onto such general forums procedures for involving students in curricular design and for creating courses based on student interest.

But sentimentality can easily replace realism here. It may be unrealistic and unfair to expect students to provide impetus for major changes in an institution or a curriculum. It is the responsibility of educators to provide, after considering students' perceived needs and what can be discovered about their future needs, the very best programs they can create. While not underestimating the value of student participation, we are unwilling to shrug off the entire responsibility onto students. They are essentially concerned with learning. We spend much time worrying about how students might create curriculum and not enough time worrying about how curriculum can, for good or evil, create students.

## 10. Parents

A further element in how a student decides on a course of study is parental pressure. Parents hold varying views on undergraduate education, some (particularly the college educated) seeing it as an opportunity to learn new things and broaden one's horizons, others emphasizing it as a stepping-stone to a career. Their views on the place of international studies in the undergraduate curriculum will also vary, depending on their background and knowledge of the world. But the canny institution will do its best to establish direct lines of communication with parents and use these to show the importance of an international perspective. If our college has a parents' day or similar activities, special efforts should be made not only to acquaint parents with the school's offerings in relevant fields but to give them a taste of the knowledge that can be acquired through these programs. Seminars for parents, brush-up sessions on languages, and the like can easily be organized. Knowledge about the world—facts and figures on interdependence, information on cultural differences or on current affairs—is invariably fascinating to the curious and can readily be converted into an object lesson in the importance of educating students for the world of tomorrow. This in turn will influence parents' signals to offspring.

### 11. Foreign Students in the United States

Ever since the end of the Second World War and the launching of the Fulbright program in 1946, the number of foreign students in the United States has been rising. This has been most dramatic over the last 20 years, when the number of foreign students rose from some 50,000 in 1960 to over 286,000 in 1980. Though this figure may seem very large numerically, we should bear in mind that the United States educates a larger percentage of its young people to the college and university level than does the rest of the world, and that therefore the percentage of foreign students relative to the total student population is lower than it might at first appear. In fact, the United States ranks twenty-first in the world in terms of the percentage of foreign students in its total student enrollment.

The foreign student population is distributed unevenly over the system of higher education. Understandably, the largest concentration is found at the major research universities, though there have been sharp increases at two-year colleges. A little over half of the total consists of undergraduates, and the most popular area of concentration for all foreign students is engineering (28.8 percent), followed by business and management (16.5 percent) (Boyan and Julian 1980: 16). There have been significant shifts in the countries of origin of foreign students, with the largest increases coming from the oil-producing countries, especially Iran, Nigeria, Venezuela, and Saudi Arabia. There has also been a marked increase in recent years in the number of women coming to study in this country. The figure now stands at about one quarter.

There are many reasons for the size of this foreign student population. As we noted, America's strength in scientific research and technological innovation naturally attracts large numbers of foreigners to our colleges and universities. Unlike many other countries the U.S. places few or no restrictions on their entry. But while this strength may be a necessary condition, it is hardly sufficient to account for the sheer weight of numbers. An additional factor, related to the U.S. technological and scientific lead, is the fact that as an English-speaking country the United States is more accessible to many foreigners than, say, the Soviet Union, Sweden, or Germany.

But considerably more important than the matter of language is the nature of the American higher education system. The invention of credits and the division of the curriculum into discrete courses —innovations of the nineteenth century—have made American university study marvelously flexible, both for students who build a program in a single institution and for those who move from one institution to another. In many countries' educational systems such flexibility is unknown. Transfer is impossible because there is no comparability. In other countries transfer among institutions is relatively easy only because all the institutions are essentially the same. The beauty of the American system is that it allows for entry to an institution at any number of points and that, despite differences in quality and programs over a vast range of institutions, all use the common coin of academic credit. While articulation between a foreign academic system and the American one may be difficult, it is certainly not impossible; and once in, foreign students can select their levels with no great difficulty.

This flexibility has made the American system particularly appealing to the newer countries. Rather than building an advanced research capability, many countries have, at least initially, relied on American resources, sending their most accomplished or promising students here. Others have sent large numbers of students at a lower level, in effect using the American educational system to supplement their own. Of late some of these countries have discovered our community college system; this accounts for the increase in that sector. In general the United States has responded well to this demand for training on the part of large numbers of foreigners (on the nature of these responses see Spaulding and Flack 1976). Many students have come under the aegis of formal exchange programs arranged on a government-to-government basis (Hayden 1980), often in the context of the U.S. foreign aid program (a dwindling number, however). Though the United States has no long tradition of welcoming large numbers of foreign students to its colleges and universities, the view has in part prevailed that higher education and the pursuit of knowledge are essentially international enterprises and that global problems require cooperative and global responses.

This noble ideal of the university open to the world—important and enduring though it may be, and worthy of defense as it surely is —has of late been severely tested. More and more Western European countries have limited their foreign enrollment, claiming that the scarce university places are better reserved for their own nationals. There have been signs of some resistance to foreign students here, particularly at smaller colleges in less cosmopolitan areas. The reality is that the nature of the foreign student population is itself changing. Though many come in on American money—either with direct grants or through financial aid from colleges and universities—the larger number come under grants from foreign governments or, to an increasing degree, on their own money. The self-supported students particularly are here to buy services—which may as well advance the development of their own countries but which are frequently available to them because they represent the moneyed elite.

We are not passing judgment; we are simply suggesting that a steadily increasing percentage of foreign students are using the American higher education system for purposes indistinguishable from those of their American counterparts. The United States is little by little shifting its priorities in this area, from a supplier of development assistance to ex-colonial and other countries to a supplier of educational services to those who can pay. This change, though it reveals all too clearly how America has retreated from what it regarded as its foreign aid responsibilities in the 1960s, does have the rather backhanded advantage of making foreign students operationally almost indistinguishable from Americans. Partly because of the flexibility of the system, because of its orientation toward the provision of services and because there is no shortage of capacity in higher education, the federal government has never imposed quotas on foreign students. The money they bring in helps sustain the system; the balance of payments between U.S. assistance to foreign students and the foreign students' assistance to the system may well show a net profit for this country, despite state and federal subsidies to higher education (Spaulding and Flack 1976: 112). Above all, foreign students help compensate for falling birthrates in the U.S., sustaining colleges short of students and keeping open graduate programs that would otherwise collapse for lack of demand.

This new situation carries its own problems. The National Association for Foreign Student Affairs (NAFSA) and other American organizations are concerned about the exploitation of foreign students by unscrupulous colleges anxious to keep their enrollments up. As the dollar drops in relation to other currencies and as wealth increases in numbers of countries, foreign students look increasingly attractive as an investment, even though they may lack the linguistic, academic, or cultural qualifications to transfer easily to an American environment. Particularly if present trends continue and personal wealth in countries like Kuwait and Venezuela, and now Mexico, continues to grow, we can expect a steady increase in foreign students. More colleges will recruit overseas and, unless this is controlled, there could be more exploitation than ever.

On the other side of the educational ledger, the influx of foreign students continues to constitute a massive brain drain from the developing countries (see Spaulding and Flack 1976: 204-60 for the considerable literature on this subject). Despite elaborate precautions instituted by the Immigration and Naturalization Service, large numbers of foreign students stay here following their training —many legally, though some illegally. In certain fields this aggravates the shortages of skilled manpower in developing countries and surpluses in the United States. In other fields the developing countries have in effect filled the gap caused by underproduction in the industrialized fields. Medicine is a case in point. According to a recent article (Link, New Delhi, June 29, 1980, reported in World Press Review, September 1980: 8), the developing countries are producing more doctors and nurses than their economies can support. "Of the 140,000 physicians working outside their countries of origin or training...120,000, or 85 percent, practice in just 5 countries—77,000 in the U.S., 21,000 in Britain, 11,000 in Canada, 6,000 in West Germany, and 4,000 in Australia." A full 13 percent of India's doctors work abroad—and no less than 88 percent of nurses from the Philippines are in foreign countries. Whether this is cause for alarm depends on one's interpretation of what is, after all, rather ambiguous data, but there is no doubt that the global market for skilled labor is taking on dimensions and convolutions unimagined 30 years ago.

Nevertheless, the foreign student population does constitute an important resource for the internationalization of undergraduate education and a unique opportunity for the promotion of international understanding. We can learn a great deal from our foreign students and their presence adds incalculable richness to American students' educational experience. It is in our interest to treat our foreign visitors well, both because of the understanding of American culture that they carry home and because we want our own students to be treated with equal courtesy abroad.

## 12. Catering to the Needs of Foreign Students

We are here concerned primarily with foreign undergraduates as part of the student mix in American colleges and with foreign graduate students as far as they interact with American undergraduates. Foreign undergraduates have certain needs to which we should pay particular attention (cf. Spaulding and Flack 1976: 295-8).

a. Foreign undergraduates require curricula that fit their needs. A large percentage of students coming to this country take preprofessional programs but others study the liberal arts. Given the enthusiasm for American education that brings them in the first place, they are disinclined to complain about programs geared to American students' needs. According to survey results and discussion at a 1979 conference titled Curriculum: U.S. Capacities, Developing Countries Needs, sponsored by the Institute of International Education, the major problem for many returning to their countries after study is a lack of preparation for applying their skills at home (Meyer 1979: 189).

Institutions with appreciable numbers of foreign students ought to provide special academic advising and perhaps modify requirements to fit their needs. We are not suggesting a relaxation of standards, but careful planning, perhaps with the aid of faculty familiar with the students' own educational systems, to build appropriate programs. Efforts might also be made to add material to some of the courses taken in large numbers by foreign students.

**b.** Every college that accepts foreign students should have a foreign student advisor who is sensitive to differences in culture and language and can help with housing, the workings of the American educational system (a total mystery to many new arrivals), health matters, and so on.

**c.** Foreign undergraduates need help with immigration regulations. The advisor should be familiar with current rules and should maintain contact with the local INS office. The institution should also be in regular contact with NAFSA and with other institutions accepting foreigners.

**d.** Foreign undergraduates need special programming. It is very easy to overprogram. We should remember that foreign students are very different: A student from Toronto probably has little in common with one from Kuala Lumpur and a student from Accra has little in common with a student from Caracas. On the other hand, students will find the United States very different from their countries and will welcome efforts to help them bridge the cultural gap. Programs may be practical and educational (simply giving information about daily life in the U.S.) or social. Host family programs and similar welcoming efforts are particularly helpful—and as enriching for the hosts as for the guests. The problem of foreign student spouses and children occurs less frequently among undergraduates, of course, but it can be a source of difficulty since spouses generally cannot work here and may lack language competence and familiarity with U.S. culture. Differences in child-rearing practices and eating habits may compound the problem.

**e.** Many foreign undergradutes need language training. At least the basic skills should be taught by qualified instructors in a properly constituted English program for foreign students. If the college does not have such a program it should either establish one or make an agreement with a nearby college that has one (the latter course may be preferable).

Good written material, sent to the student before departure, can allay fears or doubts and help the student gauge expenses. A hospitality program on arrival will speed integration. Foreign students already on campus can help the new arrivals settle in and provide the kind of advice they may hesitate to ask of a foreign student advisor. It is, by the way, helpful if the student can deal with the advisor at this initial stage in the student's own language. The journey is traumatic enough, and an early talk with the advisor or even with an experienced undergraduate or graduate student in a familiar language helps eliminate misunderstandings and inspire confidence.

To what extent should we regard the foreign student as separate and special, to be treated differently from Americans? As noted in the section on study abroad, integration is, in principle, preferable to special treatment. This does not mean students will not need special help; but they should be housed with American students rather than together in their own quarters, integrated with American students in classes, and so on.

Foreign students will come into frequent contact with faculty and administrators who have no particular interest or training in dealing with them. It is important to convey to these Americans that foreign students are highly valued members of the community and that they are worthy of patience and understanding. They may indeed be outstanding individuals, and certainly are not without initiative. We emphasize the point because at the most trivial level foreign students are a nuisance: They often take longer to grasp instructions, they have difficulty with forms, they may be confused by regulations. This means they take longer to deal with than their American counterparts. Since their difficulties are especially great when they first arrive, and that is the time of year when administrators are most harried, it is no wonder that they may be treated a shade unfeelingly. Even students entirely proficient in English have problems: British bureaucracies and forms are simply different from American ones. The terminology is different. And what is the Chinese student to make of requests that he record his first name or last name?

### 13.   The Foreign Student as an Educational Resource
Foreign students also represent an important resource for the institution they attend. Some, of course, come as half of an exchange pro-

gram that sends American students to their institution, and hence they are part of an important and mutually beneficial activity of the two institutions and, in a sense, have an obligation to both places. But regardless of the reason for their visit all foreign students carry cultural values and an outlook on the world (to say nothing of specific knowledge) that can help American students understand cultural differences and increase their awareness of the beliefs and aspirations of people whose way of life is different from theirs. Over the years many educators have puzzled over how best to tap this educational resource. Everyone agrees that foreign students are an important educational asset, but little has been done to put this belief into practice.

Pioneers in this regard have been a group of faculty at the University of Minnesota, which launched its Learning From Foreign Students program in 1974 (Mestenhauser 1976). As it evolved, it offered five approaches to the use of foreign students in the classroom (Mestenhauser and Barsig 1978): new courses intitiated by faculty with the active participation of students from the countries or regions studied; the use of foreign students as specialists or informants in relevant parts of existing courses—languages, religions, comparative education, and so on; foreign student interviews as elements in course work (to supplement or replace term papers, for example); independent study with foreign students, under faculty supervision; and laboratory or field work, with foreign students as subjects or informants in such areas as anthropology, education, or social work.

Minnesota also operates a pilot program for the training of foreign students as teaching assistants. There are many advantages for both foreign and American students in the employment of foreign students in the classroom, but there are problems as well. Students may lack English proficiency and teaching experience and may have different expectations in the classroom from those of American students. These problems are too frequently ignored, causing American students to resent foreign students in general after such poor experiences. The Minnesota program addresses these issues and provides a model to prepare foreign students for American teaching.

The Learning From Foreign Students program, and others across the country it has spawned, will likely work best in large institutions where foreign graduate students can work with American undergraduates—though undergraduate-to-undergraduate relationships are possible, too. The strength of these programs is that they recognize that foreign students have something special to offer—that they are more than simply outsiders in the system. Success depends on the careful selection of foreign students: Not all are suitable, since teaching talent is required. Furthermore, there is a potential ambiguity between foreign-student-as-informant (a role that, without skilled supervision, can easily become foreign-student-as-curiosity) and foreign-student-as-teacher.

Curricular planners will be able to create many variations on the Minnesota model. As conceived by Mestenhauser, the program draws on foreign students as volunteers, but they can be drawn into the teaching process as professionals, again with careful supervision. Recently several programs and experiments have begun along these and other lines, some sponsored or funded by NAFSA.

Even without a formal program, administrators and teachers can work to bring foreign students into academic contact with Americans on an ad hoc basis. A well-organized office of international programs can serve as a kind of broker between willing students and faculty able to use them in the classroom. Good publicity on initial efforts will bring further requests. These efforts can also be fruitful in informal programming—including foreign students in discussions on world affairs, involving them in programs on global problems, and linking them with the kinds of symposia and conversations we wish to generate in our efforts to internationalize the curriculum.

At the University of Pennsylvania the International Classroom program sends screened foreign students primarily to elementary and secondary schools to tell pupils about their countries or about some aspect of their way of life. Teachers request students from a certain area or with a special set of interests, for single or multiple visits, usually coordinated with pupils' class work. Visits are also used in problem situations—to ease locally related racial tension and to broaden understanding in times of international crisis. A new development is the use of International Classroom participants in social studies and language classes at the college level. This popular program is an easy and mutually interesting way of helping foreign students and Americans learn from one another. With the aid of a federal grant an effort is being made to duplicate the project across the country.

It should be emphasized that we must not expect too much from our foreign students. They are often no more or less thoughtful than their American counterparts, their hold on American customs and language may be weak, and their views on the world may be simply so different from the received opinions of Americans that the gap in perceptions is not easily bridged—especially if the students lack the conceptual vocabulary to do so. And there is no reason to expect the foreign student to be more tolerant and understanding than we are.

But if we enter this field with realistic expectations and a willingness to experiment, the rewards can be great.

Ultimately the main value of foreign students as teachers may lie in their informal relationships with other students. Opportunity should be provided for them to make their presence felt as part of the campus environment. In fact, the more the American students recognize the environment as international—rather than as an American place that foreign students share only on sufferance—the more we can create an atmosphere conducive to our main goals.

Frequently foreign students will be employed in roles identical to those of Americans—as dormitory counselors, teaching assistants, and so on. Here cultural differences can be a disadvantage. It is important to create adequate employment opportunities for foreign students and to draw on their talents in imaginative ways. While they should be given equal chances to secure jobs, it may be better to diversify the options than press foreign students into roles for which they are ill suited. Many make admirable and effective residence counselors, for example, but some lack awareness of the nuances of American culture.

Departments often treat teaching assistantships as just one more source of graduate student support, sending into the classroom foreign students who are competent mathematicians or chemists but whose knowledge of English or of American teaching styles is so rudimentary that little learning takes place and students become disgruntled. This may be the greatest misuse of the talents of foreign students, since it discourages teachers, creates negative feelings among students, and impedes undergraduate learning. There are times when foreign students are different and we must recognize this. We should not, of course, cut them out of opportunities or consign them to second-class citizenship, but find positions in which their strengths can contribute to their education and ours.

## 14.  The Foreign Researcher

Large numbers of foreign postdoctoral researchers come to this country every year for short or long periods (NAS 1969), generally to work at the major research universities (though a surprising number turn up at liberal arts colleges and other smaller institutions). The nature of their work is such that they are often isolated from the mainstream of university life and have few opportunities to interact with faculty outside their fields, or with students. Though the main reason for their presence is their study, they can often be drawn into social and academic programming. This population, which often includes highly talented and knowledgeable individuals, should be not only attended to but courted as an educational resource.

### 15. Alumni

Students become alumni—and alumni are an important potential source of support for international studies. Few institutions systematically cultivate contacts with foreign alumni, even though foreign students returning to their countries often hold high positions there. Alumni officers' reluctance to become involved is unfortunate but understandable. Foreign alumni are seldom large contributors; currency restrictions may limit their ability to send money abroad, or they may be less wealthy than their American counterparts. Furthermore, alumni giving is a largely American phenomenon, culturally alien to many foreigners. As a group foreign alumni seldom appear at campus reunions, as they are cut off by distance and cultural differences. And their diversity (their only point in common is their difference) makes them a difficult group to service and communicate with. But foreign alumni can be immensely useful as sources of contacts, recruiters of new students, and sources of assistance for study programs abroad. Area studies and language programs can benefit particularly from such ties; and foreign alumni may also offer good connections with foreign governments and assist as brokers in international research projects. (On developing a foreign alumni program, see Goetzl and Stritter 1980.)

What is true of foreign alumni is often true of Americans. They occupy positions that bring them into frequent contact with other countries—in government, business, or education. It is a good idea to comb alumni lists for potential international contacts and to work out ways of drawing on talents. It may be possible, by putting like-minded internationalists among the alumni into contact with one another, to build a network of support for the international element in undergraduate education and to keep its members informed of new developments on campus. Publishing articles on study abroad or other special programs in general alumni publications will also create support.

An increasingly popular element in alumni programming is alumni education. Alumni summer colleges have sprung up on a number of campuses and many institutions run special study-travel programs, sometimes accompanied by faculty, in Europe and elsewhere. International studies is a particularly fruitful area for these activities since it cuts across disciplines, relates directly to world problems, and often involves new knowledge. Foreign alumni might well play a role in both travel programs and those on the home campus.

Alumni education continues to be viewed first and foremost as a device for promoting alumni activity—that is, as a branch of alumni affairs rather than of education. But the time may be approaching when the continuing education of former students becomes part of the American college's mission. Then international studies will have an important role. Perhaps language study will be one of the first areas of activity since the refurbishing of old language skills revives a valuable link, especially for older people, with the larger world.

## 16. Legislators

State legislators' influence on a college, especially if it is part of a state system, can be decisive. Legislators are not a constituency we naturally associate with international affairs, but perhaps for that reason they need careful cultivation. To an ever-increasing degree the economics of the states have their international dimension. American agriculture is deeply involved in international markets, foreign investment in this country increases steadily, there are growing problems with competition from foreign goods, and the search for overseas markets has become an imperative for much of American industry. Recent influxes of immigrants have made cultural and language differences, social friction, and problems of education and labor a reality even in small communities. State legislators are suddenly obliged to know and understand world affairs to a degree quite unknown a few years ago.

This actually helps the curricular planner at work on international programs. Though international affairs lack an obvious and vocal constituency, they are increasingly recognized as important at every level of government. Since colleges and universities are among the top repositories of such expertise, they can fruitfully interact with government officials, legislators, and others—also at the state level. Devising effective ways of carrying out this task should be on the agenda of every state university, if only to demonstrate to the legislature the importance of support for international studies and its relevance to state government. Legislators should also be persuaded to promote and support state programs in international education and programs for the international exchange of people and ideas.

Much of this effort will be channeled through the campus office or official charged with state relations. This person might consider bringing state legislators to the campus to learn more about the institution's international programs or for special briefings on relevant topics. And legislators with international expertise might be asked to participate in programs connected with the internationalizing of the institution—such as, special symposia and conferences.

# 8

# The World on the Campus: The Campus as an International Environment

# The World on the Campus:
# The Campus as an International Environment

## 1. Administering International Programs

We have considered how our general internationalizing effort
might be carried through—with a collegewide or universitywide
committee, a statement or series of statements on the importance of
the international dimension in higher education, and so on. We suggested that a member of the administration supervise the program
and we emphasized the need to exert continuous pressure on all sectors of the institution to achieve results. We will now consider the
permanent structures needed to handle the international affairs of a
college or university and, briefly, the impact a strengthened international effort might have on the parts of the institution that support
the curriculum (libraries, etc.).

The President's Commission on Foreign Language and International Studies discussed in its report the administration of international
programs in colleges and universities:

> The Commission recommends that American colleges and universi-
> ties demonstrate and implement their commitment to international
> studies and programs by centralizing them at a high level in their in-
> stitutional structure. Such an international studies office would
> have direct access to the central administration and sufficient staff
> and resources to have leverage throughout the institution. It is also
> important that this office be broadly inclusive, so that foreign lan-
> guage and international studies, student and faculty exchanges, and
> foreign assistance projects and contracts are coordinated and mu-
> tually reinforcing rather than separate and competing. Crucial to all
> this is the leadership that the president of the college or university
> provides by encouraging and supporting international programs.

We cannot emphasize too strongly the importance of such consolidation. As the commission points out, the aspects of international affairs with which a college or university involves itself can be mutually reinforcing. Foreign students can help with advice on study
abroad; foreign faculty can assist with foreign students; area
studies and other international programs can be tied in with inter-

university agreements in areas not specifically concerned with international studies. Above all, a single office can be charged with general cognizance of all aspects of the international contacts of the institution and all lines of communication on such matters can be required to flow through it. A comprehensive international effort requires this kind of clarity (cf. Heenan and Perlmutter 1980: 153).

One of the more disquieting discoveries we made in writing this book is that offices of international programs are held in low esteem on many campuses, sometimes by international studies specialists themselves. Often they are perceived as just a student service or a branch of housekeeping services. International programs staff are often poorly paid and frequently the growth in their numbers and support services has not kept pace with the increased international involvement of their institution. Any structure that relegates concern with the international links of a college or university to some corner of the office of a dean of students is wholly out of tune with our sense of necessary priorities of both society and higher education. When we outline an international programs office, we have no such peripheral model in mind.

As the studies of Norman Palmer, Chadwick Alger, and others have indicated, the sheer quantity of international contacts that a community or institution carries on is formidably large. Institutions that do not already have a central office charged with international contacts (and even some that do) should begin by compiling an inventory of contacts and resources. This could be computerized for easy access and printout and might list the following information for a country or region:

a.  **Curriculum**. Courses dealing in whole or in part with the country or some part of it, including language courses. Programs or departments concerned with the country.

b.  **On-campus expertise**. Faculty and others who have studied in the country or hold degrees from its universities. Faculty who have taught or had extended stays there. Faculty who regard themselves as experts on some aspect of the country. Research projects and dissertations in progress. Trustees and others with contacts in that country.

c.  **Nationals**. Faculty, administrators, and students who are nationals of the country. Alumni (with addresses and any other relevant information). Visitors from the country who have recently come to the campus, with the reason for the visit and a contact person on campus.

d.  **Ties with institutions**. Current students who have studied or are studying in the country, with their temporary affiliation. Study programs sponsored by the college or university. Formal contracts or agreements with universities in the country, with names of on-campus administrators, administrative committees, and so on.

**e.  Languages.** Members of the college or university who can speak or understand languages spoken in the country.

**f.  Local resources.** Relevant details of library and museum holdings on campus or in the vicinity. Local institutions with special expertise or contacts (voluntary organizations, consulates, other colleges and universities. etc.).

Even the assembly of such data may prove difficult. Faculty are curiously reticent about revealing their overseas links, perhaps because they fear they will have to exploit them on behalf of the institution. Once the information is collected, however, it will probably reveal to these same faculty new opportunities for contacts or cooperation. The very act of assembling the information will help establish its assembler as a local expert and may convince others in the institution of the value of communicating up-to-date information about their international contacts. Above all, it will establish a base on which to construct an international programs office.

This office will not handle all the international contacts of the institution. These will continue to be made by faculty, departments, and others on a bilateral basis, though the office may give advice or technical help. Formal agreements or contracts with foreign institutions should be channeled through the office, and there should be procedures and checklists to ensure that they are consistent with the institution's policies and serve its needs in the best way. Agreements should also be carefully checked to make sure they will not lead to later administrative headaches or financial liabilities. There should be complete clarity on who is responsible for what, and who is charged with supervision of the agreement. Procedures are needed for regular filing of reports with the office of international programs. All agreements should also include clear provisions for renewal and cancellation.

The office of international programs should have direct contact with any office (or individual) on campus charged with responsibility for campus visitors, and should assist as the need arises. It might propose help with arrangements for foreign visitors; it could maintain written information on the institution in major foreign languages. Contact might be arranged between foreign visitors and American students or faculty. Aside from the intrinsic value of such meetings, they serve as reminders of the college's international dimension. A similar liaison might be maintained with the alumni office; the office of international programs might assist in programming for foreign alumni.

Among the numerous other offices with which contact might be maintained are the news bureau and the office of intercollegiate athletics. News about the institution can be channeled to the foreign press, possibly in foreign languages (thereby increasing its chances of publication), and news about international contacts, foreign visitors, and so on might go to the national and local press. The office of athletics might be encouraged to make contacts with counterparts in other countries and the international programs office could assist with travel arrangements and hospitality.

The international programs office should maintain links with the admissions office. The problem of evaluating foreign credentials is ongoing and complicated. On the one hand, the people in international programs will probably know the strengths and weaknesses of certain foreign institutions and where to get further advice if it is needed. On the other hand, the admissions office needs ultimately to evaluate foreign students in relation to general admissions criteria.

Cornell University, by the physical and organizational proximity of its international services and foreign admissions offices, appears to have avoided the usual lack of coordination between admissions procedures for foreign students and the services they need after they have been admitted. Too often, knowledge of foreign educational systems and specific institutions that can be gained through the international programs staff remains unused because of poor communication between the two areas. One possible solution is the part-time association of an international programs staff member with the relevant admissions committees. The Institute of International Education and other organizations such as the American Association of Collegiate Registrars and Admissions Officials (AACRAO) publish reference works and provide assistance in evaluating foreign credentials, but sometimes a talk with a professor or graduate student from the country can settle a seemingly unanswerable question.

The international programs office should have general responsibility for assisting foreign students, researchers, and faculty since some expertise—on immigration regulations, for example—is required, and staff members must be particularly sensitive to foreign visitors' special needs. But there should be good links with the student affairs staff and student residences, and with academic advising services. Staff members should be prepared to assist departments and schools on immigration problems. The extent of the international programs office's involvement in programming noncurricu-

lar international events on campus depends on the extent of its association with the relevant offices, but some contact would probably
be helpful. It can also assist students with noncurricular international travel unless some other agency is already handling this well.

There are important advantages to housing study-abroad programs in the international programs office: They can be linked with
other overseas activities; advice on selecting a program requires
special knowledge; many of the administrative and technical problems associated with a program are common to all. But policy decisions should be made in the academic area and there should be no
doubt that final control lies with the faculty. It is very advantageous
if the office is directed by a tenured faculty member, especially one
respected by colleagues in languages, international studies, and so
on, not least because the risk of disagreements over jurisdiction is
thus reduced.

The international programs office, at least if its leadership is
drawn from the faculty, should be charged with the general coordination of area studies programs, language programs, and so on,
even though final responsibility may lie elsewhere. Interdisciplinary
area studies programs may be coordinated by, for example, a faculty committee on which the administrator for international programs
sits ex officio, and the existing mechanisms of the operation can be
used for administering the program. This plan would facilitate the
creation of area studies programs with innovative academic and
nonacademic dimensions and ease the difficulties of interdepartmental programming. There is also an increased possibility of program evaluation, and of adapting successful elements from one program to another while avoiding pitfalls that have become apparent
through experience.

With such responsibilities it is important for the international programs office to be in touch with those in the institution who handle
relations with the federal government. If possible, the director of the
office should have direct access to relevant sections of the State Department, USICA, the Department of Education, and so on, and
should bring interesting government programs and funding opportunities to the attention of the faculty, encouraging their participation
and providing technical help. Another task likely to require liaison
with the federal government is faculty exchange, which should also
be housed in the international programs office.

While all these activities are essentially routine, there is also considerable scope for entrepreneurship and imaginative programming. They are operational manifestations of the institution's com-

mitment to international affairs which requires constant reaffirmation and cultivation on every level. The international programs office should be charged with promoting, either directly or through other administrative offices, the wide array of activities and consultations that we envisage as part of the general internationalization of the institution. It might be, in effect, the executive office of our campuswide committee. It should have enough funding to support worthy projects and seize initiatives, and it should have direct access to the chief academic officers and deans.

## 2. Libraries

The expansion of contacts with other countries and the shifts in academic priorities will certainly affect support services surrounding the academic programs. Building a collection of foreign publications, for example, will impose on the library new and punishing costs, since these are expensive to obtain and catalog (some of the problems are outlined by Carter 1979). We have advocated several courses of action that involve foreign and foreign language printed materials. But the inclusion of readings in languages other than English in course assignments, the use of materials published overseas and by non-American authors, and the development of courses in area studies all depend somewhat on the availability of library resources. Their importance cannot be overestimated, and fundamental to any effective internationalization effort is an assurance that at least minimum standards for library acquisitions and maintenance be achieved. Unfortunately, librarians usually must fight for funds, and the conflicting demands put on them can make it politically difficult to establish a system of priorities. For this reason the strategy of improving cooperation between libraries at different institutions has become increasingly important since the end of the period of rapid expansion of libraries that spanned the late 1960s and early 1970s.

This cooperation carries several dimensions: Libraries with significant collections on a geographical or topical area need to share with those that have different specialties. The Research Libraries Group, with 22 members in the Northeast, is an example of a relatively newly formed association that allows improved access to collections. Sharing among major libraries is also accomplished through cooperative acquisition and reproduction programs such as those of the Center for Research Libraries in Chicago and the Association of Research Libraries—which has, for example, a particularly valuable center for Chinese research materials (ACE 1975: 22). Cooperative possibilities can best be exploited through investment in on-line computer data management systems. By this means interlibrary loan systems are made more efficient and more satisfactory for the user. Without such help the institutional library system will find itself in a hopeless struggle to keep apace.

Smaller institutions face special problems. While sharing responsibility for specialized materials among the libraries is essential, the student at a small college who must run from library to library to acquire relatively ordinary foreign language materials or foreign publications is easily discouraged. Even the smallest and least pretentious library should keep some holdings in languages taught or used at the institution, and major works relating to all foreign areas should be available, whether or not there are courses in these areas on campus. Nor should acquisitions be limited to literary works. Foreign language materials should range across the disciplinary spectrum and should include newspapers and periodicals, so that language students can link their study with other curricular and personal interests and faculty can assign foreign texts also in nonlanguage courses. It may be advantageous in smaller libraries to maintain an additional card catalog that is organized by language.

The needs of area studies specialists in literature and history may be easier to serve than those of scholars interested in the sciences or social sciences (ACE 1975: 82). This seems particularly unfortunate in view of the needs of our overall internationalization effort, since the ability to study current affairs is a key element in the whole process. It is perhaps in these areas that the greatest effort is needed to make accessible the best of the scholarship of other nations—in translation, if necessary. Problems other than financial are involved in acquiring foreign publications: In some countries insufficient numbers of copies are printed to allow export of most works; in others currency restrictions require exchange arrangements that can be hard to negotiate. The whole academic community is probably insufficiently tuned to research in other countries, and we are all guilty of laziness in this respect. The scarcity of translations of major foreign texts suggests as much.

## 3. The Campus Bookstore

Important as library resources are in terms of day-to-day visibility, it is perhaps in the campus bookstore that foreign publications are hardest to ignore. Here the situation is often close to scandalous. Many bookstores function like those unassociated with educational institutions: They are run for profit (or at least enjoined to avoid losing money) and not for the benefit of their customers' education. In recent years more than one store has abandoned even a token stock of foreign books on the ground that low demand makes them uneconomical. Books in languages other than English are then only ordered when assigned as texts or specially requested. In such cases even reference books and dictionaries are usually in diminished supply. Since professors rarely assign texts in foreign languages except in language and literature courses, the printed word in the bookstore is likely to be exclusively the English word.

The failure to provide students with easy access to the staple products of foreign publishers is counterproductive on a number of levels. While it is not possible to keep comprehensive stocks of foreign books in a campus store, at least a token selection of the more important and staple items might be available—for the major languages and for those of the largest groups of foreign students. If students of French want to read the same kinds of popular novels in French as they read in English (or, better still, those two or three works currently gripping the hearts and minds of half the student population of France), it should be possible to do so. *Madame Bovary* may be accessible in some corner of the library (though, unfortunately, not to own and scribble in), but not the latest Pierre Nemours or Asterix. And a selection of Livres de Poche, or of the *Que sais-je* series, should surely be available, along with Bachelard or Levi-Strauss or Foucault. Why assume that everything worth reading is written in English—that while a language may be worth studying, it should not be supported in other ways, too? Classrooms are not everything. A commuting school without a parking lot or a residential school without a dormitory would be an oddity indeed. A school in which languages are taught without the wherewithal to use them is, or ought to be, thought equally odd and maladjusted to its task.

There are, of course, difficulties involved in ordering and obtaining foreign books. They are awkward to deal with and making selections is a problem. But regular consultation with foreign faculty and students or with relevant committees and departments could ease selection. As for obtaining the books, the problems are doubly difficult for the individual customer, and surely a campus bookstore should try to help precisely in such troublesome areas as these. We might add that a policy of waiting until orders are placed, rather than stocking the books in the first place, is tantamount to giving up on foreign books altogether, since foreign orders take months to fill.

The burden should not fall exclusively on hard-pressed bookstore managers. Under the right kind of pressure intelligently applied, they could probably be persuaded to ease up on one losing proposition (in some other part of the store) and invest in another. But ideally, college subsidies should be available to encourage managers to stock foreign books in reasonable quantities. With cooperation from literature and language and international studies teachers, a community of students who consider reading fiction in a second or third language an appropriate pastime could be created. As the market grew, the financial loss would diminish. This would, of course, happen all the more rapidly if the bookstore became known in the community for this policy and teachers, immigrants, and others turned naturally to it for their purchases.

It is not merely stocking such books, but locating them that should be carefully considered. It may be a mistake to segregate literature by language; possibly the literature and fiction section of a campus bookstore should be multilingual (though reference lists would need to be available by language). Thus a student looking for the latest Harold Robbins might be tempted by a Spanish text sufficiently appealing at first glance to be worth the extra effort. This would certainly be a change from rows of Dumas in one section, Thomas Mann in the next, Garcia Lorca segregated in a third, collectively forming a section to be carefully skirted between economics and geology.

Even more important than books are newspapers and magazines, since a language student who would balk at fiction in any language might be willing to try Der Spiegel or Paris Match. In many American cities and surely in most smaller towns (except occasionally in an ethnic neighborhood) foreign magazines and newspapers are not available at all if not on campus. While they may be hard to obtain, they are needed in an international campus environment. If foreign students know that newspapers in their language are available, they are likely to buy them. So will American students required to do so as part of courses with an international dimension. A cafeteria where students read Le Figaro and Frankfurter Allgemeine Zeitung (to say nothing of Asahi Shimbun or Izvestia) is a common sight in Europe; in this country it would be cause for comment. Even for students who are less adventurous World Press Review, the Economist, and other English-language publications giving a non-American perspective on the news should be available, if not in the bookstore then in the library—or, preferably, in the student union or international programs office.

## 4. Audio-Visual Resources

If we attract more students to language programs, the increased enrollment may necessitate expansion of the language laboratory, which can perform a valuable ancillary service for all language courses and can act as a central element in some.

But the use of audio-visual materials in language learning can go beyond the aids we traditionally associate with language laboratories. A good audio-visual center will, for example, collect materials for self-instruction in languages not normally offered in the curriculum. It will gather tapes and records of general interest. In fact, a systematic effort should be made to build the foreign holdings in the campus audio-visual center and the record library.

Recent technological advances have made it far easier to pick up television stations over long distances. There are now ways of gaining direct access even to satellite broadcasts. Videocassette programs can also be obtained. This means that most colleges can have access to foreign television. An evening of French commercials or an Italian soap opera can do wonders for linguistic knowledge.

In many parts of the country students have access to one or more of the 270 commercial radio stations that broadcast in Spanish, 226 of them with time slots allocated for broadcasts in other languages designed to interest ethnic minorities (Simon 1980b: 144). Students should be alerted to this programming and encouraged to use it as an aid to language learning and also for the cultural background it provides. Unexpected instances can be found: For example, the local Argentine community in Philadelphia provides an occasional broadcast of tango music with explanatory material. Where these stations cannot be picked up, there may be a college station with room for language teaching programs or for programming with international content. International folk music programs can draw on the expertise of members of the university or college and can provide an introduction to another culture and another language. Programming on international politics, where there is less than adequate coverage on local public radio stations, can be combined with in-depth examinations of the background of current events. Islamic law, the electoral systems of other nations, indigenous cultures threatened by industrialization, can provide topics for radio discussion or lectures. This might be suggested or mandated listening for students taking related courses.

Public radio and television are probably underutilized as an educational resource. For instance, the WGBH Boston series *World* presents a variety of approaches to issues important in other parts of the globe. These programs—as well as special presentations such as "Death of a Princess," which inspired considerable controversy over its treatment of Saudi Arabian mores—should be brought to students' attention as a matter of general interest, not simply as an adjunct to their courses.

There are numerous possibilities for commercial and short-wave radio in the classroom, particularly in foreign language teaching. News broadcasts in many languages can be used both for practice in aural comprehension and for their content and the perspective they provide (for a bibliography of articles on creative ways to use radio in language teaching, see Melpignano 1980: 389-390).

## 5. A Cosmopolitan Campus

Except in rare instances, high school graduates do not select a college on the basis of its cosmopolitan environment or international programs. Yet the contacts students make outside the classroom and the extracurricular programs they are exposed to as undergraduates will influence what they choose to learn, how they learn it, and how they ultimately use it. The nature of the campus environment is more than tangential to any consideration of the internationalizing process.

How does one create a campus atmosphere in which international perspectives play a salient part? What makes for a cosmopolitan environment? What factors make students wish to become more knowledgeable about the world outside the campus and beyond their country? Above all, is it possible to change the feeling of the environment, and how, apart from the ways already described, might that be done?

Many of the factors that make a real difference are basic. Consider language. Large numbers of people across the world take linguistic diversity for granted. They are used to dealing with languages they barely understand, confronting the incomprehensible as best they can. Their surroundings are rich in incentives for language learning: If they need to understand something, they work at doing so. Diversity of language should be built into the environment of the American student. Ideally, it should be impossible to spend a day without encountering something written or spoken in another language. Progress across the campus should be a series of challenges, an obstacle course, of foreign phenomena, just as it is for the foreigner in an American institution. Little by little, challenges become pieces of furniture, familiar items in an accepted ambiance. What contributes most strongly to cosmopolitan diversity—apart from the presence of foreigners, whether as students, visiting scholars, or short-term visitors—is that unobtrusive evidence of involvement in the world that is found where the international dimension is taken for granted.

But the nature of the institution is often crucial in determining the resources available and the kinds of programs that will work. The smallest, remotest campus with the most homogeneous student body may have resources within itself or readily accessible that can bring to the attention of students and faculty those issues of interdependence that underlie the need for internationalization. Beyond that, it is frequently *awareness* of resources that is lacking; an inventory of possibilities, even a more modest one than that proposed earlier in this chapter, can unearth the potential for surprisingly varied and flexible extracurricular programming that is international in character.

In fact, the taking of an inventory may, as in the case of curricular programming, be a good place to begin. It will reveal at once people active in, or potentially useful for, creating awareness of international concerns; programs and activities that contribute to the cosmopolitan nature of the community; and resources that bring people on campus into contact with foreign languages and cultures and with world affairs. Some of these programs and resources exist because of international dimensions of the curriculum; others because of the nature of the local community or the student body, or the location of the institution. It is not the existence of such resources but their effective exploitation that is frequently problematic. Perhaps a student activities council can be persuaded to working toward fuller use of the resources, with the cooperation of advisors on international programs and interested faculty. Funding (even if small) for extracurricular activities, and assigning it along with an appropriate mandate to an administrator, may bring a similar result.

A committee responsible for internationalizing the curriculum and campus should also cover extracurricular concerns. This would centralize information about all international aspects of campus life, and thus increase the chances of producing well-integrated and coherent projects with substantial commitment from those involved. The same mechanisms used for publicizing and developing curricular innovation could then be exploited for extracurricular programming. This is not, of course, the only method of organizing portions of the environment for a good internationalization campaign, but for a new effort it is a means of securing cooperation and visibility.

When we speak of internationalizing the campus environment, we are saying that the experience of living or studying or working on campus should be as international and cosmopolitan as possible. The existence of other countries and cultures should be so much in evidence that it is taken for granted. At every turn we should encounter these realities and our senses should constantly receive messages to reinforce our general impressions. Nothing is irrelevant: Everything, down to the simplest matters of campus housekeeping, can be internationalized. The purpose of the entire effort is, of course, to support and strengthen an internationalized curriculum—by allowing students to carry into the classroom experience gathered outside and by causing them to think seriously about taking courses with an international component.

The possibilities are limited only by the imagination. Language coffee hours, notices in Arabic of Muslim prayer meetings, T-shirts printed with "I Love New York" in Japanese, postcards of foreign (preferably non-Western) art, displays of Chinese jewelry on sale, an adequate selection of foreign records, posters from the campus energy conservation committee bidding one to "Do It in the Dark" in half a dozen languages—the list goes on. All such touches are as possible in two-year colleges as in major research institutions.

We should also not forget the campus press. In addition to serving the functions already noted, college newspapers can feature an international dimension if there is the impetus to do so—such as news of foreign visitors, articles by foreign students, a column in a foreign language, or commentaries on foreign affairs. It is often in small ways that students begin to feel, day by day, that their institution is a member of the world and that they have relevant obligations and privileges.

Let us look at some of the more elaborate programs with an international dimension that can help to transform the campus.

## 6.  Traditional Programming

There are numerous traditional programming possibilities that can heighten awareness and bring to the campus a range of cultural phenomena from other parts of the world. These are generally related to the arts and there is a strong chance that at least some are already exploited, at least sporadically, on most campuses. Musical performances and visual exhibits require only passive participation from students, but their importance should not be underestimated; interest in another culture can often be sparked by appreciation of its art forms. Such programming can be divided into exhibits, performances, and films, Since they present different kinds of experience, they need different modes of organization and exploitation.

### a.  Exhibits

Exhibits require space, security, and well-informed presentation. They may be materials collected in an ad hoc fashion for a single occasion by the person responsible for the event, or a predetermined selection of materials on tour as a package. The huge success of the exhibits of the Tutankhamen artifacts nationwide and of the China show indicates the extent to which the American imagination can be caught by artifacts and historical and archaeological materials from other cultures. A major university may have its own resources for fashioning permanent or short-term exhibits. Such courses as Native American studies, anthropology, and archaeology frequently include visits to artifact displays at local museums and galleries, but these exhibits' impact on people with no prior knowledge or interest can also be great if the organization and explanatory materials are well done. Curricular and noncurricular programming can, with careful planning, come together around such events.

Finding suitable space for exhibits is rarely difficult. Even the necessity of placing materials in well-trafficked areas can be an advantage, providing security risks are not high. What to exhibit presents a far greater problem, if this is the question facing a committee charged with internationalizing the environment. Depending on resources, objectives, and the area of cultural interest, traveling exhibits can sometimes be secured through professional groups such as the Asia Society or through Washington agencies such as the National Council for the Traditional Arts and the Folklife Program of the Smithsonian Institution. But since this is likely to be costly, it should only be attempted as part of an integrated program focused on a certain culture or part of the world. Exhibits can be best used to draw students toward new awareness of other highly developed cultures in conjunction with courses in language or area studies, and sometimes with the existence of a local or student population from the area. For example, the Smithsonian prepared a Southeast Asian exhibit directed toward cities and towns that had received Southeast Asian refugees. Seen in conjunction with courses and other programming, such an exhibit is relevant to the lives of students in a community faced with absorbing a new ethnic population.

Exhibits can be effectively assembled and presented on campus with the help of students from overseas, members of the community, and perhaps students in the fine arts. We have seen, for instance, a highly effective and attractive exhibit of Polish traditional costumes presented along with a dance performance on campus. The better the explanatory materials that accompany these exhibits, and the better the integration of different but related events, the greater the impact on the environment. Incidentally, all materials in the Polish exhibit were owned by members of the community and it cost nothing to mount.

Because of the importance of coordination, those concerned with programming should know what is happening locally. An exhibit on Ukrainian church art and history can then be combined with a local visit from, say, the Ukrainian national folk dance ensemble.

### b.  Performances
Internationally related performances vary enormously in their power to draw an audience, and thus in their attractiveness to student activities councils and other such committees. At the moment Irish traditional music is fashionable on the East Coast: Almost any Irish performer can attract capacity audiences, huge numbers of students among them. Students and members of the Irish-American community are joined by a common enthusiasm for step dancing and Gaelic. But this situation is unusual. Most performers of foreign materials have to fight for an audience, on or off campus, and it is once again probably through effective integrated programming that performance events have real impact. Publicity is extremely important. On campuses with substantial music, theater, or dance departments it may be easier to persuade students of the value of such performances, but they will probably be most successful if presented in conjunction with language programs that have strong cultural dimensions, such as those at Middlebury College. This is, of course, particularly true of theater. Drawing an audience for a foreign language play is difficult but not impossible, especially if the language is widely taught and other colleges or high schools are included. One idea is to invite an amateur troupe from a foreign university with which one's institution has links and perhaps organize a tour of other colleges for it.

Simply presenting a series of performances by, say, Balkan folk musicians will not make a campus environment more international. Performances are symptomatic, rather than causal, in respect to the interests and awareness of the campus community. It is not sufficient to set up concerts, or a series of craft exhibits, and cite these as the successful creation of an international dimension. They must be used in conjunction with curricular programming and exploitation of community resources to produce any significant results.

### c.  Film Series
Almost every campus has a film society and many institutions of all types offer courses in film. International film series are best used in conjunction with related materials or with discussion groups that help students integrate their experience of the film with a comparatist approach and also with an understanding of the culture that informs the film.

Many important foreign films, both classic and new, are available for rental, often at moderate cost. However, a hodge-podge of foreign films is likely to leave even a devoted audience of regular movie goers frustrated and confused. Cinema, perhaps more than any other art form, lets us exist for a while in another environment, another culture; but the different aesthetics of, say, Brazilian magical-realist or German new wave movies can be hopelessly disconcerting just as they can be startlingly illuminating. A series of, say, Latin-American films can open a faithful audience to an understanding of life on the continent and, particularly if Cuban films are included, to questions about political issues of interdependence. But if the films are merely screened, with no explanatory materials, related courses, or discussion opportunities, they may be incomprehensible, alarming, or irrelevant—at best, confusing. In order to help increase awareness and understanding, a film series—whether comparatist or area focused—must be supported by intelligent planning and preferably helped along by considerable expert guidance.

Films, especially foreign ones, are perhaps underused as an educational tool at the university level; they are certainly not employed with as much imagination as could be wished. A range of foreign films could counteract the ethnocentrism that so often characterizes issues-oriented courses. Extraordinary and powerful films from many countries, including the Third World, offer new perspectives on, for example, hunger, human rights, colonialism, and industrialization. Rarely used in teaching, these can do more than any lecture to break down stubbornly unicultural perspectives.

Why don't teachers use these materials more frequently? Probably because it is easier not to. If we are to forge strong links between programming of this kind and curricular activities, two principles are crucial: faculty involvement and careful planning. Wherever possible, faculty should be included in programming decisions. In fact, the offices concerned with programming might work through deans and department chairs to establish liaison with key departments and perhaps create departmental committees to help design and execute programming relevant to their specialties. Faculty can also be drawn into discussion groups following performances; the preparation of program notes, catalogs, or articles on special events; and the hosting of visiting performers. The more such events can be tailored to existing curricula, the easier these links will be. But that requires a great deal of planning and an easy and cooperative relationship between faculty and programmers.

Performances do not necessarily require outside professionals to come to the institution. Language teaching can itself resemble theater, and it is but one step from such a method to the performance of plays (Melton 1980). Even if the results are avowedly, not to say appallingly, amateur, they can be valuable aids to teaching —and there may even be a few hardy souls (perhaps from other courses in the same language) willing to come and watch. We do not recommend full-scale productions, but relatively simple and entertaining short plays—in which, for example, class A presents a play to class B and class B reciprocates. More promising from an audience's point of view are amateur music or dance performances, especially if linked to a genuine attempt to discover and experience (and learn about) the culture in question. Again, the more the faculty can be involved in such efforts, the better.

### 7. Programs on Current Events and Global Issues

If exhibits, professional performances, film series, and the like constitute traditional extracurricular programming, there are many possible additions that involve active rather than mere audience participation from members of the institution. For example, student interest in newsworthy events—international crises, the Olympic Games, and so on—may be exploited with conferences and seminars, in relation to a variety of courses, designed to improve understanding and promote active discussion and analysis. Debating societies and other organizations can be encouraged to address international rather than local and national concerns; participation in conferences can be made mandatory for students in certain courses —particularly history, political science, government, or international relations. Well-organized and publicized seminars of this kind may also, particularly on isolated and residential campuses, be developed on a dormitory basis as part of a series or as a special activity. Where organizers are attuned to the issues that catch students' imagination or curiosity and can attract prestigious speakers from the faculty and from outside, response may be very good—as it is to such freshman seminar series at Yale and Brown.

The Model UN format—often used in high school instruction on the nature of the United Nations—and other simulation exercises can work well for undergraduates if presented in conjunction with academic programming. This approach offers a particularly good opportunity for students to research in depth the issues surrounding questions of international significance, not only from the American standpoint but from that of other nations. In some areas public radio stations broadcast portions of UN debates on issues significant to the United States. Where this is so, or where field trips to the UN are possible, a module can be developed that provides a clear understanding not only of the United Nations but of such complex issues as the North-South debate and the population question, which continually recur in relation to specific events internationally. The United Nations Association can assist in planning programs of this kind.

An interesting experiment in nontraditional programming was developed at the University of Nebraska at Lincoln in conjunction with an effort to introduce an international and interdisciplinary dimension to the curriculum. Focusing on international terrorism, five courses led up to a two-day simulation of a terrorist takeover. Students and faculty from other institutions, a consultant, and the FBI participated in the event. Students had been extensively prepared for the simulation with readings and discussions. The necessary element of surprise was built into the simulation by staging the takeover—by a theater group—in the middle of what was billed as a briefing session. During the simulation students failed notably to apply what they had learned during the preparation period; during later debriefing sessions they came to terms with this. The outcome of the experiment seems to have been that students not only gained knowledge of the phenomenon of international terrorism but about the problems of transferring classroom knowledge to real situations. (For other examples of simulation programs see Snow 1977: 65-78).

Though a good deal of work and planning is required for events such as this, the results may easily justify it. Once again the value of integrating curricular planning with special events is clear. It is worth pointing out that not all our programs have to be created anew. Every campus has its student activities or special programs with an international flavor, and it may be that with more publicity or attention they can have a greater impact on the campus. In principle, the more we internationalize in one area, the stronger the international influence in another: We strengthen the hands of others already involved in international activities. We should do everything we can to support student activities that are international in nature —UN clubs; travel clubs; clubs for languages; clubs and organizations concerned with hunger, human rights, or the environment (if their interests extend beyond the United States).

There are also possibilities for programming aimed at the campus and outside community that is largely unrelated to academic programming. Examples from the University of North Carolina at Charlotte for 1975-76 included a Great Decisions Banquet with a former ambassador to the UN as speaker (on Great Decisions see chapter 9);

an international festival organized by the foreign language department in conjunction with ethnic and community groups from the area, attended by an estimated 8,000 people; a 5-week symposium on The Comparative Role and Status of Women and Men; and a 2-day symposium on Alternative World Futures. A strong commitment by the institution and the appointment of a director of international studies preceded a successful application for funds from the then U.S. Office of Education. These activities are part of an ongoing movement to strengthen the Center for International Studies at UNCC and develop an undergraduate major plus outreach programs within and beyond the campus. The centralization of international programming, at UNCC as elsewhere, provides integration and maximum visibility for special events.

For the small institution seeking to develop fundamental programs of international content, using existing language departments and, if possible, local ethnic communities under the auspices of a committee, can probably yield the best results—at least if a single area of concentration is selected and efforts are focused on developing strength in a single culture area rather than on diversification. But awareness of global issues does not require expertise in a particular area, and the absence of such a concentration does not necessarily negate the benefits of extracurricular programming for international awareness. The best programming is sensitive to the nature of the constituency, the institution's resources and environment, and the strengths of the curriculum.

## 8. Residences

Probably the most highly developed language house programs are those in which only the mandated foreign language may be spoken within a residence hall and all social programs for the hall involve the language and elements of an associated culture (Binzen 1978). Folk dancing, balalaika classes, the films of Eisenstein, and the novels of Tolstoy and Doestoevski may provide the bases for in-house programming in a Russian language residence hall. Study-abroad programs during the summer may be the culmination of the academic year's living-learning program and provide the final immersion experience for which students have been prepared. Such projects are most successful on isolated campuses, but are by no means impossible on the urban residential campus. Here, a degree of commitment can be exacted from residents as a requirement for living in the hall and perhaps in connection with credit for levels of proficiency attained and for independent study projects. While the classic examples are at colleges such as Middlebury and Earlham, where there is a special commitment to language and international studies, they exist on most residential campuses that have strong language programs.

Another living-learning project which can be implemented on campuses where there are foreign students is based on the model of an "international project" or on the more elaborate international houses—such as those in New York near the Columbia campus and in Philadelphia, Chicago, and elsewhere. An international house may be a short-stay hotel for foreign visitors as well as a residence for American and foreign students. An international residence hall located within the university can function in the same way, as an environment in which students from around the world are induced by proximity to accept cultural differences and develop tolerance and understanding of alien ways of living. The objective is to help foreign students interact not only with other foreigners but also with Americans, and to let American students share living space with foreign students and increase their own awareness of cultural (as opposed to interpersonal) variables in social interaction. Students with an already developed interest in international affairs are more likely to be attracted to such a project, but it would be productive to encourage engineering or science majors to participate. Cultural, informational, and even curricular programming in such projects can contain strong international elements. These are probably best worked out on a thematic or issues-oriented basis; in such a residential environment they can be combined with adventures in cuisine, dance demonstrations, and slide shows usually found in these settings.

International living-learning centers exist at a variety of campuses, including Syracuse, Cornell, and SUNY at Stony Brook. Programming and success vary greatly, but in general selection of residents and the creation of mechanisms for ensuring continuity seem to be crucial (Hoopes 1976: 137-146). With enthusiastic residents and effective methods of governance, programming seems to present few problems, becoming a natural outcome of the mix and interests of the students.

This last point is the most important. The environment in which the students in an international project live is, in effect, naturally international. Projects and programs of this kind constitute a model of what we would like to achieve on a campuswide basis, and they should be viewed not as enclaves in an otherwise American setting but as catalysts for programs and activities across the campus. It is important that foreign students not be confined exclusively to international residences but that a fair proportion be scattered across the campus.

## 9. Bringing Americans and Foreigners Together

Is it better to provide a supportive environment for foreign students by designing special programs for them and by letting them live together, or is it better to encourage integration? Probably neither option can be applied singlemindedly; a combination responds best to students' needs and temperaments. Where there is a substantial population of foreign students, for example, nationality groups are likely to be formed. While they exist primarily as support systems for the students, they can also work to disseminate information and awareness about other cultures and about issues of global concern. Financial support for student activities could be available to such associations, just as it is to any other student group. Students who join are usually willing and eager to share aspects of their culture with the rest of the community; if the administration cooperates with their initiatives, they will be likely to provide assistance as well as original and useful programming suggestions.

On campuses with small foreign student populations a composite international students' association will take the place of nationality groups. The association at the State University of New York at Buffalo works to protect the interests of foreign students and to promote intercultural understanding. Their publication *Intertwine* is distributed free across the campus and contains articles on global issues, personality profiles, poetry, a correspondence column, and information about programming. It is worth special investment to ensure that foreign students participate and express their opinions in internationally related seminars and conferences. It is often in such contexts that American students have their initial firsthand experience of the perspectives natives of other cultures bring to issues of international importance.

Interaction between foreign and American students has become the focus of what might be called the applied end of the field of intercultural communication. The scholarly component of this field is derived primarily from anthropological and communications theory and its humanistic orientation is toward communication across racial and cultural boundaries. The Society for Intercultural Education, Training and Research (SIETAR) has a series of readings in intercultural communication, several volumes of which are concerned with applications to social interaction. The intercultural communication workshops (ICW) is an event often replicated on campuses and is designed to help foreign students adjust to the United States and to help Americans understand basic issues in cultural relativity. Such workshops require trained facilitators and a degree of commitment from participants. They are perhaps most effectively used with American students planning to study overseas plus foreign students studying here. ICWs held at the University of Minnesota as part of orientation programs for foreign students were rated very highly for their effectiveness in changing preconceived ideas about another culture (Hoopes 1976: 4-5).

In recent years a number of textbooks have appeared (Asante, Newman, and Blake 1979: 9) and facilitator training can be arranged through SIETAR for foreign student or study-abroad advisors with an interest in the area. Workshops can also be oriented toward specific concerns: At the University of California at Los Angeles in spring 1980 a program arranged for the Latin-American Studies Department in conjunction with Latino students was timed to coincide with a seminar for NAFSA Latin Americanists at the University of Southern California, thus providing a week of academic and culturally oriented events open to members of neighboring academic institutions. Students participated and also acted as resource people.

The terms "intercultural communication," "intercultural programs," and the like, have become catch-alls for any effort to communicate with foreigners in the United States. It is no doubt extremely useful and important (morally as well as practically) to increase one's sensitivity to cultural differences and to learn how one's own behavior can be influenced negatively by cultural biases. Efforts along these lines are, however, subject to abuse. There is a tendency, for example, to reduce the problems of communication across cultures to a set of stereotypes or norms that are only marginally less misleading than the stereotypes they are intended to replace. It is debatable whether the intercultural workshop designed to eliminate such stereotypes as "All Ruritanians are dirty" or "All Ruritanians eat weird foods" is really useful if it simply replaces these judgments with the observations that "In Ruritania everyone is about 15 minutes late for appointments" or "In Ruritania it is considered bad form to eat with a fork." When a Ruritanian turns up for an appointment at the international programs office on time, should we conclude that his conduct is unacceptably assertive? Behavior is a kind of language and we learn and absorb new patterns in new circumstances. But, as with language, some people behave with an accent, some behave like native speakers. We should avoid jumping to conclusions, but we should not try to account for people's behavior exclusively in terms of their cultural difference.

A second problem involves what is often regarded as one of the premises of intercultural understanding—that it is important to empathize, to get inside the skin of someone else. Most communication is not total. We keep a great deal to ourselves and we communicate only what we choose. There is nothing wrong with that. Under the guise of honesty we may impose ourselves on others and do violence to the delicate, and restrained, processes of communication. Many foreigners may already feel burdened and confused by the so-called openness of American communication patterns. It is simply one way of communicating and may not be superior to others. Thus we should avoid proselytizing. All this is not to suggest that intercultural studies have no place in our priorities or that we can learn nothing from them. If they educate us in objectivity and skepticism and the ability to reserve judgment, they are immensely useful. But we should beware of assuming cultural difference where there is none, and we should beware of using foreign students for our own psychological explorations.

While foreign students are long-term residents on campus and continuously contribute to its life, most institutions are also visited occasionally (or, in the case of major research institutions, almost constantly) by foreign visitors who plan shorts stays at the institution or in the area. But visitors from overseas who come to the United States as academics have capabilities in their fields of specialization and as experts on their culture and society. The Institute for International Education, aware of the importance that scholarly contact internationally can have for individual departments and researchers, has created a Speakers' Bureau. At minimal cost it handles requests for visiting foreign scholars to speak on their field at any academic institution that requests their services. It has long been possible for enterprising administrators to contact Senior Fulbright Award holders in their area and request their services as guest lecturers. It is much less common to find foreign scholars, or their spouses, involved in direct interchange with students about their own country and its educational system and values. Where there are student clubs based on interest in international affairs, visitors may benefit from an informal social event in which they can meet American students, while the students can converse with a representative of a culture they are interested in. It is especially helpful to provide facilities for short-term stays in campus residence halls; students are often delighted to act as guides and experts on their own environment while practicing a second language or entertaining an expert in their major field of study.

Major institutions will also receive delegations from other countries and foreign universities. For example, delegations from the People's Republic of China have become a common sight on American campuses. They are usually treated with much respect and ceremony, and rarely meet anyone outside the faculty and administration. Where receptions can be arranged to include students, a good deal of pleasure and interest is often shared by foreign dignitaries and young Americans, as mutual fascinations with sport, modes of dress, travel, and language emerge from what has often become a solemn dialogue on academic potential and research trends.

And it is neither pure chance nor some strange kind of academic osmosis that brings delegations to one campus rather than another. Often these visits result from contact by individual faculty or through such organizations as the National Academy of Sciences. But numerous delegations of other types also move around this country—on fact-finding trips, goodwill visits, and so on. Institutions interested in receiving more visitors should contact the relevant divisions of USICA and such nongovernmental organizations as the National Council for International Visitors (or local Councils for International Visitors, where they exist).

## 10.  From Planning to Action
While much of what we have described can be initiated by students or faculty, a systematic attempt at internationalizing the environment will require more concerted action. Perhaps at the urging of our International Committee, a group of students might be persuaded to form an international action group to improve the international dimension in various small ways. Similar efforts are possible at the faculty level. But student affairs administrators should take on some of this task—and they will need to be convinced of its importance.

The second (and more subtle) method of persuasion is to enlist student affairs administrators' participation in what is a well-publicized endeavor. Presented with an image of themselves as key cooperators in an effort that is painted as a major component of a changing or developing institutional identity, and under the leadership of senior administrators whose power is recognized and accepted, even the recalcitrant may become tractable. As the international nature of the campus becomes a well-advertised fact, built into catalogs, student newspapers, commencement speeches, and reports to the trustees, newly hired personnel will take it as a matter of course and resistance will wane before a fait accompli.

# 9

## College and Community

# College and Community

## 1. U.S. Organizations and Government Agencies

No college or university is an isolated community. Scholars and students interact with the people around them, faculty and administrators are members of the larger society as well as that of their institution, and campus programs also serve a larger audience. Even the college most isolated from its neighbors has ties, through its students and faculty, with distant communities; and faculty are part of an international network of knowledge. In this chapter we shall examine what outside agencies can do to strengthen international programs and give greater emphasis to international matters in the curriculum. We shall then look at how the college can serve the community by becoming a kind of international resource for it.

If there is one truism about American higher education, it is that everything has been tried somewhere before. There is a whole literature on ways of internationalizing or globalizing the curriculum. This book is only the latest addition. (There is a national directory of model programs in the same series.) Members of organizations, among them the International Studies Association (ISA), are constantly on the lookout for new ideas which they publicize through their journals. ISA normally runs several panels on curriculum at its annual convention. The Council on Learning takes an active interest in such matters through *Change* Magazine. The Consortium for International Studies Education, based at Ohio State University, is developing a comprehensive series of curricular materials on major world problems, and members of other organizations, such as the Council for International Studies and Programs (CISP) and the Consortium on Peace Research, Education and Development (COPRED) are engaged in related efforts. The work of Global Perspectives in Education (New York) is directed primarily at elementary and secondary schools, though many of its publications have a bearing on higher education. Global Perspectives is concerned not simply with international studies but with a comprehensive infusion of global attitudes throughout the curriculum. Global Education Associates (New Jersey) also works in this area. Among other organizations concerned principally but not exclusively with elementary and secondary education is the American Council on the Teaching of Foreign Languages (ACTFL), which publishes a journal, *Foreign Language Annals*, and curriculum guides (see ICIE 1977; Weston 1979-80). The Association of Departments of Foreign Languages, an arm of the Modern Language Association, performs a somewhat similar function for higher education through its *Bulletin*.

In reviewing programs and ideas from other institutions, it is important to remember several educational programs outside the framework of higher education proper. The Defense Language Institute, for example, takes care of the language needs of the armed forces, employing some 500 faculty to teach over 30 tongues at its headquarters in Monterey, California, and also running nonresident language courses. These courses emphasize basic, practical skills —the kind of language training ideally suited also to students in professional programs at colleges and universities (Department of Defense 1979). The Foreign Service Institute (FSI) conducts similar training prorams for diplomatic personnel and also publishes much of the curricular material that it uses. The FSI has developed, for example, a "testing-kit" project which uses a criterion-referenced testing system for evaluating language proficiency. After a workshop organized with participants from academic institutions and the ETS in 1979, it was concluded that this method of proficiency testing could be adapted for college students at all levels to add significance to the letter grades usually assigned (see Frith 1979: 12).

The Peace Corps pioneered the teaching of numbers of lesser known languages, especially African languages, again for essentially practical purposes. An organization that has moved toward conventional higher education from its beginning as essentially a training program for overseas experience is the School for International Training of the Experiment in International Living. Like the Peace Corps, the Experiment provides cultural as well as language training; although it is accredited to award degrees, emphasis is placed on "life training." The Experiment does not aim at preparation for immediate service overseas, as the Peace Corps does, but graduates frequently work in the field of international affairs.

Regardless of an institution's size and the nature of its curricula, it will probably have numerous ties with the federal government. Efforts should be made to understand the extent and nature of these ties, working with the individual or office on campus responsible for federal liaison. There should be many ways to build on established personal connections to strengthen the international aspect of these links. The institution's local congressman or senators or the entire state congressional delegation can help forge ties with the government at various levels. Linking these people with programming and keeping them and their aides abreast of on-campus efforts at internationalization is definitely advisable and may pay dividends. They might be invited to visit the campus occasionally and college personnel might visit them in Washington as the need arises (contacts between middle-level administrators or individual faculty and congressional aides are easy to maintain and can grow into informal relationships of great mutual value). The college should follow the projects of federal legislation relevant to international education with great care (through the *Chronicle of Higher Education* and through such Washington organizations as the American Council on Education, the American Association of Community and Junior Colleges, the American Association of State Colleges and Universities and others) and express its opinions on appropriate issues. It is a good idea to form a small, informal committee attached to the international programs office to follow the international aspects of the institution's federal connections. The committee can review pending legislation, formulate positions on that and other issues, and follow up on funding opportunities.

Because of its situation at the very center of international affairs in the government, the State Department can be helpful in numerous ways. It is particularly advisable for area studies programs to establish informal contacts with the foreign desks for their areas, especially if communication can be two-way. USICA handles the federal government's programs for cultural and educational exchange, a source not only of funding but of contacts with foreign visitors and institutions. It is primarily as a source of funding that the Department of Education may be helpful, though its international education specialists also provide advice and publications on the educational systems of other countries and offer assistance on the entire range of international programs, including student exchange, study abroad, and overseas employment. Other government offices with extensive international ties include the Agency for International Development, the Department of Agriculture, the National Academy of Sciences, the National Institutes of Health, and the National Science Foundation.

The United States National Commission for UNESCO is a semigovernmental body that serves as a point of contact between nongovernmental organizations and private citizens' groups in the United States and UNESCO itself. It has taken a particularly active role in human rights, publishing materials and disseminating information (e.g., Buergenthal and Torney 1976). The commission will help organizations (and colleges) in this country plan and execute programs and activities associated with UNESCO's programs in such fields as literacy, the natural sciences, and communications.

Many of the more important educational organizations maintain special offices devoted to international activities and services (Burn 1980a: 150). For example, the Division of International Educational Relations (formerly the International Education Project) of the American Council on Education (ACE) has been a leader in the lobbying effort for area studies centers and other international education programs. Recently a number of organizations in the foreign language field, under the influence of the report of the President's Commission on Foreign Language and International Studies, have established a Joint National Committee for Languages, whose Washington Liaison Office is specifically intended "to create a national constituency for the promotion of foreign language training," and to work with, among others, the United States Congress. In May 1980 the formation of a National Council on Foreign Language and International Studies was also announced. This organization, which has received financial support from a number of private sources and from USICA, aims "to focus public attention on the nation's declining competence in foreign languages and the urgent need for improved understanding of international affairs." It was first proposed by the President's Commission. The council will commission reports from a panel of experts on what information about foreign areas is needed in the United States, and hopes to make recommendations on the need for language training and other issues.

The range of organizations interested in aspects of global studies or world problems is enormous. Some are long established and have well-known and respected programs. Others have grown up recently. Among them are national membership organizations like the United Nations Association (UNA) and the Asia Society; independent bodies like the Foreign Policy Association (FPA) and the Institute for World Order; and university-based centers or consortia such as the Center for Teaching International Relations, at the University of Denver, and the Center for International Studies, at the University of Missouri. The field is constantly in flux, with new consortia or cooperative programs starting up, others dropping by the wayside, still others continuing quiet efforts in some corner of the field.

In principle we should encourage faculty to keep in touch with and participate in these activities, since much of the most interesting thinking on international issues takes place within such organizations. Their programs offer numerous opportunities for the enterprising internationalizer. Their leaders can be invited to the campus, faculty can be sent to their conferences, their publications can be used as a basis for debate and discussion. The Great Decisions Program of the FPA is particularly useful on this last point: Its publications are designed to stimulate and promote debate on foreign policy issues. The program also provides opinion ballots which are tallied and the results submitted to the media and political leadership. Radio stations and the UPI Focus series carry materials designed to supplement the program, which can be used by individuals or by groups, including classes and international studies associations.

The United Nations Association does much of its work through local chapters, which can, of course, be set up on campuses. Founded to promote the United Nations ideal and to disseminate information about the UN, the UNA serves as a convenient link with the UN system. Its own publications focus on aspects of world problems, on special campaigns or celebrations of the UN, and on U.S. policies on UN issues (see, for example UNA 1979). The association also helps establish contact with UN offices and disseminates many UN items (including films, posters, etc.).

## 2. Internationally Based Organizations

Though the UNA is an obvious point of contact with the UN, one can deal with it directly through its Department of Public Information (DPI). The UN is only dimly understood by many Americans, and efforts to make its work better known on campus might help make students more aware of the problems of creating international institutions and the nature of the pressures on them. Much of the work carried on through the UN's offices in New York, Geneva, and Vienna, and through its specialized agencies, is essentially nonpolitical. The enormous array of UN publications available through the headquarters in New York attests to this. Both the UN and UNESCO produce a great deal of material of interest to curricular planners, some of it relatively unknown in this country. UNESCO's publications on the teaching of human rights are particularly informative (e.g. Vasak 1978, UNESCO 1980).

The fact that the United Nations has its headquarters in the United States opens numerous other possibilities for contact. Study visits to UN headquarters can be arranged for students, perhaps in conjunction with courses on the UN or on topics with which the UN is concerned. Visits might include not only a tour of the facilities but briefings and discussions with UN officials and at the United States Mission. Both the DPI and the U.S. Mission can help make arrangements. The UN system contains a remarkable range of talent and interest, and a chance to meet its officials will help make its work real to students. The U.S. Mission may also be able to set up contact with other UN missions, or arrangements can be made with them directly.

In addition, the DPI will help identify suitable speakers on UN topics to visit campuses. Perhaps a college can invite a UN official to stay for several days as a kind of resident fellow. The visit could serve as a focal point for discussions on the UN and could be tied in with courses and with work in the community or the schools. The organization's events and celebrations, such as UN Day in October or Human Rights Day in December, can be occasions for special activities on campus. Programs, activities, or courses might be tied in with the UN's special years, such as the Year of the Handicapped in 1982 or Youth Year in 1985.

Since the World Bank and the Organization of American States have their headquarters in Washington, they are also accessible as educational resources. The interests of the World Bank extend beyond financial matters into a range of issues associated with economic development. Much of the Bank's resources go into agriculture; its other special interests include energy and transportation. The Bank has a particularly imaginative and effective office of public information.

The Organization of American States is the oldest of the large regional organizations. Its concerns include many of the areas covered by the UN and its specialized agencies, including education and culture, science, development assistance, human rights, political affairs, and, through the Pan American Health Organization, health. Since much of its business is carried on in Spanish, language learning could be linked with visits to, or study about, the OAS.

One of the most important resources available in Washington to international programmers is the diplomatic community. Most embassies are not only very willing to provide written materials about their countries but may have exhibitions and films available for loan. The cultural attaché in an embassy may be a useful contact on performing arts groups visiting the United States, and the education attaché (often the same person, at least in the smaller embassies) may help with student and faculty exchanges and other contacts with universities or research institutes in the country in question.

Embassies will often provide speakers or put inquirers in touch with visitors from their countries. Since they can help in so many ways, it is a good idea to maintain regular liaison with the more interesting embassies, perhaps making a point of inviting ambassadors from key countries to visit the campus and involving them in appropriate programming. Through these contacts a college may get to hear about particularly attractive cultural activities in time to arrange for them to come to the campus.

Several embassies (the Romanian, for instance) take a special interest in promoting study of their countries in the United States. Others, such as the Nigerian, maintain liaison offices in Washington and New York to handle exchanges with the United States. Many countries have tourist offices here and are happy to work with colleges on planning student visits, both curricular and noncurricular.

Also worth consideration are study visits to international organizations in other countries. The best time to visit is probably during the winter break, when programs are moving ahead at greatest intensity, committees are in session, and so on. The summer is the least busy time for most of the major organizations and many of their officials are traveling. A visit to Paris might concentrate on the work of UNESCO; a trip to Brussels could take in the complex workings of the European Communities. Both visits could be conducted in English but linked with courses in French—a language advantageous in dealing with the European Communities. Geneva is a center for a number of international organizations—several sections of the United Nations, housed in the old Palais des Nations of the League of Nations; the International Telecommunications Union; the International Labor Organization; the World Health Organization; and the World Intellectual Property Organization.

The International Association of Universities, based in Paris and closely associated with UNESCO, helps foster interuniversity cooperation and publishes papers on cooperation and university reform. UNESCO has done a lot to promote international educational cooperation—much more than some of its critics acknowledge. Recently its efforts in higher education have included extensive work on the comparability of degrees and it has supported such efforts at international coordination of entry-level programs as the International Baccalaureate (cf. Peterson 1972). It has also taken an active interest in student exchanges, both as a practical question and as an element in the promotion of international understanding (Eide 1970).

There have been several successful language programs in this country that use foreign radio broadcasts as an instructional device.

Many European stations beam programs to North America that are well within reach of the right equipment. Some foreign radio stations will provide tapes of their broadcasts. In addition, numerous foreign language radio stations and programs originate in this country (Keller and Roel 1980; Simon 1980b; and see previous chapter).

In this survey of internationally based resources available to campuses we should also mention international nongovernmental organizations (NGOs) and international business. Though many international NGOs are based in New York or Washington (upwards of 100 in New York and perhaps 65 in Washington; see UIA 1977), the majority are headquartered in Europe, with the largest concentrations in Brussels, Paris, Geneva, and London. They vary from modest enterprises to large organizations like the International Confederation of Free Trade Unions (in Brussels) or the International Red Cross (in Geneva). As with national NGOs there are numerous ways of cooperating with such organizations and their national affiliates:

**a.** Curriculum development in international and global studies. Several international NGOs are active in this.

**b.** Study or youth exchange, or voluntary service (the Coordinating Committee for International Voluntary Service, at UNESCO, is the umbrella organization in this field).

**c.** Work with development programs, educational development, and relief activities in developing countries.

**d.** World order activities in such fields as human rights, the rights of minorities, the migration of labor, disarmament, international law, international organization, peacekeeping work, and so on.

**e.** Research, particularly in social sciences and education.

Many international NGOs have formal relations with major intergovernmental organizations. The conferences of NGOs in Paris, and in New York and Geneva, are particularly active in promoting joint NGO action and cooperation with the United Nations system. NGOs in general are often free to take international action and to promote new initiatives that governments, for political reasons, may be unable to undertake, and hence they can often spearhead important changes of international policy. The UN and its member states are well aware of this asset (and occasionally, from their point of view, liability) of NGOs and hence promote close links with the UN system. Most major international conferences sponsored by the UN (such as the Women's Conferences in Mexico City in 1975 and Copenhagen in 1980, the Habitat Conference in Vancouver in 1976 , and so on) include a so-called NGO Forum, and NGOs generally also organize conferences in connection with special sessions of the General Assembly of the UN (such as those on disarmament in 1979 and development in 1980). These conferences and special events are accessible primarily through NGOs themselves, but individual participation is sometimes possible.

Increasing interest in the role of multinational corporations in international relations, evidenced by, for example, United Nations studies on the subject (UN 1978), is making these corporations more sensitive to the need to present their case. Hence they may be drawn on for speakers, written materials, and the like. American firms' search for world markets is also expanding the opportunities for contacts between international studies specialists and the business world. Good contacts with business leaders can result in internships in international business either here or overseas, and work abroad opportunities are available through AIESEC and other organizations (see chapter 6) or through cooperative education programs linking the U.S. and other countries (see, for instance, Slessarev 1978).

### 3.   State Governments

The interest of state governments in world affairs varies considerably. Maintaining contact with state officials is important for all institutions, whether state supported or not. Not only do state governments have a financial influence on many institutions but their policies on international education and international affairs can have significant effect on teacher-training programs and other curricula.

Both a cause and a result of much state-level interest in global education was the Task Force on Global Education, established in 1978 by the U.S. Office of Education and Commissioner Ernest L. Boyer. Its report, which appeared in 1979, stimulated several statewide programs for the internationalization of education at all levels. Strong support for innovation has recently been forthcoming in states as disparate as Michigan, Utah, North Carolina, California, Oregon, and Minnesota. Not only can colleges and universities benefit from such initiatives but they can help shape the direction of programs and provide intellectual support.

Perhaps the crucial factor in the creation and success of statewide initiatives is the attitude of the highest state education administrator. Where this support is forthcoming, the results can be impressive. In Illinois, for example, a task force on foreign language and international studies (inspired by plans for President Carter's commission) helped motivate probably the most far-reaching policy statement by a state board of education. The recommendation "that

Illinois schools provide the opportunity for every student to acquire foreign language skills and an appreciation of international issues and other cultures in a well-articulated, interdisciplinary sequence beginning in the early elementary years" is backed up by a wide-ranging program to help school districts with its implementation. Identifying financial support for new programs, organizing planning seminars, and finding community and organizational resources are some of the activities undertaken by the state. Illinois provides an impressive example of state involvement in international education. There is great concern for articulation between secondary and higher education and for the entire state educational system to move toward increasing the international awareness and related skills of its students.

In addition, several states have established commissions on foreign languages and international studies to continue at their level the initiatives of the President's Commission and to work on implementing recommendations. The question of international and global education has been addressed by many state boards of education; for example, a strong statement on international education was included in the Master Plan for Higher Education in Pennsylvania. In February 1979 the Florida board of education approved a resolution in support of teaching the concept of global interdependence.

In New York state there has been since 1961 a State Education Department Center for International Programs and Comparative Studies. Its operations have included the preparation of materials, the reception of foreign visitors, a pilot project in self-instructional language study, and advocacy of study-abroad programs. Funded in its later years entirely by discretionary federal funds, the Center was finally asked to make a presentation to the Board of Regents and was authorized to request a small allocation from the state budget. These may be seen as encouraging signs, though the professional staff of the Center has been radically reduced.

Social studies and language specialists in the education departments of such states as Maryland, North Carolina, and Indiana believe that implementation of any plan depends greatly on the enthusiasm and energy of the superintendent or commissioner. It is therefore vital that impetus come from colleges or universities, whether private or within state systems, to bring to the attention of state authorities the importance of the effort and to offer cooperation in outreach programs and curricular development. A growing interest in international commerce in many states increases the likelihood of cooperation between state government and institutions. Several states even maintain overseas promotion offices to help facilitate foreign trade.

There also are, of course, great pressures on state governments to ignore international concerns. Legislators are elected by local constituents with local concerns who can organize themselves in a way that no advocate of international relations could possibly do. The government of which they are a part is constitutionally set up to deal with local and regional issues.

Nevertheless, pressures can be brought to bear on state governments from the other direction. In several states there are statewide organizations of colleges and universities (and sometimes elementary and secondary schools) such as the Kentucky Council on International Education and the Pennsylvania Council on International Education. These bodies are useful for sharing information and planning interinstitutional cooperation. Many states have statewide or regional consortia—the Southern California Conference on International Studies, for example, or the vigorous Pacific Northwest International/Intercultural Education Consortium. These organizations can assist in resource sharing and undertake activities in concert (study programs abroad, for example) that might be beyond the means of a single institution.

## 4. Local Contacts
Paradoxically, many local organizations are far more attuned to international affairs than most state governments. We include not only the obvious organizations such as local Councils for International Visitors, World Affairs Councils, or chapters of the United Nations Association, but service organizations (such as Rotaries and Lions), local churches, immigrant groups, chambers of commerce, and city governments.

An active international programs office on campus will, of course, maintain contacts with local organizations involved in international programming. Many areas have their own Councils for International Visitors, which often act as local agents for government-sponsored visits by foreign delegations and dignitaries, as well as serving numerous less formal needs. In an area without a CIV, a college can perform some of its functions and should work through the National Council for International Visitors (formerly COSERV) to that end. Cooperation between a college and a CIV can be beneficial in numerous ways, since the college can help host visitors, cooperate in host family programs, provide translators and interpreters, and introduce visitors to faculty and students.

The National Council of Community World Affairs Organizations links local and state organizations in all parts of the country. Many less populous states have statewide councils (Alaska, New Hampshire, Vermont, and Rhode Island, for example) but large cities tend to have their own. World Affairs Councils (WACs) carry on extensive local programs, often involving visiting speakers of national or international eminence, group visits to other countries, conferences and seminars, and so on. The nonpartisan councils work to educate and inform the public and makers of public opinion about issues in world affairs. Many cooperate with local teachers and school systems. The largest program is in Philadelphia, and San Francisco and Boston have important models in world affairs education. Colleges and universities can establish links with WACs for joint programming and the two can work together on hosting visitors and bringing them into contact with both the public and the campus community. Since the councils often bring together the more enlightened civic leadership in a locality, there may also be ways of working together to make the internationalizing of the campus simply one aspect of a larger internationalizing effort extending into the city as well.

Because Rotary International operates an extensive scholarship program for international exchanges, there is an immediately practical reason for cooperation—in selecting students to go overseas and in hosting Rotary Scholars here. Particularly in areas away from major cities, Rotary and Lions clubs may help program visits by foreigners and can also assist in contacts abroad. Local churches may offer similar possibilities, at least as far as visitors to the area are concerned.

In many urban centers and some rural areas there are local chapters of national organizations run by and for members of ethnic minorities. One is the Polish American Congress, an umbrella organization paralleled by others that serve other nationality groups. These organizations are often supplemented at the local level by mutual aid societies and social clubs. Frequently their leaders are delighted to cooperate with academic institutions where an interest is shown in their culture. Apart from including native speakers who may agree to involve student learners in various activities, these nationality groups frequently have members who are knowledgeable about every aspect of their culture and willing to help organize cultural activities on campus. They may also arrange for their compatriots to come to colleges as visiting lecturers. Sometimes, as with the Polish, Italians, and Ukrainians, secular groups coexist with church-based groups. Where campus programming is to be developed in an area with a sizable ethnic community, cooperative arrangements are worth investigating.

Some areas of the country have substantial numbers of recent immigrants, primarily from Southeast Asia, Haiti, and Cuba. These people's situation is radically different from that of the descendants of earlier immigrants. Many come as refugees or to escape overwhelming economic disadvantages. They enter this society with difficulty, bringing few possessions. Respect and understanding from members of the community are of immense value and may encourage them to cooperate in academic and extracurricular programming built around the study of their culture and language. Where there are agencies that mediate between immigrants and the community, such as those service organizations affiliated with the American Council for Nationalities Service, their staff will often help with liaison as well as with information about recent immigrant populations in the area.

We have recommended compiling an inventory of international resources on and off the campus. The very act of assembling it will suggest other ways in which off-campus organizations can help. It will also probably turn up library and museum collections and other repositories of information relevant to curricular programming. Cooperation among college libraries in a locality can help strengthen the resources available to undergraduates, though cooperation can seldom be as comprehensive or total as we might wish.

## 5. Personnel Development

We have explored how the faculty's energies and skills can be redirected toward the international area. We have considered how administrators might be effectively motivated. But there is a level of technical expertise necessary for the administration of certain international services that may require the help of outside experts.

In areas of programming concerned with services to foreign students and scholars and with study abroad, one of the most valuable tools for administrators and their support staff is the professional network provided by the National Association for Foreign Student Affairs. NAFSA has a number of institutionalized methods for personnel development as well as for ensuring the life and growth of this network.

Its five divisions specialize in foreign student advising, admissions, study abroad, English as a second language, and community programs. Divided nationally into 12 regions, the organization spon-

sors and acts as a centralizing agency for national, regional, and local activities, including annual conferences with participants from
all divisions and from every level of the university and community.
Task forces on special interest areas (women, two-year colleges,
etc.), commissions (on standards and responsibilities, liaison, information, etc.), and committees (on regions of the world) cut across divisions and help create a unified and professional attitude toward
the field.

NAFSA also provides funding for professional development for
administrators. In-service training grants are available during the
first two years of an individual's professional involvement in the
field and are designed to send administrators to comparable institutions with similar programs for exposure to a successful model.
Grants are available in all five divisions. There is also a consultation
service: An experienced professional is selected by NAFSA to assess a program or an office and write a comprehensive report. This
free service can be valuable to a new administrator in the field who
is faced with the seemingly impossible task of creating a functioning
unit and who wishes to avoid the mistakes so often made in organizing international programs on campus.

A third facet of the NAFSA field service program is funding for regional workshops. These are usually designed by a senior NAFSA
member for local participation and topics vary from local concerns
to matters of international interest. They provide a forum for learning and discussion that can also bring new resources to participants' attention and radically improve the quality of services offered on a local level. They also provide an opportunity for newcomers to the field to interact with knowledgeable senior professionals and to learn to regard them as their best resource in their own
development. As with other NAFSA activities, partial funding is
sometimes available to enable newcomers to attend their first workshop. There are also occasional NAFSA special interest workshops,
often focusing on some aspect of a world region.

The NAFSA cooperative project focuses on innovative programming ideas, usually with a relatively broad-based application, such
as outreach activities to provide certain kinds of programming for
foreign students on an area basis in Boston, New York, and Philadelphia. Administrators with an interest in consortial arrangements for
such programs can explore this funding possibility where financing
seems otherwise impossible.

NAFSA is not the only organization with a concern for the professional development of administrators in international programs. The

Institute of International Education runs periodic workshops, usually primarily concerned with the Fulbright exchange programs, and publishes materials useful for developing expertise, particularly on foreign educational systems. And the American Association of Collegiate Registrars and Admissions Officers, through the National Liaison Committee on Foreign Student Admissions, cooperates in workshops held outside the United States at which admissions officials can observe the education systems of other countries. The reports of these workshops provide a valuable tool for those concerned with foreign student admissions.

Though most of the opportunities for professional development are coordinated by nongovernmental organizations such as those mentioned, much of the funding comes indirectly from the federal government. The State Department also directly sponsors a National Foreign Policy Conference, designed for leaders in higher education. Coordination of this event is provided by the American Association of Colleges for Teacher Education, and its purpose is to provide briefings on the effects of American foreign policy and its impact on American higher education. Other conferences provide valuable opportunities for administrators to keep in touch with current issues and meet colleagues who share their interests.

## 6. Serving the Needs of the Larger Society: Outreach

"What was until recently the American Century has turned into the Global Century," declared the Council on Learning, in launching its project Education and the World View. "To prepare an informed citizenry for this vastly changed global climate becomes of necessity a high priority for this nation, and for its educational systems especially." This high priority is more than a matter of making the nation's colleges and universities genuinely expressive of the shift in global power and values: It involves also making higher education a bellwether for the entire nation, communicating its internationalism to the society. As we consider how the college can draw on outside resources, we must also consider, perhaps primarily, how the college can serve the needs, perceived or unperceived, of society.

In an essay published in 1968, Robert Hutchins set out his ideas of the "learning society"—one in which education takes place not only through formal educational systems but simply as a fact of life, and in every facet of that life. The learning society, he wrote, "would be one that, in addition to offering part-time adult education to every man and woman at every stage of grown-up life, had succeeded in transforming its values in such a way that learning, fulfillment, becoming human, had become its aims and all its institutions were directed to this end." Hutchins saw technology as providing humans with enough leisure to make this feasible: "A world community learning to be civilized, learning to be human, is at least a possibility. Education may come into its own." Hutchins's vision, a dozen years later, may seem hard to accept as we battle with the problems of the here and now. But that positive vision has been transformed into a matter of dire necessity.

In many respects the United States comes closest to Hutchins's idea, even if it still falls far short. Here the acquisition of knowledge and participation at least in formal education throughout life is widely accepted. Education continues to be a passport to success and status in the United States. To an increasing degree it is also considered a legitimate activity for one's own moral and spiritual enrichment.

Torsten Husen, in his book also titled *The Learning Society* (1974), points out (page 82) that a survey of adult education undertaken by the University of Chicago in the early 1960s "found that more than one out of every five adults had taken part in organized studies after leaving regular school.... The subjects were equally divided between the bread-and-butter type on the one hand and the generally broadening and recreational on the other."

Many colleges and universities carry on some form of continuing or part-time education. The dividing line between conventional and full-time education and various kinds of continuing education has become harder to draw. This outreach may simply involve allowing a certain number of continuing education students to take regularly offered courses, or setting up a program of courses essentially similar to those in the college's regular curriculum, perhaps offered at special times or in different locations. But in addition to these conventional forms, continuing education has blossomed to include a whole range of in-service programs for teachers and members of the health professions, intensive programs for business people, and so on. More and more older people are taking courses, often specially designed for them, and many others are participating simply to learn about the world or themselves.

Since continuing education reaches a large and varied audience beyond the campus, its programs must express the global and international view we are seeking to propagate throughout the system. While much of this change might happen naturally through successful efforts at the department level, it may be necessary to work with continuing education teachers to find ways of reaching this nontraditional audience with new ideas. We might create a committee to examine continuing education programs from the internationalizing perspective.

The committee may want to encourage new courses and programs specifically on international studies and related fields. Courses on global problems, and some created to explore world trouble spots or to examine the economy or politics of a region. If offered in the traditional form, these courses will attract interest but they will not bring in a new clientele. Other formats might attract people who do not normally participate in continuing education programs. A weekend program on the Middle East, for example, could bring in business executives and teachers as well as regular continuing education students. A series of lunchtime sessions on the role of multinational corporations in development might be taught in the business district of a large city and aimed directly at business people. It could be run under the sponsorship of the chamber of commerce or a group of business enterprises.

Cooperation with a local organization is a particularly efficient way of affecting the community, since ideas, information, and attitudes filter down not only to participants in a course but, through them, to the organization. A course on the United Nations offered in cooperation with the local UNA becomes an extension of the UNA's programming and can have a ripple effect throughout the UNA chapter. Church groups or local charitable organizations can sponsor a course on world hunger, literacy, or world health. The fact that such courses are offered with the assistance of outside organizations does not compromise their objectivity. If the UNA wants to learn about the United Nations system, or a church about the politics of hunger, the college should be able to help. In fact, its failure to provide such a service may be a failure in a part of its mission.

For this reason colleges might put the knowledge of their experts at the service of the community by offering single sessions or short series, without credit, on world problem areas or regions in the news. Full-blown courses might also be developed. In these and other ways the continuing education program could become a kind of experimental workshop for the college's regular programs. Consideration might also be given to various kinds of diploma programs, consisting of groups of courses on global issues or in some branch of area studies.

We mentioned in another context refresher courses in languages for people who graduated from college some years ago and have not used the tongues they studied. Languages offer special opportunities for imaginative experiment and for reaching out to new audiences. In the continuing education field they might be linked with organized foreign travel or tied in with church groups or Rotary clubs. Service organizations especially are increasing their international spread rapidly. In fact, Lions International has long recognized that almost all its growth is in non-English-speaking areas of the world. Language learning is therefore a logical response to development in these organizations themselves—though it may be difficult to put this idea over to some local clubs.

Particularly important in this outreach effort is teacher education. Several institutions, among them Florida International University and the University of Denver, run successful in-service training programs that convey principles and concepts and methods of global education. Depending on the nature of the institution, a concerted effort might be made through a department or group of departments to create a strong program, perhaps drawing on the expertise of education specialists as well. Close cooperation with local school districts is of course a necessity, and the state department of education might be involved as well. As more and more school systems, organizations, and publishers become interested in global education, there are increasing numbers of fully developed curricula and textbooks, so that it is no longer necessary to start such programs from scratch.

Work with school systems need not be exclusively in terms of accredited courses. It may even be preferable to follow other routes. Despite programs like those at Denver and in Florida, university involvement in curricular reform in the schools has not always proven constructive or useful (Fox 1979), and it may be that developing strategies for self-help will be more effective in the long run. This is itself an argument for avoiding the curriculum development component of in-service offerings by universities and colleges and for concentrating on subject matter rather than method. Other activities to consider include the use of foreign students in the classroom (see our earlier discussion on this subject), cooperation with global education programs aimed at the schools and run by World Affairs Councils or other local organizations, and overseas trips or study programs specifically for teachers (perhaps based on existing study programs abroad whose facilities are used during the school year by an institution's full-time students). Many institutions with strong teacher education programs already have lines of communication to school systems—and student teachers can be involved in various roles. But even those without teacher education programs might consider ways of involving students in their efforts to reach out to the schools.

Other types of outreach appropriate to a college will depend on its location, size, and academic programs. There are obvious dangers in casting our institution in the role of crusader—in treating the internationalizing mission too solemnly. It has no monopoly on international contacts, as the studies of Chadwick Alger and others have made abundantly clear. But it does possess resources otherwise unavailable to the community and it should find ways to put those resources at its disposal. Our inventory of international resources, for example, need not be confined to on-campus use but could become a local data bank for others in the community interested in international affairs. Perhaps it could be expanded through the cooperation of other colleges in the neighborhood and published in abbreviated form as a handbook. Our international experts would, in effect, be putting themselves at the disposal of the community.

This is only one of the many ideas discussed earlier that could feed back into the community. And much of that community consists of constituencies predisposed to accept such cooperation. International cultural events can benefit the community as well as the campus environment. Feeding the college's international resources back into the community is likely to work best if there is already good integration between community and college, with faculty active in community groups and noncollege people readily accepted on campus. This is a strong reason for encouraging faculty to participate in international activities in the community. Since international events—from the energy crisis to the problem of Cuban and Southeast Asian refugees—have an increasing impact on the community, rational discussion and understanding of international affairs are needed. Communities have an understandable tendency to react negatively to all intrusions from outside and avoid confronting unpleasant realities. Faculty can play an important part in encouraging humane and unprejudiced efforts to address these realities and to prepare communities for change. While they are far from all-wise and all-seeing, faculty do possess information of special value in this process. In fact, they may even have a certain obligation to offer this information to the community.

We referred in an earlier chapter to the importance of maintaining links with the press. An obvious element of outreach already highly developed in many institutions is radio and television, including on-campus stations. International affairs are readily adapted to these media. Faculty might also be encouraged to prepare brief background papers on major news events or world problems for press distribution. Radio and television can, of course, be drawn into continuing education activities.

Our overall goal is to offer college resources to the community so that the internationalizing of campus and curriculum will extend outward. As all internationalized elements within the college can prove mutually reinforcing, so our internationalized college and our internationalized community can work together for mutual benefit.

# 10

## Financing
## International
## Programs

# Financing International Programs

## 1. Reordering Priorities

We have emphasized throughout this introduction to the trials and pleasures of internationalizing the curriculum that what is in essence required is a change of heart. We are asking that faculty, and others connected with the academy, look at their task in a new light: Our society's problems have ceased to be local and national and have become global. We need a new, internationalized curriculum to deal with these new imperatives.

While it might be engaging to consider what a radically reorganized curriculum might look like (and it would probably be dissimilar from efforts to create core curricula, such as Harvard's), we are here more concerned with incremental change. We would like to see a revision of syllabi in courses and a shift in balance in individual programs to take the international dimension into account. We propose the simplest and least threatening set of reforms not because they are a wholly adequate response but because we might be able to create consensus around them and begin to move our academic institutions closer toward the realities of today and tomorrow.

If such a change of heart were possible—if, as in Bellamy's *Looking Backward*, people could simply alter their way of conducting business because it was logical to do so—most of the changes we call for might not now require expenditures at all. Revising a syllabus or even reorganizing a program seldom entails significant additional costs. But the truth is that a social organization can rarely be changed by appeals to logic alone, even though the organization regards its behavior as logical. Structures create patterns of behavior and systems of rewards and sanctions that endure long past the point at which logic might decree their abolition. Changing them therefore requires outside intervention to readjust the rewards and sanctions.

What this means in practical terms is that change costs money.

We have repeatedly proposed setting up this or that fund, this or that system of grants, to induce changes in behavior and create a system more in tune with present needs. Where might this money come from? Three types of financing are required: (1) incentive financing to give released time or special grants to faculty or to provide more money to departments or administrators as a reward for changing their behavior; (2) money for curricular additions, library collections, offices of international programs, study-abroad programs, aid to foreign students, and so on; and (3) funding of marginal activities such as increased international programming, subsidies to bookstores, travel for faculty, and so on.

Though it may be difficult to achieve because of internal opposition, funds for the first category are best raised by substitution. As long as new money is being put into the system, there will be considerably less incentive to stop using the old for the same purposes. Why should a faculty member apply for a summer grant in curricular planning when there is a grant already available to support his or her research? The grants in curricular planning will end up going to those whose research proposals are not good enough to win funding and who are relatively marginal in the faculty's scheme of things. By the same token, unless administrators face the risk of actually losing funds unless they change their behavior, there will be little incentive to pursue new funding.

Since in any case putting wholly new money into the system is not feasible for most instituions, it is best to redirect present funding toward international programs by taxing existing programs and services. This is inevitably a painful process, involving a careful assessment of priorities. In fact, even beginning it implies prior agreement on the primacy of internationalization. The sequence begins, then, as a logical debate on the responsibilities, character, and capabilities of the institution in an increasingly interdependent world. It leads to a debate on the relation of this priority to others and the establishment of internationalization as a major area for development. The logical debate is then translated into a set of financial mechanisms that skim off an internationalization fund for reinvestment in the system. This fund will be spent primarily for specific programs in the international field but might also be used to reward administrators whose areas have made special efforts to internationalize their activities at acceptable budgetary levels.

The institution may have little or no funding to finance faculty research. Hence there is no research money to direct specifically into curricular development. Even here it may be better not to use completely new money but to reorganize priorities to create a fund. The institution might be tempted to look for nonrecurring funding from outside, but this is unsatisfactory; though we are reshaping a curriculum into something new, it will not be static. It will require further injections of money to create courses responsive to changing needs and to permit faculty to keep up with new developments and new areas of knowledge.

## 2. New Investments

Our first category of financing was concerned with the globalizing or internationalizing of the entire curriculum. The second category involves new programs or facilities specifically concerned with aspects of international studies. Creating new academic programs from the beginning (i.e., hiring faculty, setting up facilities, and so on) is probably beyond the means of most institutions. More probable is a reordering of internal assignments. We cannot emphasize too strongly the importance of consultation and collective action here. Particularly since a new program must work hard to gain acceptance under any circumstances, its members should feel they have a strong stake in its success. In some instances new programs will be split off from existing ones to create new departments or interdepartmental units. This arrangement carries not only academic but administrative costs, which may be hard to recoup from other sources. It is preferable to make its administration the responsibility of an existing department.

Before embarking on such a plan, it may be worth seeking a small planning grant—from the National Endowment for the Humanities, for example—to assess the costs involved and launch the process of consultation. NEH makes planning funds available to appropriate fields (it defines the humanities quite broadly). Other possible sources include the Department of Education, particularly its Fund for the Improvement of Postsecondary Education. (Admittedly, all such funding opportunities are highly competitive.)

It may also prove advisable to amalgamate departments (see chapter 4). Administrative costs might be saved by linking language laboratories and language departments more closely, or by using the administration of language or area studies programs to handle certain aspects of study abroad.

If there is still a need for new money, the various government programs might be examined. The new guide, "International Education Programs of the U.S. Government: An Inventory" (Wiprud 1980), produced under the auspices of the Federal Interagency Committee on Education, provides basic information for institutions planning to seek federal assistance in internationalizing their programs. Department of Education funds are spread over various categories, mostly derived from Title VI of the 1958 National Defense Education Act and now funded under the reauthorized Higher Education Act. This includes, as well as the provision for language and area and international studies, the new provision mentioned earlier for promoting cooperation between international business and institutions of higher education.

The erstwhile NDEA programs have undergone some vicissitudes since 1958, particularly for some years during the 1970s, when continuation of funding did not always seem assured. The budget line has, however, suffered no precipitous decline since the original appropriation. Amendments to the Act in 1972 expanded the scope of the program by adding money for problem-oriented and topic-oriented centers at the graduate level and for undergraduate international studies programs directed primarily to general education (although the total amount for the standard language and area studies programs was somewhat reduced). During this period funding for summer institutes was eliminated. The 1980 reauthorization increased funding in some categories and, significantly, extended grant eligibility for international studies centers to undergraduate as well as graduate programs, but are likely to be reduced by the Reagan administration.

Funding has also been made available for the new Citizen Education for Cultural Understanding program, formerly financed under Section 603 of NDEA and now included in Title III of the Elementary and Secondary Education Act. This makes grants available "to any public or private agency or organization to increase the understanding of students in the United States about the actions and cultures of other nations, and to enable these students to make informed judgments with respect to the international policies and actions of the United States." Competition for this funding has been fierce, with applications far exceeding resources.

Other sources of money for international programs include the Ethnic Heritage Studies Program (established under the provisions of the Elementary and Secondary Education Act of 1965 and amended in 1972 and 1974), and funding available through USICA's Private Sector Programs. In recent years the National Endowment for the Humanities has significantly increased its grants for international and global studies. The recent trend in government funding is clearly toward global and international education and away from traditional area studies programs. To an even greater degree the government is putting colleges and universities into competition with other types of organizations, thereby broadening the scope of innovation and perhaps avoiding spending limited funds on maintenance of existing curricular structures. Needless to say, this is a mixed blessing for hard-pressed colleges, especially since there have been drastic reductions in government funding for all aspects of international studies (President's Commission 1979; Burn 1980a; Berryman and others 1979).

For a number of years private foundation spending for international studies was high. The Ford Foundation's International Training and Research program, the leader in the field, spent an average of $18 million a year from its inception in 1952 to its termination in 1967 (Burn 1980a; Berryman and others 1979). The Rockefeller Foundation and the Carnegie Corporation were already in the field in the 1940s (McCaughey 1979: 37). The seventies were a relatively bleak period, but there have been signs of a renewal of interest on the part of foundations, and Ford, Rockefeller, Sloan, Exxon, and others have begun to support worthy international projects in more significant numbers and amounts. The Exxon Education Foundation is supporting the "Dartmouth Method" of foreign language teaching initiated by John Rassias. The Kettering Foundation is concerning itself with aspects of global awareness at the community level. A coalition of foundations, consisting of Exxon, Ford, Rockefeller, and Hewlett, joined forces with USICA to fund the National Council on Foreign Language and International Studies.

But again, significant external funding for the development of new fields or programs will have no lasting effect if it does not lead to real changes in structures and the fuller integration of these new programs into the system. Many experts have pointed out that NDEA funding of area studies centers in effect obviated the necessity of facing up to the question of academic priorities, since the new money was simply added on to the old and the previous structures were barely changed or threatened by the addition of new programs. The problem was compounded by the fact that the universities were then in rapid overall expansion.

Of course, it was NDEA's intent to buy services from the universities largely without asking them to reexamine their priorities, and to that extent it was entirely successful. Justifiably or not, the U.S. Congress believed in 1958 that the Soviet Union was pulling ahead in scientific research and world influence and it wanted an immediate response, not a debate on priorities. In later years the Administration became disenchanted with NDEA and its necessity, and it was kept alive primarily by intensive lobbying of Congress.

Mayville (1980) has argued that distortions in academic priorities caused by federal funding are in part a result of the academy's inability to make decisions about its intellectual goals. Certainly the federal government has shown relatively little concern about formulating a coherent higher education policy and has generally shied away from comprehensive and non-specific funding efforts. In the case of institutions with a clear mandate in a certain area, funds may be available for development of a particular kind. Departments of agricultural studies at land-grant institutions can, for example, seek Strengthening Grants under Title XII through the Board of International Food and Agricultural Development for faculty research abroad, developing the international dimension of the curriculum, and other related efforts. But in general, the burden very much rests on the colleges to define their priorities and institutionalize them.

Nonrecurring funding, or funding whose future is uncertain, at most allows an institution to spend money on a temporary program and decide at the same time whether to institutionalize it. But a careful decision on institutionalizing, with general agreement on concomitant sacrifices, is an absolute necessity. Even if money is recurring, it is better to identify what would be sacrificed if it ceased to recur, before some catastrophe necessitates sudden decisions. In short, outside funding should always be accompanied by a kind of environmental impact statement prepared by financial experts within the institution, with recommendations on how to deal with questions of priorities and institutionalization.

Funding from all sources for a new program should be completely adequate. Scrimping and saving to start a program creates a protective reaction among existing programs; they may band together to resist the newcomer and hence ensure the failure of the whole initiative. Giving a new program adequate funding may allow it to buy services from old programs and reverse the dependency (thereby offsetting the liability of newness). It also creates a set of vested interests in the new program that will help make it desirable. A rapid survey of educational innovations at the University of Pennsylvania in the early seventies reveals that programs funded at the highest level have survived, while those with less funding, though their initial impact may have been far greater, have faded.

Demonstrable commitment by the institution can ultimately be decisive in obtaining outside funding. Another strategy for introducing new programs, useful for large institutions where there is a marked reluctance to add to the roster of programs already functioning, is to begin in a small way and then seek assistance on the basis of demonstrable success. A center for, say, Middle Eastern studies requires sizable investments; but a committee on Middle Eastern studies, with work from a few dedicated individuals using only available departmentally allocated resources, can coordinate a limited basic program. Faculty with some skills in a related area can be enlisted, occasional workshops and seminars organized, special events publicized. The possibility of a new minor or major program can be broached. When it becomes clear that faculty resources exist, that there is student interest, and that a fully developed center would only require funding for support and services, administrative money is far more likely to be attracted both from within and outside the institution.

### 3. Support Services

In our second funding category we included not only academic programs per se but libraries and administrative offices. Funding library acquisitions is an ongoing and difficult problem, for continuing collections as well as new ones (ACE 1975). As we have noted, library costs are advancing by leaps and bounds, and the cost problem is especially severe with foreign materials. Some government programs and foundation grants do include small amounts for library resources. Most new programs of the type we envisage should have limited effects on library needs; on the other hand, our general advocacy of greater attention to foreign texts in all fields, our emphasis on the availability of foreign periodicals, and so on, are bound to have their consequences in budgets and acquisitions priorities.

A recent survey of colleges' and universities' structures for managing international studies and programs (Watson 1980) reveals that only 25 percent of institutions running study-abroad programs administer them through the same office that handles foreign students. We have stressed the importance of drawing the international responsibilities of an institution together under the same management. We pointed out that such programs can be mutually reinforcing and that they can give greater visibility to the international dimension of the institution. But we did not mention that centralization and consolidation may also produce administrative savings, which can be reinvested in strengthening the operation overall. In principle, it should cost little or nothing to centralize, especially if this can be done without sacrificing faculty liaison and the voluntary help of faculty and students in various phases of the administration. The same is not entirely true of new study-abroad programs, which require considerable investment and, if they are academically sound, are seldom self-sustaining. These programs are better launched on a cooperative basis.

### 4. Foreign Students
The recruitment of tuition-paying foreign students is another area in which the whole question of priorities must be addressed, at least if the institution accepts significant numbers of foreign students. There are many external programs of financial support, most run by foreign governments or through such organizations as the United Nations Development Program; but these are, of course, subject to the normal vicissitudes of such money.

Certain countries, such as Nigeria, Venezuela, and Saudi Arabia, are systematically investing large sums in educating their young people in the United States. As an alternative to developing their own academic institutions, this is sometimes a financially sound project. Students selected for scholarships to study here are adequately supported financially, usually for the duration of their programs, and have a wide variety of academic interests. The Venezuelan government agency responsible for placing students and administering their awards, Fundacion Gran Mariscal de Ayacucho (GMA), is open to placement suggestions from colleges that offer appropriate programs, particularly at the undergraduate level and in technical areas. Courting foreign students who have secured outside funding entails, of course, a moral obligation to give them the education they need as well as adequate support services.

Funding is also available in the form of Fulbright scholarships awarded by binational commissions, Rotary scholarships, awards by the American Association of University Women and by International Telephone and Telegraph, and fellowships from USAID and from the World Health Organization. With the exception of Rotary, all these agencies are primarily concerned with graduate programs; undergraduate funding is very limited. Except for institutions with very low tuition, it is important not to overestimate the ability of most foreign undergraduates to finance their American education without some assistance. But minor awards for foreign undergraduates, preferably in the form of tuition waivers, can bridge the gap between the impossible and the possible for talented students.

### 5. Ancillary Programs
We described our third category of funding as marginal and included increased international programming, subsidies to book-

stores, and travel money for faculty. We used the term because these are ancillary to programs and relate less to academic priorities than to the academic setting; but they are central to our overall goal of internationalizing the institution. Precisely these kinds of additional funding, in this world of marginal economics, may produce the decisive changes in campus attitudes that we advocate. Again, we emphasize the importance of reordering internal priorities to produce the funding needed. We have discussed the possibility of creating new administrative funding by reductions in existing budgets. Administrators should be encouraged to seek outside funding or new sources of revenue not so much for internationalizing as to reinstate activities that may have suffered financially.

A great deal of international programming can be self-sustaining or even profitable. Alumni trips abroad, for example, or on-campus conferences or special events, can bring in significant money. So can the imaginative organization of student travel. An entire area relatively unexploited by American institutions is the short-term foreign academic market. Many institutions run profitable programs in English for foreigners (of varying quality, we might add), though even in this area there may be room for innovation. These activities might, for example, prove exportable: American institutions could run summer programs in other countries, using study-abroad facilities there. And more foreign tourists visit the United States every year; summer academic programs taught in foreign languages, using fluent faculty and advanced graduate students, could be established on American campuses, primarily for adult learners. While many young people interested in the United States have some command of English, the same is not true of older generations, particularly that large number of retired people who now visit the United States from Europe and the Far East.

For certain kinds of campus programming, funding may be available from USICA or the National Endowment for the Arts. Particularly if the community is involved, sources of state funding may be tapped or an activity may be fundable through the state committee on the humanities (bodies set up to channel certain types of NEH funding through the state to the public). There may also be ways of attracting foreign support for certain activities (embassies may be helpful here) or of raising money from local groups or individuals. It is important to remember that more and more federally funded academic programs call for community involvement. One of the links between the academy and the community may prove to be various types of semicurricular or noncurricular programming. Even if they are not eligible for funding in a grant program, they may constitute an institutional contribution that will tip the scales in favor of the proposal. And it may be beneficial for the college to make a joint proposal with a community organization for external funding, either curricular or noncurricular.

Our strictures on the dangers of outside funding do not mean we disapprove of the entrepreneurial ingenuity of international programs offices and centers that have raised often impressive amounts of money from outside sources to support and strengthen international programs. (The University of North Carolina at Charlotte, for example, has raised half a million dollars to support the programs of its Center for International Studies.) But our main concern is with long-term change and permanent shifts in focus. The main task is still before successful programs—namely, to institutionalize present successes and make them permanent parts of the academic and campus landscape. Only then can one consider the task of internationalizing complete.

# 11

## Change and
## Transformation

# Change and Transformation

## 1. Structures and Outcomes

We should not fault curricular planners too much for having failed to anticipate the technological revolution of the past 35 years and the accompanying political realignments. The world has moved faster and less predictably than most of us could have imagined—primarily with respect to shifts in the center of political power. In other respects change has been less sudden. For all our failures, and in large measure through the use of technology, we have made significant progress in the battle against abject helplessness: There is less hunger in the world than there might have been without our efforts, there is markedly less disease, and we have done a great deal to build the international institutions needed to regulate our environment in positive ways and to contain the dangers of war. Yet at the same time we see new problems arising and old ones taking new forms. The problem of refugees, and the related issue of the international migration of persons, takes on new dimensions. Problems of natural resources, of armaments, of education, of human rights continue to plague us. These are not isolated issues; they are part and parcel of the new world in which we live, with its changed parameters and aspirations.

When we speak of internationalizing the curriculum, it is, above all, the technological revolution—international in scope, and carrying all kinds of implications for world communications, for the addressing of world problems, and for moral values—that we must take into account. Though the study of technology itself is important in this context, it is primarily the impact of technology on other aspects of human life that requires our attention. We have tried to outline some of the ways in which a beginning can be made by working at the level of undergraduate education. We have been concerned with helping more young people to become expert in international affairs, use international expertise in jobs and daily life, and provide leadership in society. But we are even more anxious to develop a well-informed citizenry, to see that every citizen, expert or not, understands the complexities of the world beyond the United States and appreciates its diversity and its many aspirations.

The effects on the community of this new emphasis on interdependence can be great, as we suggested, because the college or university does not exist in isolation but in relation to a network of high schools, government agencies, local institutions, and so on. Successful campaigns for change in the undergraduate curriculum may be influential in a much wider sphere. In reviewing our discussion, we note that two themes recur in many different contexts. One relates to people and the other to structures. Without leadership, without the courage to try new things and the willingness to defend them with the highest educational principles, change is impossible. But even the strongest leaders are unlikely to prosper amid organizational structures inimical to their goals. Where the structures are wrong, imaginative leadership will appear less often and the mortality rate of initiatives that manage to emerge will be higher.

The academy certainly contains all the skills, intelligence, delicacy of perception, and willingness to accept new ideas—all the ability to take intellectual risks—that is needed to realize our imperatives. Most academics accept that the world will continue to undergo far-reaching changes that will force nations into ever greater contact and oblige them to create the spirit and the institutions of cooperation or face possible annihilation. And most academics would agree that it is the academy's job to help prepare citizens for this new world. But when it comes to putting this belief into action, the flesh of the body academic proves weaker than the spirit. Individual idealism tends to give way before collective inertia: The structures created by the academy to carry on its business too frequently prove fatally constrictive and the old patterns prevail.

Academic conservatism is hardly unique. Organizations and groups of individuals create institutions and structures primarily to perpetuate behavior; often these structures continue to perpetuate the behavior long after it ceases to be productive, reinforced all the while by an ideology that has grown up around both structures and behavior and by sets of thoroughly vested interests. However, institutions and structures also help define the extent of tolerated deviance—and in certain respects deviant behavior has found a haven in the academy. What we seem to have lost is the ability to bring the fringes into a productive relationship with the center—to change the behavior of the center through the influence of the fringes. In a way the academy has worked all too well as an institution: It has accepted and tolerated deviance by containing and isolating it.

But while we might find much to criticize about the way American higher education does its business, its amazingly varied history and its present diversity suggest that it is far from immovable. Furthermore, much can be achieved without a radical realignment of structures; the productive use of those structures can bring about certain outcomes. We do not particularly favor the dismantling of department structures, at least in the larger institutions, even if such a move were possible. The classification and exploration of knowledge should, we believe, have a disciplinary base: It is mere wishful thinking to suppose that discrete methodologies are not important.

On the other hand, it is part of the academy's function not only to teach people how to manipulate and apply methodologies—a task for which the departmental system is well suited—but how to address problems by choosing among and synthesizing divergent methodologies. It is as much the academic's business to rise above his or her discipline—or to step outside it—as it is to labor away inside the discipline without ever coming up for air. This means that the structures must encourage both types of behavior, and that there must be communication between the multidisciplinary study of problems and phenomena on the one hand and study within disciplines on the other. We have contended, first, that the present and future problems of human existence are receiving insufficient attention in undergraduate education (partly because problems in general do not receive the formal attention they need, the emphasis falling on disciplines); and, second, that the study of these problems should affect the subject matter taught and the attitudes expressed within the programs in the individual disciplines.

## 2. Some Principles for Action

Our focus has not fallen on reform of the structures of undergraduate education, despite our strong emphasis on the ways certain structures generate particular results. We have preferred to emphasize what is immediately achievable even in the context of present ways of doing things. Readers may be willing to take steps larger than those we advocate and to buck trends more decisively. But we repeat that we advocate lasting change—that which touches the most recalcitrant member of the community as well as the one who is already convinced. We are concerned with uniting people in an intellectual endeavor.

The considerations on which most of our argument have been based can be summarized as six principles for action. We hesitate to

describe this as an action-oriented agenda or a call to moral arms.
We have had too many of those, and there is too much education for
the quick fix. We prefer to see this as an appeal to the best tradition
of American education, which has emphasized, often against considerable odds, preparation for life in the largest sense. We have little
sympathy with two kinds of shortsightedness that sometimes prevail
in American higher education. The first puts too much emphasis on
the immediately practical; the second assumes that if something was
good enough for previous generations it is good enough for ours. The
latter is often governed by a cyclical philosophy: If we wait long
enough, whatever it is that we do will come back into style. Both
views lack a sense of the middle ground. Education is always a compromise—between teacher and student, eternal verity and career
option, the theoretical and practical, thought and feeling, specialized and general. Hence the educational enterprise must be constantly in change, adapting to the imperatives of the present without
surrendering to them totally. Educational institutions are social and
cultural institutions, not moral absolutes.

Given that these institutions contain certain structures, many organizing sectors of knowledge into rather tightly closed units resistant to change, what can we do to alter the perspective on knowledge conveyed to students through undergraduate programs? How
can we make this perspective more international and global? Our
principles for action:

    **a.  The effort at internationalization should itself be com-
prehensive.** It might begin with the recognition of two basic
realities: first, that the academy has a responsibility to prepare people for a world radically different from that of 30 or
40 years ago, and a responsibility to study the problems of
that world; second, that we know enough about this world of
today and tomorrow to build a curriculum based on a recognition of these new realities. The first half of this statement
would probably draw universal assent. The second, perhaps
because it implies action, might not. Nevertheless, it is probably worth the effort to try; after all, much is at stake. Recognition of these realities might begin with imaginative and realistic senior administrators, or with adventurous faculty, or
with the questions of students. It should be translated into
an institutionwide effort to shift priorities. The entire campus should be involved—physical environment, student population, programming, and administrative style, as well as
the curriculum itself. All these should reflect the cosmopolitan and international nature of the institution. Classroom
work should extend naturally outward to form a part of students' daily lives: Those who have learned French, Japan-

ese, or Swahili must have easy occasions to speak and read their languages. There should be opportunities to study and explore world issues outside the classroom as well. Above all, no student should be unaware that life on campus is closely connected with what happens beyond local and national parameters.

Making this effort institutionwide will require the vigorous support of senior administrators and at least a persuasive group of faculty opinion makers, the more senior and prestigious the better. Wherever the priorities of the institution are expressed—in personnel policy, the physical environment of the campus, departmental support, residential living, libraries, admission and degree requirements—the criterion of internationalization should be injected. How do these priorities help reinforce the internationalization of the curriculum? How do they help highlight the nature of global problems in today's world? How do they show the campus community the importance of global issues? How do they project this message beyond the walls of the academy? The secret is to pinpoint the places at which priorities are expressed and to work on modifying the priorities. The more comprehensive the effort, the more progress in one area will contribute to progress in others.

In this respect it is important to remember that undergraduate education is intimately related to elementary and secondary education, as well as to graduate education. It inherits its students from the former and teaches them largely in terms of the structures of the latter, even in institutions without graduate programs. Planning for change at the undergraduate level must consider these other levels.

**b. The undergraduate curriculum is central to the entire effort.** It can be argued that the forms and priorities of graduate education have tended over the years to shape the undergraduate curriculum, and that the large research universities have deeply influenced the priorities of other types of higher education. There are reasons to believe this situation may be changing; in any case, the education of undergraduates consumes more of the resources of higher education, at a larger number of institutions, than does the education of graduate students in the conventional disciplines. Furthermore, the present lack of academic jobs has shifted the advantage from graduate to undergraduate education. At one time the undergraduate programs could employ whomever the graduate programs produced. Now departments can pick and choose and can in some measure dictate to the graduate programs what their students should be taught to prepare them for teaching (witness the growing emphasis on composition in the training of graduate students in English, for example). Finally, more undergraduates today are turning for further study not to conventional graduate school but to professional education. All these factors are weakening the grip of graduate education on the undergraduate curriculum and are opening new opportunities for reform at the undergraduate level. A determined effort here could in turn affect both graduate education and priorities in elementary and secondary education.

c.   **The mode of learning should transcend disciplines and boundaries.** If students are to gain coherent knowledge of the major global issues of today and tomorrow, they must understand both the nature of the scholarly disciplines and the ways in which the methodologies of the disciplines can be brought to bear on the issues. In effect, then, they must transcend disciplinary limitations. Furthermore, the disciplines must take the whole world for their province, transcending their own geographical and conceptual limitations. Today's world is notably more interconnected than that in which most of us were educated; and the world of tomorrow will consist of still more complex interconnections. Though our political institutions are likely to change only very slowly to take these new realities into account, and hence may lull us with an illusion of stability, humankind's ability to adapt these institutions to new needs and build new institutions to cope with new realities may determine its ability to survive. So education has a double task: not only to inculcate in young people a sense of global imperatives but to give them the knowledge and intellectual agility to create institutions that go with this sense of the global. This implies a rethinking of priorities on the part of a faculty that was educated according to other values. It also implies subtle changes of attitude even in disciplines that at first sight have no specific relevance to international affairs.

d.   **In many institutions the key element in the formation and conduct of the undergraduate curriculum is the power of the departments.** Since the shape of the curriculum is determined somewhat by the distribution of resources within an institution (one cannot teach microbiology if there is no microbiologist, and one cannot hire a microbiologist if there is no new money and the controllers of the purse strings are unwilling to give something up; on the other hand, one can teach more psychology if there are plenty of psychologists), we must either reorganize the structures through which resources are distributed or work on the priorities of the existing structural units. In general, we favor the second approach. We can convince departments to realign their priorities in two ways: by sanctions or by persuasion. The latter is likely to be more enduring in its effects. Rather than creating external structures to counter the power of departments, it is better to create internal structures to move the departments into a greater degree of interaction. Thus it is better to locate new programs within existing departments than on an interdepartmental base (if, of course, the departments are willing to accept them), since in this way they harness the proprietary sense of departments to serve the ends we favor. By the same token, it is better to convince departments to realign courses or create new ones within the departmental structure than to ask them to cooperate in programs wholly outside it. We do not disapprove of various kinds of general education courses or cross-disciplinary area studies programs and the like; but the more we can convince the departments to absorb these responsibilities and make them their own, the better off we shall be.

e.   **In making the changes we propose, consultation is absolutely essential.** When we suggest using the existing structures of higher education to achieve new ends, we have in mind not only departments but traditions of faculty governance and long-standing notions about the nature and function of undergraduate education. Though departments may be disturbingly powerful in that they can prevent the synthesis of knowledge in the classroom that we advocate, their philosophical position is weak, since so many institutions cling philosophically (if not operationally) to a belief in the value of the liberal arts and academic generalism. This provides a point of entry for questions within the disciplines about their relation to more general concerns. Through this device we can hope to convince the departments to look more closely at how their disciplines overlap. Perhaps we can also convince them to cooperate on examining problems that transcend disciplines. While much can be done before the fact to influence its setting and terms, the process is essentially one of persuasion. Creating settings for consultation requires commitment and planning. Academics like to talk about ideas; we should try to create an arena for such discussions. And we should give the discussions a larger sense of direction that will lead ultimately to the building of consensus and to decision and change—processes perhaps less central to the analytic academic mind.

If students are to learn how to synthesize the diciplines, the faculty must do the same more effectively. There must be a general lowering of the barriers of intellectual protectionism and a recapturing of the spirit of liberal education in new terms. The disciplines of philosophy, anthropology, and biology (among the humanities, social sciences, and natural sciences) will have an especially important role.

**f.  Concentration of effort and activity is the most effective way to bring about broad-based change.** The general transformation we advocate can perhaps be best achieved through centralization of effort and activity under a committee of faculty and administrators responsible for all aspects of the campaign. This may be the best way to bring change that consists not of isolated modifications but of comprehensive realignment of programs. A committee of this kind is most likely to accomplish the difficult task of bringing together the various sectors of the campus.

In all phases of this enterprise enlistment of faculty cooperation is crucial. Faculty are the key resource, since their knowledge, skills, and commitment will ultimately form the particulars of a new curriculum and carry it into effect. Consultation with faculty before decisions are made and consideration of their needs and goals is fundamental. Equally important is the commitment of high-level administrators. As we have mentioned, an institution's investment of resources and energy is essential to the success of any program. The most effective large-scale efforts to internationalize institutions have been backed by the deepest institutional investment. There is no way around this consideration. An administration reluctant to make a commitment may try to convince those involved to seek outside money. While funding is, of course, helpful, it will achieve little if it is unaccompanied by an internal sense of mission.

These, then, are the practical considerations fundamental to an effective effort to bring the world into the undergraduate curriculum. Past and present changes in our society have brought us to a point where, if we take seriously our responsibility to prepare students for present realities, we must bring new perspectives to our teaching. Blocks to learning about this new world must be overcome. Those in a position to influence the thinking of young people are best placed to overcome these blocks.

As Cyrus Vance suggested in another way, it is the essence of education that it induces not only action but reflection. It encourages us to inquire into the fundamentals of issues and it dares us to imagine new futures. It is concerned not only with that middle range of things that are more readily manageable, but with the global and the particular. In that sense international education has always been important. We cannot hope to understand ourselves if we do not understand others and we can have no perspective if we do not understand the contextual interrelationships.

At this stage in our history greater emphasis on the global and international is, in the most practical sense, now an imperative. The life for which our students are now preparing will involve a constant awareness of global issues. We are concerned that these issues operate not as the threat of the unknown but as an inspiration, and that they be understood on their own rather complex terms, not merely as theaters for the American vision.

# References

**Alger, Chadwick F.** *Foreign Policies of United States Publics.* Columbus, OH: Transnational Cooperation Program, 1975.

**Alger, Chadwick F.** and **David G. Hoovler.** *You and Your Community in the World.* Columbus, OH: Consortium for International Studies Education, 1978.

**Altbach, Philip G.** *Comparative Higher Education.* London: Mansell, 1979.

**Altman, Edward A.** and **Janet R. Marks.** "Foreign Exchanges." *MBA,* vol. 13, no. 1, Feb.-Mar. 1979, 24-35.

**American Council on Education.** *Library Resources for International Education.* Washington, D.C.: ACE, 1975.

**Asante, Molefi, Eileen Newmark,** and **Cecil Blake.** *Handbook of Intercultural Communication.* Beverly Hills, CA: Sage, 1979.

**Association of Commonwealth Universities.** *Commonwealth Universities Yearbook 1979.* London: ACU, 1979.

**Bantock, G. H.** *Dilemmas of the Curriculum.* New York: John Wiley & Sons—Halstead Press, 1980.

**Barnet, Richard.** *The Lean Years.* New York: Simon and Schuster, 1980.

**Baron, Marvin.** *The Relevance of U.S. Graduate Programs to Foreign Students from Developing Countries.* Washington, DC: NAFSA, 1979.

**Barrows, Thomas S., John L. D. Clark,** and **Stephen F. Klein.** "What Students Know About Their World." *Change,* May-June 1980, 10-17.

**Barrows, Thomas S., Stephen F. Klein,** and **John L. D. Clark,** with **Nathaniel Hartshorne.** *What College Students Know and Believe About Their World.* New Rochelle, NY: Change Magazine Press, 1981; E&WV Series V.

**Barrows, Thomas S.,** et al. *College Students' Knowledge and Beliefs: A Survey of Global Understanding.* New Rochelle, NY: Change Magazine Press, 1981; E&WV Series VII Final Report.

**Benton, William.** "English Spoken Here, There and Everywhere." *Think,* vol. 33, no. 1, Jan.-Feb. 1967, 19-23.

**Berard, Marie-Alice.** "40% des jeunes americains prennent Israel pour un pays arabe." *Le Figaro,* Paris, March 1979.

**Berryman, Sue** and others. *Foreign Language and International Studies Specialists: The Marketplace and National Policy.* Santa Monica, CA: Rand, 1979.

**Binzen, Peter.** "Taking the Middlebury Pledge." *Change,* 1978, 42-44; Report on Teaching 5.

**Black, Robert.** "Education for the Global Century: Findings from the Council on Learning Survey of Undergraduate International Education." Council on Learning, May 19, 1980.

**Black, Robert.** "Effective Programs in International Studies: Strategies From the Council on Learning National Survey." In Anne Paolucci, ed. *Problems in National Literary Identity and the Writer as Social Critic.* Whitestone, NY: Griffin House Publications, 1980, 59-66.

**Black, Robert.** "Educating for the World View: Successful Strategies for Undergraduate Education." Paper delivered at 22nd Annual Convention of International Studies Association, Philadelphia, 1981.

**Black, Robert** and **George W. Bonham.** "The Council on Learning Project on Undergraduate Education: Education and the World View." *Annals of the American Academy of Political and Social Science,* 449, May 1980, 102-113.

**Black, Robert** and **George W. Bonham,** eds. *Education for a Global Century: Handbook of Exemplary International Programs.* New Rochelle, NY: Change Magazine Press, 1981; E&WV Series III.

Bonham, George W. "The Future Forsaken." *Change*, October 1978, 12-13.

Bonham, George W., ed. *The Great Core Curriculum Debate*. New Rochelle, NY: Change Magazine Press, 1979.

Bonham, George W. "What Global Knowledge Is Enough?" *Update I*, Council on Learning, Fall 1979.

Bonham, George W. "Language and Global Awareness." *ADFL Bulletin*, vol. 10, no. 4, May 1979, 5-7.

Bonham, George W. "The New Necessities of National Survival: Education and the World View." *ADFL Bulletin*, vol. 11, no. 4, May 1980, 34-35.

Bonham, George W. " Education and the World View." *Change*, May-June 1980, 2-7.

Born, Warren C. and Kathryn Buck, ed. *Options for the Teaching of Foreign Languages, Literatures, and Culture*. New York: American Council on the Teaching of Foreign Languages, 1978.

Botkin, James W., Mahdi Elmandjra, and Mircea Malitza. *No Limits to Learning: Bridging the Human Gap*. Oxford: Pergamon, 1979.

Boyan, Douglas R. and Alfred C. Julian. *Open Doors: 1978/79 Report on International Educational Exchange*. New York: IIE, 1980.

Boyd-Bowman, Peter. *Self-Instructional Language Programs: A Handbook for Faculty and Students*. Occasional Publication 20, University of the State of New York, Foreign Area Materials Center, and the Council for Intercultural Studies and Programs, July 1973.

Brod, Richard I. "Options and Opportunities: New Directions in Foreign Language Curricula." *ADFL Bulletin*, vol. 10, no. 4, May 1979, 13-18.

Brod, Richard I. *Language Study for the 1980's*. New York: MLA, 1980.

Brod, Richard I. and Jeffrey H. Meyerson. "The Foreign Language Requirement: Report on the 1974-75 Survey." *ADFL Bulletin*, vol. 7, no. 1, 1975, 43-8.

Brownell, John A. *Japan's Second Language*. Champaign, IL: NCTE, 1967.

Buergenthal, Thomas and Judith V. Torney. *International Human Rights and International Education*. Washington, DC: U.S. National Commission for UNESCO, 1976.

Bullard, Betty M. "A Promising Agenda: International Studies in Elementary and Secondary Education." *Annals of the American Academy of Political and Social Science*, 449, May 1980, 91-101.

Burgin, Ken. "How English is Cornering the Language Market." *Times Higher Education Supplement*, March 1980, 10.

Burn, Barbara. *Expanding the International Dimension of Higher Education*. San Francisco: Jossey-Bass, 1980. (a)

Burn, Barbara. "Study Abroad and International Exchanges." *Annals of the American Academy of Political and Social Science*. vol. 449, May 1980, 129-140. (b)

Callahan, Patrick, ed. *Comparative Foreign Policy Notes*. (De Paul University), Autumn, 1979.

Carlson, Catherine Allen. "Foreign Languages: Can U.S. Foundations Help Bridge the Gap?" *Foundation News*, July-August 1980, 8-15, 39-40.

Carnegie Commission on Higher Education. *A Classification of Institutions of Higher Education*. Berkeley, CA: Carnegie Commission on Higher Education, 1973.

Carnie, John. "Children's Attitudes to Other Nationalities." Norman Graves, ed. *New Movements in the Study and Teaching of Geography*. London: Temple Smith, 1972.

Carter, William E. "International Studies and Research Library Needs." *President's Commission on Foreign Language and International Studies: Background Papers and Studies*. Washington, DC: Government Printing Office, 1979.

Chaliand, Gerard. "Ideology and Society." *The Pentagon Papers*. Boston: Beacon Press, 1972, vol. 5, 82-90; Senator Gravel Edition.

**Christensen, Cheryl**. "World Hunger: A Structural Approach." Raymond F. Hopkins and Donald J. Puchala, ed., *The Global Political Economy of Food*. Madison: University of Wisconsin Press, 1978, 171-200.

**Cleveland, Harlan**. *The Third Try at World Order: U.S. Policy for an Interdependent World*. Philadelphia: Aspen Institute for Humanistic Studies, 1976.

**Cleveland, Harlan**. "The Internationalization of Domestic Affairs." *Annals of the American Academy of Political and Social Science*, 442, March 1979, 125-137.

**Cleveland, Harlan**. "Forward to Basics: Education as Wide as the World." *Change*, May-June 1980, 12-22.

**Cleveland, Harlan**. "The Future of International Governance." In Frank Feather, ed. *Through the '80s: Thinking Globally, Acting Locally*. Washington, DC: World Future Society, 1980, 141-149.

**Commission on the Humanities** (Rockefeller Foundation). *The Humanities in American Life*. Berkeley: University of California Press, 1980.

**Conner, Maurice W**. "New Curricular Connections." June K. Phillips, ed., *The Language Connection: From the Classroom to the World*. The ACTFL Foreign Language Education Series, 9. Skokie, IL: National Textbook Company, 1977, 95-121.

**Council on Learning**. *Update I*, Fall 1979. *Update II*, Spring 1980. *Update III*, Spring 1981.

**Council on Learning**. *The Role of the Scholarly Disciplines*. New Rochelle, NY: Change Magazine Press, 1980; E&WV Series I.

**Council on Learning**. *Education and the World View*. New Rochelle, NY: Change Magazine Press, 1980; E&WV Series IV.

**Council on Learning**. *Educating for the World View: Global Understanding and the Curriculum*. New Rochelle, NY: Change Magazine Press, 1981; E&WV Series VI (workshop kit).

**Council on Learning**. Recommendations of the E&WV National Advisory Board on Undergraduate International Education, April 1981.

**Cousins, Norman**. "The Promise of a University." *CASE Currents*, vol. V., no. 8, September 1979, 6-10.

**Dathorne, O. R**. "Literary Studies in a Broader Context." In Gilbert A. Jarvis ed. *Responding to New Realities*. ACTFL Foreign Language Education Series, 5. Skokie, IL: National Textbook Co., 1974, 189-218.

**Dell, David J**. "Readings for a Global Curriculum." *Change*, May-June 1980, 70-76.

**Department of Defense**. *Foreign Language Training in the Department of Defense*. A report submitted to the Committee on Appropriations, House of Representatives, U.S. Congress, by Assistant Secretary of Defense, February 1979.

**Egerton, John**. "International Outreach from Kentucky." *Change*, May-June 1980, 51-53.

**Ehrlich, Paul R., Anne H. Ehrlich**, and **John P. Holdren**. *Ecoscience: Population, Resources, Environment*. San Francisco: Freeman, 1977.

**Ehrman, Edith**, and **Ward Morehouse**. *Students, Teachers and the Third World in the American College Curriculum: A Guide and Commentary on Innovative Approaches in Undergraduate Education*. Occasional Publications, No. 19, University of the State of New York, Foreign Area Materials Center, and the Council for Intercultural Studies and Programs, November, 1972.

**Eide, Ingrid**, ed. *Students as Links Between Cultures*. Oslo: Universitetsforlaget, and Paris: UNESCO, 1970.

**Eliot, Charles William**. *A Turning Point in Higher Education: The Inaugural Address of Charles William Eliot as President of Harvard College*, October 19, 1869. Cambridge, MA: Harvard University, 1969.

**El-Oteifi, Gamal**. *Call for a New Information Order: Preliminary Remarks*. International Commission for the Study of Communication Problems, 33. Paris: UNESCO, 1979.

**Fascell, Dante B**. "The Helsinki Accord: A Case Study." *Annals of the American Academy of Political and Social Science*, 442, March 1979, 69-78.

**Fersh, Seymour**. "Worldwide Dimensions Enrich Community-Based Education." *Community and Junior College Journal*, vol. 49, no. 6, 1979, 14-19.

**Fishman , Joshua A., Robert L. Cooper**, and **Andrew W. Conrad**. *The Spread of English.* Rowley, MA: Newbury House, 1977.

**FitzGerald, Frances**. *America Revised*. Boston: Little, Brown, 1979.

**FitzGerald, Frances**. *Fire in the Lake*. Boston: Little, Brown, 1972.

**Fox, Melvin J.**, ed. *Language and Development: A Retrospective Survey of Ford Foundation Language Projects 1952-1974*. New York: Ford Foundation, 1974.

**Fox, Melvin J.** "Indiana Language Program and Washington Foreign Language Program." In *President's Commission on Foreign Language and International Studies: Background Papers*. Washington, DC: 1979.

**Frith, James R.** "Testing the FSI Testing Kit." *Bulletin of the Association of Departments of Foreign Languages*, November 1979, 12-14.

**Garraty, John A., Lily Von Klemperer**, and **Cyril J. M. Taylor**. *The New Guide to Study Abroad 1978-1979*. New York: Harper & Row, 1979.

**Goetzl, Sylvia** and **Jill D. Stritter**. *Foreign Alumni: Overseas Links for U.S. Institutions*. Washington, DC: NAFSA, 1980.

**Goodman, Thomas H.** "Esperanto: Threat or Ally?" *Foreign Language Annals*, 11 (1978), 201-3.

**Grant, Steven A.** "Language Policy in the United States: Report to the Task Force on Government Relations." Richard I. Brod, ed. *Language Study for the 1980's*. New York: MLA, 1980.

**Gray, Andrew Ward**. *International/Intercultural Education in Selected State Colleges and Universities: An Overview and Five Cases*. Washington, DC: American Association of State Colleges and Universities, 1977.

**Gumperz, Ellen M.** *Internationalizing American Higher Education*. Berkeley: University of California, 1970.

**Hanvey, Robert**. *An Attainable Global Perspective*. New York: Center for Global Perspectives, n.d.

**Harf, James E.** "Undergraduate International Studies: The State of the Art and Prescriptions for the Future." In *President's Commission on Foreign Language and International Studies: Background Papers and Studies*. Washington, DC: U.S. GPO, 1979.

**Harry, Ralph** and **Mark Mandel**. *Language Equality in International Cooperation*. Esperanto Documents 21. Rotterdam: Universal Esperanto Association, 1979.

**Hayden, Rose L.** "Funding International Education Programs: An Unmet Agenda." Statement before the Senate Appropriations Subcommittee on Labor/HEW, September 21, 1977.

**Hayden Rose L.** " 'In the National Interest': International Education and Language Policy." *ADFL Bulletin*, vol. 6, no. 3, March 1975.

**Hayden, Rose L.** "The World and Us." *AGB Reports*, March-April 1979, 3-7.

**Hayden, Rose L.** "U.S. Government Exchanges: The Quest for Coordination." *Annals of the American Academy of Political and Social Science*, 449, May 1980, 114-128.

**Hayden, Samuel L.** "Foreign Languages, International Studies and Business (A Dubious Savior)." *Annals of the American Academy of Political and Social Science*, 449, May 1980, 141-150.

**Hayden, Samuel L.** and **Leslie W. Koepplin**. "International Business and International Studies: Prospects and Mutual Benefit." In Thomas M. Stauffer, ed. *Agenda for Business and Higher Education*. Washington, DC: ACE, 1980.

**Heath, Shirley Brice**. "Our Language Heritage: A Historical Perspective." June K. Phillips, ed. *The Language Connection: From the Classroom to the World*. Skokie, IL: National Textbook Co., 1977, 23-51.

**Heenan, David A.** and **Howard V. Perlmutter**. *Multinational Organization Development.* Reading, MA: Addison-Wesley, 1979.

**Hildebrand, John**. "Friends World College: Offbeat and Upbeat on Long Island." *Change*, July-August 1980, 15-7.

**Hill, A. David**. "A Survey of the Global Understanding of American College Students: A Report to Geographers." *The Professional Geographer*, vol. 33, no. 2, May 1981, 237-245.

**Hill, James W.** "A Series of Exchanges." *Change*, May-June 1980, 53-54.

**Hodges, Luther H., Jr.** "On Commerce and Language Study." *ADFL Bulletin*, vol 11, no. 4, May 1980, 36-37.

**Hoopes, David S.** *Readings in Intercultural Communication, Vol. 5.* Pittsburgh: Intercultural Communications Network, SIETAR, 1976.

**Howard, Michael**. "Empathy With the Enemy." Rev. of Ken Booth, *Strategy and Ethnocentrism* (London: Croom Helm, 1980). *Times Literary Supplement*, June 13, 1980, 663.

**Husen, Torsten**. *The Learning Society.* London: Methuen, 1974.

**Hutchins, Robert M.** *The Learning Society.* London: Pall Mall Press, 1968.

**Interorganizational Commission for International/Intercultural Education.** *Directory of Resources in Global Education.* Washington, DC: November 1977.

**James, Nancy Ann**. "The Faraway Classroom." *Change*, May-June 1980, 58-59.

**Jencks, Christopher** and **David Riesman**. *The Academic Revolution.* Garden City, NY: Doubleday, 1968.

**Johansen, Robert C.** *The National Interest and the Human Interest: An Analysis of U.S. Foreign Policy.* Princeton, NJ: Princeton University Press, 1980.

**Kanter, Rosabeth Moss**. "Changing the Shape of Work: Reforms in Academe." In Rosabeth Moss Kanter, Morton Darrow, and Michael Maccoby. *Current Issues in Higher Education.* Washington, DC: ACE, 1979.

**Kay, Martin**. "Automatic Translation of Natural Languages." In E. Haugen and M. Bloomfield. *Languages as a Human Problem.* New York: Norton, 1974.

**Keller, Edward** and **Ronald Roel**. "Foreign Languages and Culture in the Media: Report to the Task Force on Public Awareness." Richard I. Brod, ed. *Language Study for the 1980's: Reports of the MLA-ACLS Language Task Forces.* New York: MLA, 1980, 78-94.

**Kelly, Thomas E.** "Interdisciplinary Studies." Gilbert A. Jarvis, ed. *Responding to New Realities.* Skokie, IL: National Textbook Co, 1974, 129-59; ACTFL Foreign Language Education Series, 5.

**Klitgaard, Robert E.** "Why International Studies? A Prologue." *Change*, January-February 1981, 28-34.

**Knepler, Henry**. "Beyond American Expressland: Training for Intercultural Communication." *Change*, February-March 1980, 25-30.

**Koen, Ross Y.** *The China Lobby in North American Politics.* New York: Octagon, 1974.

**Kuhne, Robert J.** and **Gerda P. Jordan**. "Integrating International Business and Language Training." *Bulletin of the Association of Departments of Foreign Languages*, vol. 2, no. 3, March 1980, 27-30.

**LaBrack, Bruce**. "Results of International Experience for U.S. Students: Bi-Culturalism or Dual Ethnocentrism." Paper delivered at 21st Annual Convention of the International Studies Association, Los Angeles, 1980.

**Lambert, Richard D.** "International Studies: An Overview and Agenda." *Annals of the American Academy of Political and Social Science*, 449, May 1980, 151-164.

**Lambert, Richard D.** *Language and Area Studies Review,* Philadelphia: October 1973; American Academy of Political and Social Science Monographs, 17.

**Lapenna, Ivo**. "La situation juridique des 'langues officielles' avant la fondation des Nations Unies." *La Monda Linguo-Problemo,* 1 (1969), 87-106.

Levenson, Stanley and William Kendrick, ed. *Readings in Foreign Languages for the Elementary School*. Waltham, MA: Blaisdell, 1969.

Levine, Arthur. *Handbook on Undergraduate Curriculum*. San Francisco: Jossey-Bass, 1978.

Levine, Arthur and John Weingart. *Reform of Undergraduate Education*. San Francisco: Jossey-Bass, 1974.

Luce, Don. "Tell Your Friends We're People." *The Pentagon Papers*. Boston: Beacon Press, 1972, vol. 5, 91-102; Senator Gravel Edition.

Luxenberg, Stan. "All the Class a Stage." *Change*, January 1978, 30-33; Report on Teaching 5.

Luxenberg, Stan. "The Community College Contribution," *Change*, May-June 1980, 55-56.

Manley, Robert H. "The World Policy System: An Analytical and Substantive Overview." *International and Comparative Public Policy*, 2, 1978, 35-138.

Masmoudi, Mustapha. *The New World Information Order*. Paris: UNESCO, 1978; International Commission for the Study of Communication Problems, 31.

Mayville, William V. *Federal Influence on Higher Education Curricula*. Washington, DC: AAHE, 1980; ERIC Higher Education Research Reports, 1.

McCaughey, Robert A. The Permanent Revolution: An Assessment of the Current State of International Studies in American Universities. A Report to the International Division of the Ford Foundation, 1979.

McCaughey, Robert A. "In the Land of the Blind: American International Studies in the 1930s." *Annals of the American Academy of Political and Social Science*, 449, May 1980, 1-16.

Melpignano, Richard J. "Commercial French Radio in the Classroom." *Foreign Language Annals* vol. 13, no. 5, 1980, 387-390.

Melton, Judith M. "Using Drama to Teach Languages." *ADFL Bulletin*, vol. 11, no. 3, March 1980, 36-38.

Mestenhauser, Josef A. *Learning with Foreign Students*. Minneapolis: University of Minnesota, March 1976.

Mestenhauser, Josef A. and Dietmar Barsig. "Foreign Students as Teachers." Washington, DC: NAFSA, 1978.

Mitzman, Barry. "Cooperation in the Pacific Northwest." *Change*, May-June 1980, 59-61.

Muller, Robert. *The Need for Global Education*. Philadelphia: Global Interdependence Center, nd (1976).

Muller, Steven. "A New American University?" *Daedalus* (AAA&S), vol. 107, no. 1, Winter 1978, 31-46.

Myer, Richard B. *Curriculum: U.S. Capacities, Developing Countries' Needs*. Washington, DC: IIE, 1979; A Report from the 1979 Conference on International Education: the Global Context, the U.S. Role.

National Academy of Sciences. *The Invisible University*. Washington, DC: National Academy of Sciences, 1969.

Nehrt, Lee C. *Business and International Education*. Washington, DC: ACE, May 1977; Occasional Papers, 4.

O'Connell, Barry. "Where Does Harvard Lead Us?" *Change*, September 1978, 35-40, 61. Reprinted in Bonham 1979a, 25-42.

Palmer, Norman D. "The International Activity of the University of Pennsylvania Faculty." Philadelphia: University of Pennsylvania, 1977; Philadelphia Transnational Project.

Palmer, Norman. "The Study of International Relations in the United States: Perspectives of Half a Century." *International Studies Quarterly*, vol. 24, no. 3, 1980, 343-63.

**Parker, William R.** *The National Interest and Foreign Languages.* Washington, DC: U.S. National Commission for UNESCO, 1954.

**Patterson, Franklin.** *Colleges in Consort.* San Francisco: Jossey-Bass, 1974.

**Pellegrino, Edmund D.**, et al. *The Successor Generation.* Washington, DC: The Atlantic Council of the United States, 1981: Policy Paper.

**Peterson, A. D. C.** *The International Baccalaureate: An Experiment in International Education.* London: Harrap, 1972.

**Peterson, John H.** "The Next Generation: International Attitudes of Secondary School Students in Kentucky." A paper delivered at the convention of the International Studies Association, Los Angeles, 1980.

**Petit, Bernard.** "Teaching Foreign Cultures: The Brockport Model." *ADFL Bulletin,* vol. 10, no. 4, May 1979, 23-25.

**Phillips, June K.** "Individualization and Personalization." Gilbert A. Jarvis, ed. *Responding to New Realities.* Skokie, IL: National Textbook Co., 1974, 219-261; The ACTFL Review of Foreign Language Education, 5.

**Pike, Lewis W.**, and **Thomas S. Barrows.** *Other Nations, Other Peoples: A Survey of Student Interests, Knowledge, Attitudes, and Perceptions.* Washington, DC: GPO 1979.

**Pool, Jonathan.** *La politika ekonomio de interlingvistiko.* Pederborn and Seattle: FEoLL, 1980.

**President's Commission on Foreign Language and International Studies.** *Strength Through Wisdom: A Critique of U.S. Capability.* Washington, DC: U.S. Government Printing Office, November 1979.

**Quirk, Randolph.** "The Importance of Exporting English." *The Observer* (London), July 9, 1978.

**Rudolph, Frederick.** *Curriculum: A History of the American Undergraduate Course of Study Since 1636.* San Francisco: Jossey-Bass, 1977.

**Rudolph, Frederick.** "The New Curricular Equation." *Education and the World View.* New Rochelle, NY: Change Magazine Press, 1981, 55-8.

**Ruttan, Vernon.** "The Green Revolution: Seven Generalizations." *International Development Review,* vol. 19, no. 4, 1977, 16-23.

**Sanders, Irwin T.**, and **Jennifer C. Ward.** *Bridges to Understanding.* New York: McGraw-Hill, 1970.

**Schulz, Renate A.** *Options for Undergraduate Foreign Language Programs.* New York: MLA, 1979.

**Schwartz, Richard H.** "Mathematics and Global Survival." MS. See *Global Perspectives,* May-June 1980, p. 4.

**Scully, Malcolm G.** "Taking Language Out of the Classroom." *The Chronicle of Higher Education,* September 22, 1980.

**Shannon, William G.** *A Survey of International/Intercultural Education in Two Year Colleges—1976.* La Plata, MD: Charles County Community College, 1978.

**Simon, Paul.** "Battling Language Chauvinism." *Change,* November 1977, 10.

**Simon, Paul.** "Understanding Foreign Cultures." *Exchange,* Summer 1978, 2-4.

**Simon, Paul.** "The U.S. Crisis in Foreign Language." *Annals of the American Academy of Political and Social Science.* 449, May 1980, 31-44.

**Simon, Paul.** *The Tongue-Tied American: Confronting the Foreign Language Crisis.* New York: The Seabury Press—Continuum, 1980.

**Slessarev, Helga.** "Languages and the International Business Connection." *Change,* 1978, 48-49; Report on Teaching 5.

**Snow, Donald M.** "Excerpts from Revolutionary Society (REVSOC) Simulation." In William D. Coplin ed. *Interdisciplinary Approaches to Cross-Cultural Social Science Education for Undergraduates.* Pittsburgh: International Studies Association, 1977.

**Spaulding, Seth**, and **Michael J. Flack**. *The World's Students in the United States: A Review and Evaluation of Research on Foreign Students.* New York: Praeger, 1976.

**Speich, Don F.** "A Long History of Global Emphasis." *Change,* May-June 1980, 65-67.

**Starr, S. Frederick.** "English Dethroned." *Change,* May 1978, 26-31.

**Starr, S. Frederick.** "Foreign Languages in the American School." *President's Commission on Foreign Language and International Studies: Background Papers.* Washington, DC: November 1979.

**Taylor, Harold.** *The World as Teacher.* Garden City, NY: Doubleday, 1969.

**Thogmartin, Clyde** and **JoAn Mann.** "Business Needs for Foreign Languages: A Survey of 219 Employers." *ADFL Bulletin,* vol. 10, no. 4, May 1979, 32-35.

**Thompson, Richard T.** "New Directions in Foreign Language Study." *Annals of the American Academy of Political and Social Science,* 449, May 1980, 45-55.

**Thompson, Wayne.** "Equal Opportunity Internationalism." *Change,* May-June 1980, 64-65.

**Tocqueville, Alexis de.** *Democracy in America.* Trans. George Lawrence. Ed. J.P. Mayer. New York: Harper & Row, 1966.

**Tonkin, Humphrey.** *Esperanto and International Language Problem: A Research Bibliography.* Washington, DC: Esperantic Studies Foundation, 1977, 4th ed.

**Tonkin, Humphrey.** "Language: Barrier, or Mode of Self-Definition?" Paper delivered at Conference of the International Society of Political Psychology, Washington, DC, 1979.

**Tonkin, Humphrey.** "Equalizing Language." *Journal of Communication,* 29, 1979, 124-33.

**Torney-Purta, Judith V.** "The International Attitudes and Knowledge of Adolescents in Nine Countries: The IEA Civic Education Survey." *International Journal of Political Education,* 1, 1977, 3-20.

**Torney-Purta, Judith V.** "Psychological and Institutional Obstacles to the Global Perspective in Education." In James M. Becker, ed., *Schooling for a Global Age.* New York: McGraw-Hill, 1979, 61-93.

**Tuchman, Gaye.** "Let's Hold Trials Here in Spanish." *New York Times,* August 28, 1979.

**Tunstall, Jeremy.** "The American Role in Worldwide Mass Communication." George Gerbner, ed., *Mass Media Policies in Changing Cultures.* New York: Wiley, 1977, 3-12.

**Tunstall, Jeremy.** *The Media are American.* New York: Columbia, 1977.

**Twarog, Leon I.** and **E. Garrison Walters.** "Mastery-Based, Self-Paced Instruction in Foreign Languages at Ohio State University." *The Modern Language Journal,* vol. 65, no. 1, Spring 1981, preprint.

**Unesco, International Commission for the Study of Communication Problems.** *Interim Report on Communication Problems in Modern Society.* Paris: UNESCO, 1978.

**Unesco.** *Many Voices, One World: Toward a New, More Just, and More Efficient World Information and Communication Order.* London: Kogan Page. New York: Unipub. Paris: UNESCO, 1980.

**Unesco.** *The Use of Vernacular Languages in Education.* Paris: UNESCO, 1953.

**Unesco.** *L'enseignement des droits de l'homme.* Paris: UNESCO 1980; Travaux du Congres international sur l'enseignement des droits de l'homme, Vienne 12-16 Septembre 1978.

**Union of International Associations.** *Yearbook of International Organizations.* Brussels: UIA, 1977.

**United Nations Association.** *United States Foreign Policy and Human Rights: Principles, Priorities, Practice.* New York: UNA-USA December 1979.

**United Nations Economic and Social Council.** *Transnational Corporations in World Development: A Re-Examination.* New York: United Nations 29 March 1978, E.C. 10/38.

**United States Office of Education**. *Task Force on Global Education: Report with Recommendations*. Washington, DC: USOE, 1979.

**Vasak, Karel**, ed. *Les Dimensions internationales des droits de l'homme*. Paris: UNESCO, 1978.

**Veysey, Laurence R**. *The Emergence of the American University*. Chicago: University of Chicago Press, 1965

**Watson, Paul**. "Report of Survey of Post-Secondary Organizational Structures for International Studies and Programs." *International Studies Notes*, vol. 7, no. 1, Spring 1980, 15-16.

**Watters, Pat**. "The Interdisciplinary Umbrella." *Change*, May-June 1980, 61-62.

**Weston, Burns H**. "Peace and World Order Education: A Needed Response to Global Peril and Change." *Bulletin of Peace Proposals*, vol. 10, no. 4, 1979, 345-355.

**Weston, Burns H**. "Contending With a Planet in Peril and Change: An Optimal Educational Response." *Alternatives*, 5 (1979-1980) 59-95.

**Whipp, Leslie T**. "Simulating World Crises." *Change*, May-June 1980, 56-58.

**Williamsen, Marvin** and **Cynthia T. Morehouse**, ed. *International/Intercultural Education in the Four-Year College: A Handbook on Strategies for Change*. New York: State Education Department—Learning Resources in International Studies, 1977.

**Wilson, James Q**. "Harvard's Core Curriculum: A View From the Inside." *Change*, November 1978, 40-43. Reprinted in Bonham 1979a, 43-50.

**Wiprud, Helen R**. *International Education Programs of the U.S. Government: An Inventory*. Washington, DC: Government Printing Office, 1980.

**Wolkomir, Richard**. "Native Speakers: Integrating the Language." *Change*, May-June 1980, 49-51.

**Wood, Richard E**. "Proceedings of the Symposium on the Teaching of Esperanto at United States Universities and Colleges." *LMLP*, 4, 1972, 159-74.

**Wood, Richard E**. "Teaching the Interlanguage: Some Experiments." *Lektos*, Special Issue, 1975, 61-81.

*The World of Learning 1979-80*. New York: International Publications Service, 1979; 2 vols.

**Ziff, Howard**. "Sharing at the Five Colleges." *Change*, May-June 1980, 62-64.

# Organizations

AACRAO
**American Association of Collegi-
ate Registrars and Admissions
Officers**
One Dupont Circle, N..W.
Washington, DC 20036
(202) 293-9161

AACJC
**American Association of Com-
munity and Junior Colleges**
Suite 410
One Dupont Circle, N.W.
Washington, DC 20036
(202) 293-7050

AACTE
**American Association of Colleges
for Teacher Education**
Suite 610
One Dupont Circle, N.W.
Washington, DC 20036
(202) 293-2450

AASCU
**American Association of State
Colleges and Universities**
One Dupont Circle, N.W.
Washington, DC 20036
(202) 293-7070

AAUW
**American Association of Uni-
versity Women**
2401 Virginia Avenue, N.W.
Washington, DC 20037
(202) 785-7700

ACE
**American Council on Education**
Suite 800
One Dupont Circle, N.W.
Washington, DC 20036
(202) 833-4700

ACTFL
**American Council on the Teach-
ing of Foreign Languages**
2 Park Avenue
New York, NY 10016
(212) 689-8021

ADFL
**Association of Departments of
Foreign Languages**
62 Fifth Avenue
New York, NY 10011
(212) 741-5592

AIESEC
**International Association of Stu-
dents in Economic and Commercial Sciences**
622 Third Avenue
New York, NY 10017
(212) 687-1905

**Amnesty International**
777 United Nations Plaza
New York, NY 10017
(212) 582-4440

**The Asia Society**
112 East 64th Street
New York, NY 10021
(212) 751-4210

CCIVS
**Coordinating Committee for the
International Voluntary Service**
UNESCO
1 Rue Miolis
75015 Paris, France

CES
**Council for European Studies**
1405 International Affairs
420 West 118th Street
New York, NY 10027
(212) 280-4172/4727

CICHE
**Consortium for International Co-
operation in Higher Education**
Suite 610
One Dupont Circle, N.W.
Washington, DC 20036
(202) 293-7120

CIEE
**Council on International Educa-
tional Exchange**
205 East 42nd Street
New York, NY 10017
(212) 661-1414

CISE
**Consortium for International
Studies Education**
223 Derby Hall
The Ohio State University
Columbia, OH 43210
(614) 422-8130

CISP
**Council for Intercultural Studies
and Programs**
60 East 42nd Street
New York, NY 10017
(212) 972-9877

COPRED
**Consortium on Peace Research,
Education and Development**
Gustavus Adolphus College
St. Peter, MN 56082
(507) 931-4300

**Council on Learning**
271 North Avenue
New Rochelle, NY 10801
(914) 235-8700

ETS
**Educational Testing Service**
Rosedale Road
Princeton, NJ 08541
(609) 921-9000

ELNA
**Esperanto League for North
America**
Post Office Box 1129
El Cerrito, CA 94530
(415) 653-0998

ESAA
**Esperanto Studies Association**
Department of Spanish and Portuguese
University of Wisconsin
Milwaukee, WI 53210
(414) 963-4257

FIPSE
**Fund for the Improvement of Post-
secondary Education**
3123 FOB 6
499 Maryland Avenue, S.W.
Washington, DC 20202
(202) 245-8100

**Ford Foundation**
320 East 43rd Street
New York, NY 10017
(212) 573-5000

FPA
**Foreign Policy Association**
205 Lexington Avenue
New York, NY 10016
(212) 481-8454

GMA
**Fundacion Gran Mariscal de
Ayacucho**
Suite 1020
515 Madison Avenue
New York, NY 10022
(212) 751-1400

**Global Education Association**
552 Park Avenue
East Orange, NJ 07017
(201) 675-1405

GPE
**Global Perspectives in Education**
218 East 18th Street
New York, NY 10003
(212) 475-0850

HEWLETT FOUNDATION
**The William and Flora Hewlett
Foundation**
Two Palo Alto Square
Palo Alto, CA 94304
(415) 493-3665

IAESTE
**International Association for the
Exchange of Students for Tech-
nical Experience**
Suite 217
American City Building
Columbia, MD 21044
(301) 997-2200

IC
**International Classroom**
University Museum
3300 Spruce Street
Philadelphia, PA 19104
(215) 243-4065

ICFTU
**International Confederation of
Free Trade Unions**
37-41 Rue Montagne-aux-Herbes-
Potageres
1000 Brussels, Belgium

IIE
**Institute of International Educa-
tion**
809 United Nations Plaza
New York, NY 10017
(212) 883-8200

ILO
**International Labour Organisation**
4 Rue des Morillons
1211 Geneva 22, Switzerland

IRC
**International Red Cross**
17 Avenue de la Paix
1211 Geneva, Switzerland

IREX
**International Research and Ex-
  change Board**
655 Third Avenue
New York, NY 10017
(212) 490-2002

ISA
**International Studies Association**
James F. Byrnes International Center
University of South Carolina
Columbia, SC 29208
(803) 777-7810

ISEP
**International Student Exchange
  Program**
Georgetown University
1316 36th Street, N.W.
Washington, DC 20057
(202) 625-4388

ISO
**International Standards Organisa-
  tion**
1 Rue de Varembe
1211 Geneva 20, Switzerland

ITT
**International Telephone & Tele-
  graph**
320 Park Avenue
New York, NY 10022
(212) 940-1000

ITU
**International Telecommunication
  Union**
Place des Nations
1211 Geneva 20, Switzerland

IWO
**Institute for World Order**
777 United Nations Plaza
New York, NY 10017
(212) 490-0010

JNCL
**Joint National Committee on Lan-
  guages**
Suite 210
11 Dupont Circle, N.W.
Washington, DC 20036
(202) 483-7200

**Kettering Foundation**
Suite 300
5335 Far Hills Avenue
Dayton, OH 45429
(513) 434-7300

LASPAU
**Latin American Scholarship Pro-
  gram of American Universities**
25 Mt. Auburn Street
Cambridge, MA 02138
(617) 495-5255

**Lions International**
300 22nd Street
Oak Brook, IL 60570
(312) 986-1700

MLA
**Modern Language Association of
  America**
62 Fifth Avenue
New York, NY 10011
(212) 741-5588

NAFSA
**National Association for Foreign
  Student Affairs**
1860 19th Street, N.W.
Washington, DC 20009
(202) 462-4811

NAS
**National Academy of Sciences**
2101 Constitution Avenue
Washington, DC 20418
(202) 393-8100

NASILP
**National Association for Self-
  Instructional Language Pro-
  grams**
c/o Critical Languages
Box 38
Humanities Building
Temple University
Philadelphia, PA 19122
(215) 787-1715

NCCWAO
**National Council of Community
  World Affairs Organizations**
President: Dr. Stanley E. Spangler
World Affairs Council of Boston
Curtis-Saval International Center
22 Batterymarch Street
Boston, MA 02109
(617) 482-1740

NCFLIS
**National Council on Foreign Languages and International Studies**
17th Floor
605 Third Avenue
New York, NY 10158
(212) 490-3520

NCIV
**National Council for International Visitors**
Meridian House
1630 Crescent Place, N.W.
Washington, DC 20009
(202) 332-1028

NCTA
**National Council for the Traditional Arts**
Suite 1118
1346 Connecticut Avenue, N.W.
Washington, DC 20036
(202) 296-0068

NEA
**National Endowment for the Arts**
1201 16th Street, N.W.
Washington, DC 20036
(202) 634-6369

NEH
**National Endowment for the Humanities**
806 15th Street, N.W.
Washington, DC 20506
(202) 724-0386

NIH
**National Institute of Health**
9000 Rockfield Pike
Bethesda, MD 20205
(301) 496-4000

NSF
**National Science Foundation**
1800 G Street, N.W.
Washington, DC 20550
(202) 655-4000

OAS
**Organization of American States**
Washington, DC 20006
(202) 789-3000

**Rockefeller Foundation**
1133 Avenue of the Americas
New York, NY 10036
(212) 869-8500

**Rotary International**
1600 Ridge
Evanston, IL 60201
(312) 328-0100

SIETAR
**Society for Intercultural Education, Training and Research**
Georgetown University
Washington, DC 20057
(202) 625-3391

**Sloan Foundation**
630 Fifth Avenue
New York, NY 10020
(212) 582-0450

**Smithsonian Institute**
Folklife Program
Room 2600
L'Enfant Plaza
Washington, DC 20560
(202) 381-4348

TCE
**Teachers' Centers Exchange**
1855 Folsom Street
San Francisco, CA 94103
(415) 565-3095

UIA
**Union of International Associations**
1 Rue aux Laines
1000 Brussels, Belgium

UN
**United Nations**
Department of Public Information
United Nations, NY 10017
(212) 754-1234

UNA-USA
**United Nations Association of the United States of America**
300 East 62nd Street
New York, NY 10017
(212) 697-3232

UNESCO
**United Nations Educational, Scientific, and Cultural Organization**
7 Place de Fontenoy
75700 Paris, France

**U.S. Advisory Commission on International Communication, Cultural, and Educational Affairs**
USICA
1750 Pennsylvania Avenue, N.W.
Washington, DC 20547
(202) 655-4000

USAID
**U.S. Agency for International Development**
Washington, DC 20523
(202) 655-4000

**U.S. Department of Education,**
**Educational Resources**
Washington, DC 20208
(202) 254-7934

USICA
**U.S. International Communication**
**Agency**
1750 Pennsylvania Avenue, N.W.
Washington, DC 20547
(202) 655-4000

**U.S. National Commission for**
**UNESCO**
Department of State
Washington, DC 25120
(202) 544-4000

UNU
**United Nations University**
Toho Seimei Building
15-1 Shibuya S-chomo
Shibuya-Ku, Tokyo 150
Japan

UNU New York Liaison Office
United Nations, NY 10017
(212) 754-5610

UNU, American Council for the
1911 Kenbar Court
McLean, VA 22101
(703) 538-4773

WORLD BANK GROUP
**International Bank for Reconstruc-**
**tion and Development**
1818 H Street, N.W.
Washington, DC 20433
(202) 477-1234

WHO
**World Health Organization**
Regional Office
525  23rd Street, N.W.
Washington, DC 20037
(202) 223-4700
(1211 Geneva 27, Switzerland)

WIPO
**World Intellectual Property Or-**
**ganisation**
32 Chemin des Columbettes
1211 Geneva 20, Switzerland

# 1981 Publications in the Education and the World View Series

## The Role of the Scholarly Disciplines

This book focuses on the potential role of the disciplines in encouraging enlarged international dimensions in the undergraduate curriculum; it also provides useful insights into campus initiatives and effective curricular approaches. **$4.95**

## The World in the Curriculum: Curricular Strategies for the 21st Century

Written by Humphrey Tonkin of the University of Pennsylvania, this volume considers concrete, feasible recommendations for strengthening the international perspective of the undergraduate curriculum at academic institutions; it provides a guide to meaningful curricular change for top administrators and faculty. **$6.95**

## Education for a Global Century: Issues and Some Solutions

A reference handbook for faculty and administrators who wish to start or strengthen language and international programs, this contains descriptions of exemplary programs, definitions of minimal competencies in students' international awareness and knowledge, and recommendations of the project's national task force. **$7.95**

## Education and the World View

A book edition of Change's special issue on Education and the World View for use by trustees, faculty, and administrators; it also contains proceedings of a national conference that considered the implications of educational ethnocentrism and action to encourage change. **$6.95**

## What College Students Know About Their World

An important new national assessment of American freshmen and seniors, conducted by the Educational Testing Service, that covers the strengths and weaknesses of American college students' global understanding; an aid to faculty and program directors, it pinpoints areas for improving international content. **$5.95**

## ETS National Survey of Global Understanding

The full report of the 1980 national assessment of 3,000 college students about world cultures, foreign languages, and contemporary world issues. With complete data, charts, and analysis. **$10.95**

**Order from Change Magazine Press, 271 North Avenue, New Rochelle, N.Y. 10801. Add $1 if billing is desired.**

All volumes in the Council on Learning's new international education series, listed on reverse side of page, can be rush-ordered through:

Change Magazine Press
271 North Avenue
New Rochelle, N.Y. 10801